ETHEREA

ETHEREAL QUEER

TELEVISION, HISTORICITY, DESIRE

AMY VILLAREJO

DUKE UNIVERSITY PRESS ::: DURHAM AND LONDON ::: 2014

© 2014 Duke University Press
All rights reserved
Printed in the United States of
America on acid-free paper ∞
Typeset in Chaparral Pro by
Tseng Information Systems, Inc.

Library of Congress
Cataloging-in-Publication Data
Villarejo, Amy.
Ethereal queer : television, historicity,
desire / Amy Villarejo.
p. cm.
Includes bibliographical references and index.
ISBN 978-0-8223-5495-6 (cloth : alk. paper)
ISBN 978-0-8223-5511-3 (pbk. : alk. paper)
1. Homosexuality on television. 2. Gays in
popular culture — United States. 3. Television
programs — Social aspect — United States. I. Title.
PN1992.8.H64V55 2014
791.45′653–dc23
2013025247

CONTENTS

I have presented material from drafts of this book to audiences at Barnard College, the Center for Lesbian and Gay Studies (CLAGS), City University of New York (CUNY), the College of William and Mary, Columbia University, Duke University, Georgia State University, Justus Liebig University Giessen, Northwestern University, Oklahoma State University, the School of Criticism and Theory, Syracuse University, the University of Arizona, the University of California at Los Angeles, the University of California at Santa Cruz, the University of North Carolina at Chapel Hill, the University of Texas at Austin, and Wayne State University. Thanks to my hosts and interlocutors at all of them for warm receptions, astonishing engagement, and wonderful questions. Similarly, stalwart conference attendees heard and responded to versions of these chapters at the Modern Language Association, the Society for Cinema and Media Studies, the American Studies Association, Visible Evidence, the International Association for Philosophy and Literature, Queer Matters, and Screen. A number of individuals made these adventures in intellectual exchange possible and delightful, among them Brian Price, Lynn Spigel, Jeff Sconce, Max Dawson, Domietta Torlasco, Michael Dwyer, Meghan Sutherland, Steven Cohan, the late and much-missed Alex Doty, Beverly Seckinger, Mary Beth Haralovich, Roger Hallas, Crystal Bartolovich, Janet Jakobsen, Paisley Currah, Patricia Clough, Rich Cante, Angelo Restivo, Tom Conley, Robyn Wiegman, Karen Krahulik, Leisa Meyer, Varun Begley, Shelley Stamp, Peter Limbrick, Patrice Petro,

A. Aneesh, Lane Hall, Janet Staiger, Ann Reynolds, Ann Cvetkovich, and many support-staff members at various institutions. I am grateful to Dean Barbara O'Keefe of Northwestern University's School of Communications for welcoming me to its faculty in the spring of 2008. I also thank the International Graduate Centre for the Study of Culture at Justus Liebig University Giessen, particularly Beatrice Michaelis, Kai Sicks, and Martin Zierold. Jackie Byars invited me to teach the summer doctoral seminar at Wayne State University, convening an extraordinary group of students (to whose thinking I remain gleefully indebted) and making possible a week of fabulous Detroit fun. Amanda Anderson's invitation to teach at the School of Criticism and Theory in the summer of 2012 came at a crucial time and put me in earshot of her laughter and insight for a good six weeks. Students at both Cornell University and Northwestern University and participants and faculty members at the School of Criticism and Theory helped me clarify and refine many of the bits and pieces, though I am alone responsible for what may remain muddied.

Many thanks to Jeff Ruoff for lending me his VHS tapes of *An American Family*, and thanks to Alex Thimons at Northwestern for his conversion prowess. Thanks to Larry Rhodes and his website Tours of the Tales for providing me with *Tales of the City* images.

My editor at Duke University Press, Ken Wissoker, once again provided steady and invaluable encouragement and advice. His friendship and companionship, along with Cathy Davidson's, have become treasures I carry with me wherever I go. In the process of publication, I received two anonymous readers' reports that were uncommonly careful; I relied on their advice in revision and thank them for treating my work with such thoughtful attention. Also at Duke, Elizabeth Ault and Sara Leone gave crucial editorial support. And to my Hunter Rawlings Presidential Scholar and undergraduate researcher extraordinaire, Celine Izsak, I cannot say thank you enough.

Portions of this work have appeared in previous venues, including "Ethereal Queer," in *Queer TV*, edited by Glyn Davis and Gary Needham; "The Halting Grammar of Intimacy: Watching *An American Family*'s Final Episode," in *Political Emotions*, edited by Janet Staiger, Ann Cvetkovich, and Ann Reynolds; "Killing Me Softly: Brazilian Film and Bare Life," in *Beyond Globalization: Making New Worlds in Media, Art, and Social Prac-*

tices, edited by A. Aneesh, Lane Hall, and Patrice Petro; and "Materiality, Pedagogy, and Queer Visibility," in *A Companion to Lesbian, Gay, Bisexual, Transgender, and Queer Studies*, edited by George E. Haggerty and Molly McGarry.

There would be no book at all without the all-around, vital support I have received over the past years from my parents, Don and Merna Villarejo, and from Hope Mandeville. My life in Ithaca is enriched by ongoing conversations with other colleagues, including David Bathrick, Sabine Haenni, Leslie Adelson, Nick Salvato, Sara Warner, Jason Frank, Lucinda Ramberg, Ellis Hanson, and Tim Murray, and many students in and around the gorges. I miss Biddy Martin but think Amherst an even better place thanks to her. I miss Anne Friedberg, who died in 2009, just as I was discovering that I not only loved her extraordinary intellect and scholarship but also had a kindred spirit. To have found a best friend in Alison Van Dyke has been the most glorious gift of increasingly middle age: walking, talking, sharing, and watching with her have sustained me beyond measure, and I am grateful to her for providing me with an aerie of my own in which to complete this book. Alison, you make me happy. And to Andrea Hammer, well, there are no words to describe our journey of survival, strength, recovery, and love. Thank you for being with me.

Conjure some funereal soundtrack to play in the background, a dirge perhaps. Analog television is dead. Long live analog television!

We have passed through the threshold of digital television, to which the entire United States converted on (the arbitrary and much-postponed date of) June 12, 2009. For a period of seventy years, from television's public unveiling at the world's fair of 1939 in New York to the conversion date in 2009, analog represented, in Raymond Williams's phrase, television's dominant "technology and cultural form."[1] Beginning in the mid-1940s, when the Federal Communications Commission granted broadcast bands to commercial television stations, electromagnetic analog signals traveled over the ether, the airwaves, to be plucked by a television antenna and converted into images on the screen by a cathode ray tube. Following the logic developed for the radio broadcast industry, in the Telecommunications Act of 1934, Congress effectively privatized a public resource—our broadcasting spectrum, our shared ether—and handed it to telecommunications monopolies, free of charge. In return, those four networks that define "network television" (DuMont, NBC, CBS, and ABC) accepted social responsibility, called trusteeship, for a public dimension of broadcast service. An enclosure of the commons of the most significant order, this privatizing gesture determines all subsequent understandings of what television might have been, be, or become: its social role, its economic status, its technological form. *Enclosure*, the term used to describe the historical process of private property asserting its right over common land, frequently references a movement ("the enclosure movement") or a moment ("the first enclosure"), but it unfolded over many centuries of what Marx would call "primitive accumulation" and continues today with new forms of enclosure (intellectual property, spectacle, war) in the service of ravenous capitalist expansion.[2]

Taking Williams's triad of social role, economic status, and technological form together: this televisual apparatus would have, by definition, to include mutating formats (that is, a technological field involving what historians of technology might call "perpetual" or "continual" innovation); national, international, and globalizing regulatory and policy frameworks; multiplying systems of delivery as a result of deregulation; and all of the transformations that followed on the anticipated and much-delayed conversion to digital television. Unlike analog signals, as you likely now know given the hoopla the conversion spawned, digital signals generate no interference or "noise," and appear, within the spectrum, as a perfect signal (which, incidentally, analog, low-fi, and alt-practices of many sorts contest). These signals also have the potential, with the increased bandwidth made available to commercial entities, "to provide new kinds of video and data services, such as subscription television programming, computer software distribution, data transmissions, teletext, interactive services, and audio signals, among others. Referred to as 'ancillary and supplementary services' under the Telecommunications Act of 1996, these services include such potentially revenue-producing innovations as stock prices, sports scores, classified advertising, paging services, 'zoned' news reports, advertising targeted to specific television sets, 'time-shifted' video programming, and closed-circuit television services."[3]

Critical media studies confronts this mutating apparatus in order to understand a set of contradictory claims about the representation of gays and lesbians on television in the United States *now*. Either, so the claims go, we're witnessing an explosion of gay TV (at the moment when *Queer Eye* coincided with *Will and Grace*, *Queer as Folk*, *The L Word*, *Project Runway*, and, lest we forget it, *Amazing Race 4*) or gay men and lesbians hardly appear at all. A study of programming for the 2006–7 season, for example, revealed that, out of 679 series regulars on scripted broadcast television, only 9, or 1.3 percent, were LGBTQ people. Well, not even people, really, as two of them appeared on animated comedies (*Drawn Together* and *Freak Show*).[4] Another version of the contradiction now circulating is the provocative claim that while television has always been *queer*, from the schoolteacher humor of Eve Arden in *Our Miss Brooks* to the camp perfection of Tony Randall's version of Felix Unger on *The Odd Couple* to the more contemporary investigation of friendship, intimacy, and masculinity on *Seinfeld*, it has only recently been or become recognizably *gay*. The presumption in some of these accounts is that there is some narrative of homosexual televisual evolution whereby the clandestine has yielded to the overt, the retrogressive has ceded to pride (and the white has blossomed into the multiracial), and so forth. If you would like to see expanded versions of these sorts of understandings of representation under the rubric of visibility politics, turn your attention to two books, Ron Becker's *Gay TV and Straight America* and the anthology *The New Queer Aesthetic on Television*, edited by James Keller and Leslie Stratyner, or to the website of the watchdog media organization, the Gay and Lesbian Alliance Against Defamation (GLAAD), who sponsored the report yielding the statistics on the programming for the 2006–7 season. Concentrating for the most part on analyses of scripted television, and furthermore on characters within series, many of these readings of television as vehicles for LGBTQ inclusion make a number of assumptions I think are, and will endeavor to show in this book to be, simply wrong: that television reflects its viewers; that television *ought* to do so; that it has an *obligation* toward diversity of representation; or that diverse representation leads to political change. One consequence of these assumptions is a set of inflated claims, conflating revolutionary or emancipatory political struggle with the appearance of queer marginalia.[5] One can also detect a certain narrowness of tone in this writing: a lack of irony, an oft-sounded note of nagging insistence or disappointment. (Let me also recognize that exceptions to these tendencies are wonderful, such as the very strong essay in *The New Queer Aesthetic on Television* by Margo Miller, which precisely resists the teleological narrative I've rehearsed in order to argue for a queer frame for television's relentless heteronormativity, or Marcie Frank's book on Gore Vidal, *How to Be an Intellectual in the Age of TV*.)

It may, however, be that it is simply difficult to practice television criticism. Mary Ann Doane (whose work on television time I treat at greater length in chapter 1) notes the difficulty of framing television as an object, its resistance to analysis.[6] Similarly, John Corner has very helpfully argued in an article published more recently in the online journal *Flow* that television presents barriers to academic criticism for several reasons: it lacks the self-conscious critical community of other arts; it necessarily attempts to engage with diverse materials, unlike the more delimited aesthetic-artistic ambitions that are the focus for criticism elsewhere; it presents dangers of subversive or hegemonic diagnoses, whereby critics are "drawn into either polemical opposition or seductive alliance with popular culture"; and, finally, the field qua field encompasses rival claims and methods. Corner suggests that television raises questions of value "of a more openly contested kind" than cinema.[7] We need not accept each of his claims equally: surely television has a self-conscious critical community in its fans; surely television is among the most reflexive of contemporary media. But because television is regarded as "inherently systemic," Corner further argues, judgments of individual programs may suffer from the "baby-with-the-bathwater" dismissal problem: if all of television is of a dubious quality, in other words, then any given program cannot be detached from the suspect whole. The opposite, and equally pervasive claim, is that every element of the system merits close attention and scrutiny for the sake simply of diagnostic analysis: I just reread a piece by Douglas Kellner in a frequently taught collection of essays on television, in which he reminds us that "*Beavis and Butt-Head* is surprisingly complex and requires a diagnostic critique to analyze its contradictory text and effects."[8] Even if it's true, doesn't it sound a bit silly? Similarly, Corner asserts that television is "rightly seen as more pervasively social" than film, "in its range of contents, its modes of address and, of course, the range and character of its delivery to audiences." As a result, television lacks the autonomy that often characterizes the aesthetic object offering itself for critical commentary or contemplation. Let me underscore this consequence. Additionally, Corner observes in television's "generic heterogeneity" a challenge to different disciplinary approaches. If a critic of the humanist stripe wishes to engage with television's "full range of output," he or she confronts those social scientists who would insist upon measuring that output with the data and methods of sociology, political science, or economics. The social scientists, in turn, according to Corner, "are often not hugely impressed by an activity that seems dangerously close to a kind of 'personal phenomenology,' in which media productions are 'read' and judged for their qualities and wider meanings largely in relation to the views, predilections and insights of the critics themselves." Corner ends up wondering how to produce television criticism better both as a discourse of knowledge and as a "discourse of cultural dispute." By this latter phrase, he might mean this: how do we produce television as a domain belonging to a larger set of questions about who we are, and who we are in relation to technics—not simply technology but an ensemble of technology, technique, and techne?

TECHNICS AND TIME ON TELEVISION

Ethereal Queer is just such an attempt to produce television as an autonomous discourse of cultural dispute and thereby to think against these often contradictory discourses of representational justice, identification, and recognition that animate most academic studies of LGBTQ televisual appearance. It is, alternatively, a prehistory of reality TV: an argument that realist paradigms underwrite much of that scholarly work on what appears queer as or on television, paradigms that in turn displace other potential genealogies of inquiry into television as a specific type of system, abstraction, and temporal object that invites reflection on facets other than televisual representation. In still other words, a preoccupation with realist representation forecloses reflection on how TV makes or takes our time.

The first impulse of this book, as the product of various reflections over the years on television, some of which appear in other venues, is to try to analyze the stakes of sexual and gender difference in the variegated history of US television as it now morphs into digital TV (hence, *ethereal* as a phase of television and as its passing). Following this impulse, I propose a more robust and rich sense of the queer archive than that which informs much current writing on TV (Becker, Keller and Stratyner, and so on).[9] There is a lot more going on in this history than the oft-repeated triad of "ignoring, marginalizing, or stereotyping" gay characters.[10]

I find delicious the graphic force of a queer archive that would (and only partially) include *Private Secretary; The Steve Allen Show; The Asphalt*

Jungle; Our Miss Brooks; Father Knows Best;[11] *Rowan and Martin's Laugh-In; All in the Family;* Charles Nelson Reilly; Paul Lynde; Agnes Moorehead (or at least her turn as Endora on *Bewitched*); Lily Tomlin; *Room 222; Sanford and Son; An American Family;* Nancy Kulp; talk television (as detailed in Josh Gamson's wonderful study *Freaks Talk Back*); *Marcus Welby, M.D.; Owen Marshall: Counselor at Law; Hot L Baltimore; Prisoner: Cell Block H; Harry-O; Soap; Maude; Carter Country; The Streets of San Francisco; Starsky and Hutch;* WKRP *in Cincinnati; The Baxters; A Question of Love; All My Children; Out on Tuesday; Cagney and Lacey;* Merv Griffin; *The Naked Civil Servant; The Golden Girls; 21 Jump Street; Thirtysomething;* all of *Melrose Place; Law and Order; Roc; Coach; Cheers; Northern Exposure; The Larry Sanders Show; The Simpsons; South Park; Ellen; Roseanne; Portrait of a Marriage; Oranges Are Not the Only Fruit; Friends; Sex and the City;* news; queer cable-news magazines such as *Network Q*; Martha Stewart (especially when wielding power tools); *Losing Chase; The Kathy and Mo Show; Tales of the City; Kids in the Hall; Strangers with Candy; Dame Edna; Jack and Bobby; Absolutely Fabulous;* Charo; *Coronation Street;* Rosie O'Donnell; documentaries screened on PBS and POV like *Silverlake Life: The View from Here, Serving in Silence: The Margaret Cammermeyer Story, Word Is Out, Silent Pioneers, Coming Out under Fire,* and *Licensed to Kill;* and the recent flurry of niche programming in addition to *Queer Eye; Queer as Folk; The L Word; Boy Meets Boy; Fire Island; Straight, Gay, or Taken?; Ru Paul's Drag Race; Rick and Steve;* and whatever the new channel LOGO digs up alongside *The Big Gay Sketch Show* and *Noah's Ark*. Not that I could tackle all of this stuff, of course, but the list represents a start at stimulating an atrophied form of historical understanding by imagining something other than representational injustice or invisibility.

Simply put, we should first stop claiming that the 1990s brought us gays and lesbians on television for the first time, after fifty years of invisibility or shame. Let's look at some of this material, much of it already compiled systematically (in Steven Capsuto's *Alternate Channels,* for example), and take it seriously as a domain for media criticism and theory. Second, I am particularly interested in elaborating the *apparatus,* the complicated temporal and spatial system that is television, asking how television's changing time and spaces organize and respond to also changing queer times and spaces. This project constitutes the core of *Ethereal Queer*.

Two genealogies inform my method. The first is a line of inquiry, which could be violently shorthanded as poststructuralism that chips away at the problematic of representation. From the Frankfurt School to Deleuze, Heidegger to Derrida and Stiegler, Lacan to Žižek, this body of work, now loosely called "theoretical" in relation to technology, challenges the hermetic, quasi-literary, and often precious approaches to television texts that seem at times to dominate academic protocols. Much of this theoretical landscape has been charted, if asymptotically, by previous scholars; Richard Dienst, for example, devotes pages to many of these thinkers in relation to television in his book *Still Life in Real Time*. But Dienst and other thinkers in this vein, like Samuel Weber, Brian Massumi, and David Rodwick, all too frequently cleave the transmissions that characterize televisual exchange from gendered and sexual life, indeed from much actual television history.[12] To take the second genealogy, following feminist scholars who have been arguing this for some decades now, I treat television as one of the—if not *the* most—gendered and sexualized repetition apparatuses of modern technoscience, *the* modern implantation of gendered and sexualized social time. It is deserving of deeper analyses of its specific function as a technology of sexual becoming and erotic life beyond the terms of *recognition* and *identification* most often used to describe relationships between spectators and particular programs. (I hope you'll see what I mean by *beyond* in each chapter's undertaking.) If much of that feminist work is more admirably historical than this project can be by virtue of my training and interests, I try to hew to its materialist and institutional emphasis, always keeping the forest of the commercial television industry in focus alongside the trees of its particularly shiny or glossy programs.

Ethereal Queer is therefore neither a comprehensive history of "gays and lesbians on American television" nor merely a set of readings of particular programs or episodes showcasing the variety of queer life on planet TV, as delightful or horrific as these may be: famous lesbian kisses on *Roseanne* or *L.A. Law*, for example, or the time Betty White slept with a woman on *The Golden Girls* (which was swell).[13] Instead, the book finds a few nodes of interest for reflection on television's own mode of existence, its way of life (and death). These nodes are located at pivotal moments when the temporality of television changes. I isolate particular rhythms of television and queer time, understanding the conjunction between the ether and queer, neither as unidirectional (as, in one direction, reflection theory would do, or, in the opposite direction, the idea of spectatorial "queering" would accomplish) nor as exactly homomorphic, but rather as coeval, producing a conjoined time. In this stew of temporal orders, textual forms, subjectivies, and identities, I argue for coimplication. On the one hand, in certain cases changing temporal orders on television enable new modes of queer representation. On the other, changing iterations of queerness lead to new televisual forms.[14]

A rather straightforward example of the former comes in chapter 1, "Adorno's Antenna": the four-network grid of 1950s television is founded on stereotypes, not simply as a pejorative form of dismissal but as a necessary shorthand crucial to the organization of social life as and through the "time slot." Understanding the structures of repetition inherent in the stereotype—through the careful and patient work of Theodor Adorno during his time in exile spent watching American television—requires a way of understanding the queer stereotype *as a temporal structure*, a way to register existential and affective connection as well as a form of temporal production of queer life in the 1950s. In subsequent chapters I address the emergence of public television's new rhythms in relation to "coming out" in the 1970s; the development of multichannel video program delivery platforms such as cable and satellite in relation to recursivity and nostalgia; and the switch to digital television through allegories of corporate culture. Adorno's work on the stereotype confirms both the ubiquity of queer representation and the difficulty of extracting images of freedom from these constraining repetitions: I should also make it clear that I don't find liberation per se in the list I've offered of the open-ended archive. By the 1970s, given the development of images of much longer duration (when the grid expanded to accommodate TV movies and multiepisode documentaries produced under the auspices of the then-new PBS), the stereotype persisted but was framed within a new temporal tension, between a flash and more sustained mode of queer appearance. If the queer characters who populated 1950s sitcoms sketch their feyness or butch gestures in broad yet largely inferential strokes, many gay and lesbian characters in 1970s actually proclaim their gayness . . . but only for a second. By the time the grid expanded to the multichannel universe involving recording and time shifting, queer life could involve returns and delays, pauses and rewinds.

Trying to find my way into television's changing mode of existence and peculiar temporalities, I find prerequisite guides in the most perceptive thinkers on *cinema*'s emergence and its reorganization of social life tout court: Miriam Bratu Hansen's readings of Walter Benjamin, Hanns Zischler's reflections on Kafka's encounters with cinema, and Philip Rosen's return to the ontology of the image through Barthes and Bazin, to name a few.[15] But historians of television—both those who take a very broad view of technics such as Siegfried Zielinski and those whose interests are more focused, such as Jeffrey Sconce—are at pains to document television's uneven penetration and historical wildness in comparison to cinema and to note, therefore, the insufficiency of the comparison. Television's national and international genealogies are all over the place; as Zielinski and Sconce both show, televisual processes coincide with those of cinema but also with multiple forms of audiovision, from ghosts to cars to embalming and video recording.[16] Certainly, many of television's foundations and inspirations are shared with those of cinema; in this sense, both exemplify arts of the nineteenth century riding the technologies of the twentieth and now the twenty-first. But many intertwine with broadcast models derived from radio, stressing the capacity of networks and the ether to stitch nations across vast territories (or "wastelands," in Newton Minow's famous phrase describing TV itself as a "vast wasteland"). Television may now be fulfilling its telos as home cinema *and* be turning the model of broadcasting on its ass, sending so many YouTube videos into the digital vortex in a frenzy of passionate production. What I try to balance is the sense in which television is constitutively excessive, frustrating most theoretical attempts to make claims regarding television as a whole (and thereby disappearing from almost all "new media" theory, which leaps from cinema to new media), and the commitment I have had and sustain here to a combination of critical theory and poststructuralism as resources in the critique of identity.

Television history zooms in to examine these uneven parameters of the apparatus's evolution. Television theory, on the other hand, tends to zoom outward, to the broadest possible considerations of television's paradoxical role, the role of technics, in relation to who we are. That paradox might be put as follows: technics, apparently a force or power in the service of humanity, becomes detached, autonomous from the instance it empowers. At the heart of this paradox, for both Bernard Stiegler (whom I read in the theoretical excursus that constitutes the short chapter 2) and his mentor, Derrida, is the relationship between technics and time. What distinguishes modern technics, or techno-logical modernity, is acceleration, speed, instantaneity; what therefore interests both Stiegler and Derrida about television is *liveness*. What is this specifically televisual liveness?

Jane Feuer's "The Concept of Live Television: Ontology as Ideology," as many readers versed in television scholarship will know, anticipates Stiegler's and Derrida's rather delayed musings on televisual liveness by several decades. In that chapter she argues that the less that television is a live medium in the sense of an equivalence between the time of an event and the time of its transmission (and now, with the capacity for "time shifting" via TiVo and DVR recorders, the time of its reception), the more television seems to insist upon the ideology of liveness (the immediate, the direct, the spontaneous, the true).[17] A circuit of mean-ings therefore lodges in the idea of the live, conflating an ideological claim for lack of mediation with a denial of death, with a boastful sense of a technical feat of presence. Or, to put it slightly differently, the "live" both describes the actuality of a convergence between global capital and digital technology *and* the ideological effect of that convergence, which is to mystify the conditions of its own emergence and hegemony. Much television scholarship on the topic of liveness (from work on anthology drama to reality TV) has subsequently been devoted to examining the interventions through which the live is produced as (an) effect, chief among which, still, is the mere declaration that it is so, whether through time coding, announcements from anchors on location, or graphic as-sertions.[18]

Hence my point of departure: the limits of Stiegler's conception of television come in this emphasis on liveness as *simultaneity*: for time on TV is also segmentation, repetition, seriality, frozen, paused, captured, looped, restored, lost, and found. At the core of the book's overall argument is the strong phenomenological claim that we live as and on television, with layers of memory and image consciousness that I will explicate, but that the specificity of the apparatus demands that this "we" be thought of in deeply gendered and sexualized terms. To put it more bluntly, television, each time we watch, takes our time in a way that enfolds all aspects of socialization. Television is time, and television is the modern apparatus casting, to paraphrase Adorno, a "spell of selfhood."[19] In each chapter, I treat a particular and historical organization of both television and queer temporalities, extending phenomenology to the specificity of the apparatus. The limits of Feuer's similar insistence on liveness as ideology come in the relentless motor of ideology critique as the primary rejoinder to the "live effect" that is televisual simultaneity; ideology critique is important, but it is not a sufficient method for moving beyond claims of representational justice. The question in each chapter, therefore, becomes one of understanding more boldly what television can think, what it is possible to think on television, not just about television, for we are "live" as television is, we live life as and through television.

LIVING AS TELEVISION

I spent my childhood in West Los Angeles, a fact that may help in less theoretical and more prosaic terms to explain my conviction that I am TV. Summer afternoons found me on my bike, riding up to the Pronto Market on National Boulevard where, in the parking lot while eating Otter Pops (a delightful form of frozen sugar water), I could regularly watch crews setting up location shoots for television serials. Once a week, in the evenings, I went to guitar lessons on Pico Boulevard, moving from our immediate neighborhood toward other "locations." A cherished family story recalls my five-foot-tall New York Jewish mother running out to the sidewalk to berate a cop putting a ticket on our '68 Dodge Coronet, which she parked legally in the same spot or two each week. Responding to the teeny ball of fury, the "cop," of course, responds: "Lady, lady. I'm an actor, not a cop. Look, look around. We're filming a movie." If you pause, you can catch the glimpse of our car in *The New Centurions*. And at Overland Avenue Elementary School, our courtyard was for a good part of one fine day occupied by Starsky and

Hutch themselves, in a scene every kid in the school strained to recognize in each week's episode.

I'll leave out the *Six Million Dollar Man* field trip, or the time we played Bionic Woman across the street from Lindsay Wagner's house. Or the constant sightings of the Partridge Family bus on the way to day camp. Not to put too fine a point on it, but my world was saturated with television. Even if I was limited by my parents to watching just an hour a day, I was inserted into its rhythms and places, in addition to its schedule.[20] If I had tuned in during the mid-1970s to a specific episode of *Starsky and Hutch* (described in helpful detail in the *TV Guide*, a text one could scour for queer reference), I might have found "Death in a Different Place," from the third season and initially broadcast on October 15, 1977 (when, incidentally, I was fourteen).

I want to notice the richness of this episode before anticipating the work of the subsequent chapters of the book, because it provides one of the best examples I have come across of the synchronization of queer and televisual time as a matter of life and death, that is, as a matter of being or becoming queer dispersed across television's many times. In its exemplarity, it is not, however, unusual in its frank examination of social issues in 1970s prime-time television. What distinguishes it from its companion "gay episodes" may be simply the sheer volume of its gayness: the proliferation of gay characters, sights, sounds, places, and issues seeps into the queerness of the buddy relationship between the two protagonists. By the time the episode is over, everything's queer.

Here is a brief synopsis. "Death in a Different Place," like most investigative dramas, quickly draws a figurative context (a heat wave equals intensified social relations). The corpse of the police lieutenant John Blaine (Art Fleming) was found suffocated in a sleazy apartment in an unspecified red-light district in Los Angeles. Blaine, a father figure to Detective Dave Starsky (Paul Michael Glaser), is last seen with a male hustler, provoking the revelation that he was or had been gay without his figurative son having a clue. Drawn into the mystery of his death and seeking personal resolution, Starsky and companion Detective Ken "Hutch" Hutchinson (David Soul) retrace Blaine's steps, including time spent at a gay bar (the Green Parrot) that features a drag-show performance by Sugar (Charles Pierce), who helps to harbor the suspicious hustler Nick Hunter (Gregory Rozakis) (see figure I.1).

I.1. Starsky and Hutch (ABC, TV series, 1975–79). Shown, from left: David Soul and Paul Michael Glaser. © ABC, courtesy Photofest.

Pierce's performance puts the transvestite back in TV. Involving a mélange of impersonation (Carol Channing, Mae West, Bette Davis) and character-driven bitchiness, Pierce's performance allows the small screen to devote a striking amount of time to queenly behavior in the episode.[21] But it gets better. Blaine, it turns out, had been in a clandestine long-term relationship (outside of his marriage to the stoic Margaret [played by Virginia Leith]) with a man who is an "out" politician. This fictional politician was campaigning, as the real Harvey Milk was in San Francisco, as this episode aired in 1977, linking gayness and political change and synchronizing a significant shift in gay politics. Add in a sequence with Starsky, Hutch, and the series regular and black street informant Huggy Bear (Antonio Fargas) going undercover at the Green Parrot and a bunch of heartfelt dialogue about Blaine's suffering in a homophobic world. The result is that the ambient gayness overwhelms the actual plot revelation of a cocaine-smuggling ring, a cop gone bad, and the lid about to blow (back to our heat wave) for the black Captain Harold Dobey (Bernie Hamilton). The buddy drama condenses all of these plot points into the melodramatic death of a gay man.

The framing of the episode with the title sequence and a coda featuring the eponymous protagonists helps the viewer to shuttle between the regularity of the homosociality in the series and the vitality of a specific gayness that it showcases through this episode. In short staccato beats, the title sequence stages its knowingness and playfulness about the relationship between Starsky and Hutch. Title sequences depend on quick visual cues (including costuming) and catchy music to attract viewers, and they, like stereotypical representations, must condense the look and characterizations of an entire series in a few brief moments. If Starsky first catches Hutch leering at a stripper, then the two soon fall into each other's arms, play on an old western set in cowboy drag, wear further costumes (gangsters, the Marx brothers), play hairstylist, and explode into one another's arms at the end of the sequence.

Seventies fashion is on fabulous display: both men wear impossibly tight and high-waisted jeans, with shirts frequently unbuttoned to reveal their chests. Starsky's sweater has a pronounced shawl collar. (Insofar as fashion always mines its past, we are back to precisely this second: my retro blue Adidas sneakers are exactly the ones Starsky wears, and Earnest Sewn has named one of its styles of jeans "Hutch." The serial was remade, badly, as a feature film in 2004.) In many of these shots in the title sequence, their clothing is highlighted precisely as costume: they are detectives who go undercover (and therefore assume a range of surprising identities), but they are also playful, talented, and mobile. Their homosocial bond recalls cinematic precedents but announces, in its explicitness and knowingness, that this is new ground.

"Death in a Different Place" makes no secret, that is, about the ways in which its gay storylines bleed through the key relationship of the series. Through Pierce's drag performance in the Green Parrot and performance of the character of Sugar, and likewise through the closeted character of John Blaine, the episode reminds its 1970s spectators of a queer past that is very much present in Los Angeles: clandestine bars, hustlers, drag queens, and not a little bit of danger (much of it engineered, as it happens, by the Los Angeles Police Department and Alcohol and Beverage Control Bureau). This gay world is not that of Starsky and Hutch, but neither is it entirely separated, as the two go undercover without trouble (and even with a little flirtation) at the Green

Parrot, and Starsky discovers that his kin bond had been with a gay man. Through another angle on Blaine, however, we meet his longtime boyfriend Peter Whitehead, "a gay candidate for a straight deal," a politicized image and one that beckons beyond the small screen, again contra the insistence that televisual gay and lesbian images "are treated as a purely personal or interpersonal phenomenon, unconnected to larger political realities."[22] Political realities are not, furthermore, external: they are processes of becoming, of change. As surrogates for the spectator, Starsky and Hutch continually evaluate what they know, what they think they know, what they learn, and how they are moved by their encounters with gay people and politics.[23]

Finally there is a short coda in which Hutch drives with Starsky lounging in the backseat (after being framed almost always together as a couple in the front seat), and the episode concludes with an overt dialogue about these processes of queer encounter, where gayness becomes a matter of calculating time:

STARSKY: You'd think in this business you'd get used to surprises.

HUTCH: Well, the day that happens we might as well throw in the towel.

STARSKY: Yeah, well it's still kinda hard to believe.

HUTCH: Starsk, it's no big thing.

STARSKY: Hey, you're not *that* sophisticated! I mean, a man preferring a man is not as casual as someone having a bad cold.

HUTCH: Is that right?

STARSKY: Yeah, I mean, I'm not taking a position for or against it, but it is something to contend with. I mean, it's not your usual everyday thing.

HUTCH: Right.

STARSKY: Hey, you want to get something to eat?

HUTCH: No.

STARSKY: Wouldn't mind something to drink.

HUTCH: Starsk, would you consider that, uh, a man who spends seventy-five percent of his time with another man has got certain tendencies?

STARSKY: Seventy-five percent, you mean three quarters?

HUTCH: Right.

STARSKY: Yeah. Sure. Why not? I mean . . . that was the case between John . . . ?

HUTCH: No. No. It's the case between you and me.

STARSKY: What?!

HUTCH: Well, figure it out. In a five day week, there are about eighty waking hours, right?

STARSKY: Yeah.

HUTCH: We work, eat, and drink about twelve of those hours.

STARSKY: Right.

HUTCH: That's sixty hours a week, seventy-five percent of the time we spend together . . . and you're not even a good kisser.

STARSKY: How do you know that?[24]

When I've shown this episode to students, we struggle to frame it. To what degree is it necessary to have seen the whole series, the whole season, or a few episodes at least to draw conclusions about its representational politics? How should we approach questions of characterization? To what degree was Sugar scripted (or just doing his thing or act)? Why did the writers (or Aaron Spelling and Leonard Goldberg, the producers) feel compelled to introduce a gay story line in the first place? Were they knowingly referencing Harvey Milk? Were Starsky and Hutch "queered" in the initial moment of reception in 1977, seen as queer buddies then as now? Does the episode reference "real" locations (the gay bar, performances) that might contribute to a genealogy of gay life in a particular time and space? And so on.

I see moments of television as helpfully producing these kinds of questions, and I see scholarly value in production histories and studies of broader swaths of television than a single episode as vital ingredients of a critical queer media studies. My own response to "Death in a Different Place" comes from and to a different place, one that is undoubtedly marked by my proximity to its own. I want to affirm the value of this sort of representational range and its limits as a response to the messy gay politics of the 1970s: this was TV responding to and setting value on life, mine included, by demonizing the murder of queers, by showcasing political responses to injustice, by "humanizing" straight responses to gay revelation through its stars (and it should be noted that Paul Michael Glaser became famous a second time through his wife's pediatric AIDS foundation). This was TV catalyzing a reconfigured relationship to femininity, if it did so entirely through "male" characters (a hustler, a drag queen, a candidate, a "father"). And this was TV offering me, a queer kid, the pleasure in some gay humor about these "buddies." This is not all about pleasure and fandom, however. This is about what sets us to work, what brings us to the table, so that we can follow the leads that make our (work) lives possible. As I watch this episode over and again (time shifting more than thirty years via DVD), I return, actually, to Sugar. I return, that is, to the violence *and* possibility of stereotypes, shorthands, false eyelashes, lots of mascara. I return to the queen, and, so, to the task of generating questions to begin to think about our lives on and as television. Let me summarize what follows.

"ADORNO'S ANTENNA"

Inspired by a strong emphasis on the evanescent and luminous nature of the temporal object that is television, I embrace the opportunity to reflect more deeply on the changing temporal structures of television in the United States. I seek in each of this book's chapters to elaborate the complicated temporal (and spatial) system that is television over the past seventy years, asking how television's time and spaces have organized and responded to queer times and spaces, and, in turn, how queer modes of becoming, being, and surviving have been televised. But I am hesitant, in chapter 1 (which I will sketch here) and throughout, to embrace the generalized academic-speak rubric of "time and space" tout court, for the perhaps obvious reason that it becomes a meaninglessly huge abstraction. Second, as I discuss at some length in the opening section of chapter 2, these form, in Deleuze's terms, a "badly analyzed composite," one rendered infinitely richer and nuanced when treated instead through the concepts of duration and what Bliss Cua Lim calls "immiscible time," by which she means heterogeneous time, or that which resists blending into (what, in turn, Walter Benjamin calls) empty, homogeneous time.[25] Third, and equally substantive, diverse scholarship enveloped by the capacious term *queer temporalities* — by turns clever and eager, reductive and breezy — has emerged and, for me, is listing uncomfortably toward the literary tides of hermetic readings and bracketed reference. Wanting to right this promising ship, a desire accompanied by a profound respect for a fledgling mode of inquiry, leads me to summarize the emerging work in this field in chapter 1, ultimately returning to, rewinding, and replaying Adorno's contributions to understanding the time of queer stereotypes in the 1950s.

Elizabeth Freeman's introduction to a foundational GLQ issue on queer temporalities helpfully glosses divergent strands of thought encompassed in this emergent literature. In the most capacious sense, *queer temporality* gestures toward "a set of possibilities produced out of temporal and historical difference," or "a manipulation of time to produce bodies and relationalities."[26] Within this ample view, time can feel embodied. The rhythms and segmentations naturalized through institutions (as Foucault would say, through implantation) become legible as effects of power and might be regridded through new schemes of affect, eroticism, and embodiment. The manipulation of time (say through surprise, shock, or elongated and slow coaxing) might reorganize body politics and sexual relations.

It is important also to note how powerfully sexuality as a field incorporates contradictory temporal models—for example, how psychoanalysis relies on a teleological model of sexual development toward heterosexual reproduction, while that other part of Freud (the part we like more) notices how, as Freeman puts it, "the past is unlikely to remain in the past."[27] Queer theorists pry open new routes for sexual and erotic life by embracing this untimeliness (uncanniness, delay, belatedness, and failure) as well as objects that might seem outside of history's march (ephemera, gossip, found objects, and so on). Reproduction, an insistent paradigm for organizing the movement of time, yields to affiliation, intergenerationality with or without offspring, lateral modes of relation. On the far end of the polemical scale, Lee Edelman refuses futurity itself, understanding it as a necessarily reproductive orientation.[28]

Not all of this work strikes me as helpful: at moments, it can look as though all nonsynchronous, discontinuous, nonteleological, or immiscible time is folded without further elaboration into the category "queer." What is striking from my perspective about these recent discussions is the almost total absence of the dominant system of temporal implantation of the past seventy years, that is, TV. (I say "almost total," because Dana Luciano's great article in GLQ on Todd Haynes's film *Far from Heaven* at least remembers for us that the husband struggling with gay desire, Frank, is a television sales executive.[29])

Absent from these queer discussions is a rich library in television studies and reflections on technology that would help to refine the specific overlap or encounter between queerness and temporality. Doane's aforementioned writing on catastrophe finds a convergence between failures of technology and resulting confrontations with death, insofar as live broadcasts of catastrophe do the very work of denaturalizing everyday logics and rhythms that these queer theorists find strategically compelling.[30] Jeff Sconce's already mentioned excavation of the fictions long accompanying the development of media technology finds fantasies of disembodiment alongside television's hyperinsistence upon presence in liveness and what he calls television's "unbordered empire of flow."[31] Elizabeth Grosz develops a concept of temporality not under the domination or privilege of the present; instead she focuses on becomings, including our becoming in relation to technological prostheses.[32] Examples could be multiplied. Synchronization, transmission, seriality, recursivity, pause and delay, rewind, repeat: how does television time organize, disrupt, or otherwise confront queer temporalities? How too does queer history, or in Carolyn Dinshaw's phrase, the queer desire for history, meet television history?

Adorno's writings in the 1950s certainly have, as though by the crankiest of gatekeepers, been reluctantly admitted to a canon of critical approaches to television studies.[33] But while they have been admirably situated, contextualized, historicized, and otherwise consigned to the past, nowhere have they been revived or exhumed in the service of particularly queer critical theory today. The work of chapter 1 is to begin the process of noticing how attuned Adorno's antenna was to gendered and sexual life on TV and how that awareness alerts us to the specific transmissions between television and queer life, particularly in the 1950s. While television in the United States has continuously obeyed the prime mandates of capitalist organization, and while the privatization of the airwaves has long been a matter of contention and state intervention, it remains imperative—and very much in the spirit of Adorno's work—to mark those occasionally contradictory, incoherent, and ancillary effects of privatization that cannot be captured merely by noting its industrial nature. These effects were keenly felt in the 1950s, the decade of television's most spectacular growth and consolidation in the United States, particularly the period from 1953 to 1955, when Adorno undertook his study of television programming. "How to Look at Television" was published in the *Quarterly of Film, Radio and Television*.[34] His article, like this book, is a study almost exclusively of American television, with all of the complications such a focus brings.

"Adorno's Antenna" revisits *Our Miss Brooks* and its queer stereotypes, for this was of course the program that inspired Adorno's writing, though it is nowhere mentioned by name. Curling around his key concept, realism, is a set of assumptions about how television's gendered and sexual stereotypes constrain freedom. Pseudorealism, one of those perverse critical coinages of Adorno's that doesn't on the face of it help matters, seems to him to be the core operation of televisual representation, essentially reflecting back to the viewers an image of their imprisonment. Vigilance in relation to stereotypes, for him, is a practice of negation, a bid for freedom: these are the crucial concepts he developed for critical theory. Curiously, these stereotypes are largely to do with feyness and butchness, as well as with domesticated femininity. (I say "curiously" because the Adorno I thought I knew didn't seem to write much about queers, and because the 1950s television world I thought I knew wasn't populated with them either.) What concerns me is the stereotype within the form of the time slot, that is, the constraints upon *sustained* queerness as a form of social life. Glimpses, furtive glances, shorthand, visual cues, slang: all of these elements of brevity and staccato appearance structured queer life in 1950s America. The question that the chapter ultimately poses is how to gain critical purchase on these elements as miniaturized or pseudo (rather than *only* maligned negative or pejorative) aspects of being and of being on television.

"EXCURSUS ON MEDIA AND TEMPORALITY"

Rather than embed extensive theoretical reflections on television temporality in each chapter, this excursus forms a bridge between my reading of Adorno and network television and subsequent chapters on public television, cable, and digital platforms. I'm primarily interested in elaborating a fairly strong version of the claim that we are television, resources for which I find in the Heideggerian phenomenological tradition, taken up in the inspirational and quirky volume R/U/A/TV? through to Derrida and Stiegler, and, quite differently, in the Bergsonism taken up by Deleuze. In the former line of inquiry, I read the third volume of Stiegler's *Technics and Time*, in which he elaborates, following Edmund Husserl, a phenomenology of the temporal object. Although his strength seems to me to lie in understanding cinematic temporality, he alludes to the workings of a much larger audio-visual field that he calls variously television, "cine-television," and so on. In reading his work, I find support for a theory of time-consciousness appropriate to the merging of the self with television. In the second line of thought, which I don't treat explicitly in chapter 2, Bergson's work on duration forms the core archive. In *Time and Free Will*, Bergson famously elaborates a conception of duration as ineffable, grasped only intuitively. While there is much to distinguish his vitalist philosophy from the poststructuralist phenomenology of Stiegler, the two share an interest in the convergence of consciousness with technology, the fusion of the "we" and our object. My aim is to give the reader a brief but substantive understanding of the theoretical frame that undergirds this book, without overloading already-dense chapters with (to me invaluable) philosophical questions, always returning to the question of who we are in relation to television.

In this brief chapter, I examine who we are in relation to other temporal objects: theater, digital art, and cinema. In encountering them, I differentiate the experience of televisual time from that of other media *and* reframe the following chapters as extensions of a theoretical conversation begun in existential phenomenology and continuing through French poststructuralism.

"'TELEVISION ATE MY FAMILY': LANCE LOUD ON TV"

Being on television has almost always involved being in a family. Moving from the three-channel flow of network programming to an environment enlarged by a fourth channel, the introduction of a deliberately alternate idiom via public television (PBS) in 1970, chapter 3 makes more explicit the ways that television shapes temporal conceptions of the family, as television similarly tackled the family head on, and, in turn, the ways that ideas about family and kinship shape conceptions of television. Reproduction, affiliation, intergenerationality, custody, pedagogy: all of these march to queer time on TV in the 1970s. And while much queer delight has rightfully focused on the 1960s—*Bewitched*, anyone?—my own antennae are tuned more to the effects that social movements of the 1960s actually had on television in the 1970s and how the consolidation of public television institutionalizes these effects structurally. Following the infamous Moynihan Report (which scapegoated strong black women for the problems of "the black family"), television programming in the 1970s relentlessly pursued revisions on and of familial life. Television retooled the sitcom and elaborated the family via miniseries such as *Roots* ("the saga of an American family") and *An American Family*. The latter, a documentary, and reality serial, becomes in large measure this chapter's focus, showing how television stretched its remit to forms of family life, including gay teenagers, occluded from television's previous representational politics. This chapter is not, however, an homage to so-called more inclusive television lifeworlds; it is rather an argument that seriality, an emergent structure for television storytelling (borrowed from the soap opera, as much as from direct cinema as well as from cinematic models), in this decade transformed the calibration of queer life and death by introducing questions of duration. Let me be plain on this and as anti-Whiggish (that is, against the notion of history as inevitable progress toward greater liberty and enlightenment) as possible: television did not get better and better; it got longer and longer. The first miniseries to air on American television, *The Forsyte Saga* (broadcast in the United States in 1969), set the stage for enormous transformations in public television in the decade to follow.

During the 1970s, overtly gay characters also began to appear on prime-time network television, as it obeyed the capitalist command to penetrate ever more deeply into American domestic life: they appeared as criminals, cousins, aunts, teachers, friends, neighbors, drinking buddies, coaches, and other tentacles to familial domesticity. It's not that they hadn't been there before; it's that they became characters rather than types, members of television families or teachers of their children rather than anonymous clerks and hairdressers. Prime-time sitcoms and drama showcased mostly one-off queer characters and a couple of recurrent ones throughout the decade: on *All in the Family* and its spin-off, *Maude*, and on *Room 222, Sanford and Son, Marcus Welby, M.D., Owen Marshall: Counselor at Law, The Streets of San Francisco, Harry-O, Hot L Baltimore*, and, of course, *Soap*, because it transformed the model of daytime soaps into a success featuring a recurring gay character. In the Norman Lear–produced vehicles (which included *All in the Family, The Jeffersons*, and *Maude* but also *Sanford and Son, One Day at a Time*, and *Good Times*), gayness becomes topical, as au courant as the Vietnam War, civil rights, feminism, the counterculture, and drug use. But even in those (self-consciously progressive) productions, most prominently *All in the Family*, television began to offer a more sustained meditation on queer attachment.

Through the character of the female impersonator Beverly La Salle, *All in the Family* erected a four-part ode to queer loss, when Beverly (a character who had appeared in two episodes, "Archie the Hero" and "Beverly Rides Again"), in the two-parter "Edith's Crisis of Faith," is brutally murdered at Christmastime (circa 1977, the same moment as my *Starsky and Hutch* episode). More than Edith's "Cousin Liz" (the title of an episode that treated the aftermath of Edith's lesbian cousin's death), "Edith's Crisis of Faith" probes the effects of homophobic violence on familial forms of love. Queer characters acquire density and, more significant, history: even in death, they leave pasts behind. To be sure, the sitcoms and dramas of the 1970s continued to trade in stereotypes, but they also circulated more lingering and intimate glimpses of queer lifeworlds for those viewers lucky enough—because there were no recording devices—to happen upon them. (A year later, in 1978, I stayed home one day from school, faking illness, to watch a made-for-TV movie, *A Question of Love*, advertised in the television listings as a "lesbian custody" topical film, just to see what these lesbians, one of them memorably played by Gena Rowlands, would do and say and feel and look like. It's not just to say that the stakes are high; it's that these contortions are so weird yet so regular and banal that I made myself "sick" to verify my becoming gay, giving myself over, as it were, to the custody of TV.)

One such sustained glimpse came in 1973 in the series *An American Family*, a breakthrough television event for PBS. Having set the context for seventies television through the sitcom and prime-time dramatic treatment of the family, I devote the subsequent bulk of the chapter to seriality as queer time in the 1970s through an analysis of the historical place of PBS and its determinations upon textual form. I am interested not in realism but in the meshes of the real, where the indexical traces surface through these ethereal transmissions, where specters haunt in the coincidence of televisual and queer time. Television's transformations in this decade—insofar as it spectacularized domestic life through these two serials, *Roots* and *An American Family*—actually may have led to transformative rubrics for gender and sexual becomings. That is, *An American Family* may have actually inspired the gay movement's new political rallying cry: come out (which I did in that decade and still do). I stress the importance of broadcast time, of the synchronization of television with perceptual bodies, with growing up and its rhythms and perceptions. I didn't see *An American Family* until recently (2007), when Jeffrey Ruoff, the author of a fine monograph on the series (*An American Family: A Televised Life*), lent me his VHS tapes. By the time I got to see him, Lance Loud, the queer protagonist of the series, was dead.

But oh how he lived on and as television! If "reality TV" was not yet the mode of production it has become (providing cheap fodder for the ever-expanding grid), *reality* was nonetheless the key term around which debates spun regarding *An American Family*. Would Pat and Bill have divorced had the cameras not been there? Did Lance come out on television or was he out all along? How representative was this American family of the aggregate? Or was it possible that the Louds were chosen for their *particular* forms of banality, excess, and indulgence? Where does responsibility lie in producing this sort of intimate and proximate television? The questions proliferate. By a long shot, the most contentious response to *An American Family* comes from Jean Baudrillard, who puts the series as the centerpiece of his book *Simulations*: the Louds exemplify what Baudrillard calls the "hyperreal," the realm of pure simulation, shorn of substance.[35] Lance, in his flamboyant gayness, signified even more excessively: he was a figure not only of hyperreality but of the death drive, the relentless path toward destruction.

I take the series up to its final moment, its final part: *Lance Loud: A Death in an American Family*, shot in 2001–2 and broadcast in 2003, a return of this American family to television after a thirty-year hiatus. As Ruoff and the few others who have written at length on *An American Family* have shown, the mode of production for the series, borrowed in part but not in whole from direct cinema, was artisanal, dependent on close relations between the makers and their subjects. The filmmakers (the husband and wife team of the Raymonds) and the Louds remained friends for the thirty years between the original broadcast and Lance's death, which he requested that they document and air as closure to and for the Louds' drama. I look closely at how the ostensible moment of Lance's coming out is constructed as a retrospective fiction, driven by the changing discourses of gay liberation, human rights, and queerness over the three decades of the seventies, eighties, and nineties, respectively. In seeing how the Raymonds shaped these fourteen hours of television (including the "final episode") from more than three hundred hours of footage, we see how new forms of queer reality and new forms of family emerged by virtue of the new horizon that was public broadcasting.

"QUEER ASCENSION: TELEVISION AND TALES OF THE CITY"

Chapter 4 uses a single series to examine the effects of new forms of sexual regulation and consequent experimentation that appear with pay cable television and its attendant time shifts. *Tales of the City*, a six-episode ensemble-cast miniseries, produced by Britain's Channel Four, Working Title Film, and Propaganda Films, debuted on PBS's *American Playhouse* on January 10, 1994. It's worth noting its British origins, in that Channel Four risked production without an American buyer, while PBS acquired the series cheaply and without jeopardy. The miniseries ran on three consecutive nights for two hours per night, earning spectacular ratings (averaging 4.3 with a 7 share) for a PBS-aired drama and in San Francisco remarkably surpassing ABC, CBS, and NBC. Two sequels, *More Tales of the City* and *Further Tales of the City*, contributed an additional twelve episodes in 1998 and 2001, respectively. They aired on Showtime, a point to which I return. *Tales of the City* also sparked outrage for its explicitness and provocations: the Georgia State Senate passed a nonbinding resolution demanding that the state's affiliates "cease airing it and never air it again," while a bomb threat in Chattanooga "emptied the local PBS affiliate the first night the show aired."[36] Based on the gay writer Armistead Maupin's column "Tales of the City," initially published in a now-defunct paper called the *Pacific Sun* and later in the more widely circulated *San Francisco Chronicle* (and later collected as serial novels), the drama follows a group of characters who converge at 28 Barbary Lane in San Francisco, a fictional address that cites the Barbary Coast, a real San Francisco neighborhood known by the beginning of the twentieth century as a hotbed of perversion, as well as prostitution, gambling, and crime.

Everything I have just described is recursive, about rewinding, re-circulating, pauses, and delays. For readers of the *Pacific Sun*, Maupin's stories of gay life in San Francisco offered a kind of running commentary, a permanent parabasis, an alternative reality to heteronormativity widely circulated elsewhere. Collected as serial novels, the stories began to generate nostalgia for readers who encountered them in the 1980s, as AIDS ravaged the very utopia traversed by the two main characters, Mary Ann Singleton and Michael "Mouse" Tolliver, in Maupin's *Tales of the City*. By the time the tales reached the small screen, the nostalgic tinge was impossible to suppress, and the melodrama began to appear more fanciful, more detached, from the lives it initially sought to document. *Tales of the City* was a period piece, and on television it moved from sentimental drama (on PBS) to sexually explicit fare for gay men (on Showtime). Chapter 4 documents the bridge from one to the other, stressing the architectures of queer life in each form.

If the previous chapters will have essentially stressed television's relentless domesticity, its focus on intimate relations and the family, this chapter stretches its focus slightly outward to understand how these televisual domestic spaces are impossibly carved (that is, they are imagined and conjured) from complicated social-spatial urban relations and migrations. In particular, dividing the chapter into four sections—walls, sidewalks, staircases, and windows—I am interested in these Western representations of queer urban life, tales of the city, that seem to celebrate the normative ideal of modern city life at the very moment when many of the world's cities abandon it. Queer cinematic and postcolonial images from the beginning of the twenty-first century largely anatomize conditions of migration and urban publicness that radically oppose the sense of bounty and happy gayness on offer in *Tales of the City*: *Macho Dancer* (directed by Lino Bracka 1988), *The Blossoming of Maximo Oliveros* (directed by Auraeus Solito, 2006), *A Thousand Clouds of Peace* (directed by Julián Hernández, 2004), *Bomgay* (directed by Riyad Vinci Wadia, 1996), and *Wild Side* (directed by Sébastian Lifshitz 2004). These kinds of analyses and alternative genealogies not of "the city" as un-differentiated urban space but of cities under siege, cities to which we are umbilically linked in global networks, powerfully chart the fraying of normative ideals of modern city life. These ideals include a sense of openness, fluidity, and coexisting unassimilated differences. These cities under siege are, to borrow Teresa Caldeira's book title, cities of walls.[37]

Historians and geographers have recently begun to chart specific his-tories of our gay cities — New York, San Francisco, London — to oppose those normative ideals from other directions, emphasizing the com-plexity of movement for queer people to and through the cities of the global North. George Chauncey, Matt Houlbrook, Morris Kaplan, and others demonstrate that the sexual binarism represented by the homo-hetero distinction is an astonishingly recent creation, distorting the cir-culation of many forms of queerness through the modern city (move-ment I designate as "sidewalks").[38] These scholars' explorations of the city and sexual difference emphasize how the nomenclature of *gay* oc-cludes the variety in types of sexual actors and practices of the twen-tieth century and leads to the misconceptions wrought by continuist history. Chauncey insists, contra the kind of history that assures us of progress across the march of time, that "gay life in New York was *less* tolerated, *less* visible to outsiders, and *more* rigidly separated in the sec-ond third of the century than the first, and that the very severity of the postwar reaction has tended to blind us to the relative tolerance of the prewar years."[39]

Sexual and spatial practices also converge along a number of social forms. Houlbrook alone lists "modern forms of expert knowledge, mu-nicipal government, the urban crowd, a mass media, consumerism, new understandings of selfhood, economic change, and the separation of public and private space."[40] Both Houlbrook and Chauncey invoke sexual topographies as practices or "tactics by which gay men appro-priated spaces not identified as gay," and also as forms of inscription, counter-mapping or cognitive mapping: "maps etched in the city streets by daily habit."[41] (Henri Lefebvre would similarly distinguish among spatial practices, representations of space, and representational spaces.)

Chauncey and Houlbrook are wonderful guides to queer cities, but despite declarations to the contrary, they are not particularly inter-ested in gender, much less women, much less transgender. What is remarkable, to me, about *Tales of the City* is that it rewrites the history of the queer city through transgendered melodrama, following Mary Ann more closely than Mouse, and focalizing almost of all of the show's intrigue on the mother of Barbary Lane, the captivating and enchanting Anna Madrigal (played by Olympia Dukakis and her alluring upper lip). To return to the central question of queer temporality, I argue that *Tales of the City* relies on its recursive return to the secret of Anna Madrigal (whose name is an anagram for the revelation — shall I give it away? — "a man and a girl") in order to reformulate a political trajectory. *Tales of the City* returns us not to "gay men," "the Castro," "sex before HIV/AIDS," or "the seventies" but to queerness as a televisual topography and temporality of expansive gendered and sexual relationality. The most insistent trope for that figuration is the staircase, relied upon to build Barbary Lane's web of connections but also to signal flights into the utopian clouds of the queer imaginary. Ascension as transgender telos!

The Showtime sequels, by contrast, build menace into their stairwells, whether in the investigation into Burke Andrew's amnesia in *More Tales of the City* (in which a staircase figures with Hitchcockian vertigo) or in the rebirth of Jim Jones, the architect of the Jonestown massacre, who is found to be alive and well and living in Golden Gate Park in *Further Tales of the City*. Showtime's willingness to take on the controversial serial is narrated as bravery: PBS shies away from scandal, and cable — O the brave new representational order! — steps in to complete the cliffhanger begun four years earlier. But there is a difference in spirit between the first series and its sequels that is difficult to explain without recourse to changes in the apparatus and in policy with the entry of multichannel program-delivery platforms. This is a change so significant that Amanda Lotz perhaps didactically insists that ad-based and subscriber-based contexts be as resolutely separated as possible in institutional analyses: "Accounting for institutional features may not be central to textual analyses, but even examinations of programs must acknowledge variant institutional contexts in a way that makes comparisons across situations problematic. The institutional certainly does not resolutely determine the textual, but it provides a significant feature that evaluations too often under-emphasize."[42] The last part of this chapter tries to detect this textual difference in the niche conception of audiences held by a corporate entity such as Showtime.

Ethereal Queer closes with an evaluation of queer futurity insofar as it will have traveled through digital circuits. While there is a great deal of hand-wringing and celebrating about digital culture, I try to situate the morphing apparatus of television again within the terms of new forms of enclosure with which I began, now closing with a meditation on melodrama as a form. If Dienst's signal contribution in *Still Life in Real Time* came in his observation that television contributes to what Antonio Negri would call real or total subsumption (in which capitalist social relations subsume all aspects of social life, so that even our capacity to pay attention becomes commodified), the challenge now is to imagine life through and in those channels in new ways.[43] The proliferation of content production through the platform YouTube, the mobility of content from platform to platform, the capacity of capitalist media to exploit new synergies and technologies: all of these indisputably will change our use and experience of television. In this conclusion, however, I am more interested in how television is already allegorizing these changes, and so I conclude with a brief speculation about the ways in which televisual melodrama reflects on the past and our future.

CHAPTER 1

Adorno's Antenna

I was giving up—*being realistic*, as people liked to say, meaning the same thing. Being realistic made me feel bitter. It was a new feeling, and one I didn't like, but I saw no way out.
—Tobias Wolff, *This Boy's Life: A Memoir*

For Theodor Wiesengrund Adorno, the "culture industry"—the unified, centralized, and highly administered system of early to mid-twentieth-century industrial production of mass culture, including print media, film, radio, and television—never appeared in its own right as an object of analysis. Instead, Adorno posed the *question* of the culture industry, as one of his editors puts it, from "the perspective of its relation to the possibilities for social transformation[,] . . . its potentialities for promoting or blocking 'integral freedom.'"[1] The disciplinary location of the subject and critic is therefore implicated in the form of appearance of the object of analysis, since both the subject and object are products of the same alienating effects of capitalist subsumption. In his writings in German and in English, with Max Horkheimer and other collaborators or alone, Adorno stressed the necessity for the dialectical analysis of autonomous art and mass culture, the necessity of thinking culture within larger rubrics of philosophy and politics to challenge the status quo, and the necessity for criticism as an essential component of cultural production. In this chapter I read closely and sympathetically one of Adorno's essays that is preoccupied with gender and sexual representation, "How to Look at Television," from the vantage point of current cultural criticism that addresses queer appearance.[2] This article is anthologized and read far less widely than *The Culture Industry* or Adorno's essay on music, "On the Fetish-Character of Music and the Regression of Listening."[3] My goal is, as his was, to urge the possibility of negation, of saying no to what is. If realism and representation regulate the terms of that negation, Adorno may have offered us, more than a half century ago, the tools we need for a change and the mechanisms we need to understand the peculiar forms of time and life that dominated television shortly after its widespread adoption. Both television theory and critical theory are transformed in the interaction.

Writing about more-recent organizations of these televisual forms of life in the guise of "liveness," Mary Ann Doane begins her observations in "Information, Crisis, Catastrophe" with an apparently simple truism: "The major category of television is time."[4] In what sense? First, time is television's "principle of structuration," in Doane's words, insofar as television's flow is segmented into changing rhythms and patterns (from the fifteen-minute time slot to the droning or mesmerizing presence of uninterrupted footage).[5] For Doane, however, this principle of structuration penetrates or organizes modes of apprehension; this is one of the signal contributions of her important article. In naming these "information," "crisis," and "catastrophe," Doane attends to the ways in which constancy (steady presence, flow), condensation (decision, resolution), and instantaneity (the moment, the punctual) characterize the three respective organizations of the televisual event. Historically, multiple and varying temporalities have structured televisual time.[6] There is no reason not to extend Doane's thinking beyond the largely nonfiction and news domain that she believes marks a limit case of television temporality, for there exist multiple temporal structures even within something as naturalized and seemingly synchronized and serialized as a situation comedy, which is the dominant form referenced in Adorno's article. The audience's familiarity with recurring characters creates a constancy that corresponds to Doane's category of information, a flow of time across episodes, in which the spectator will bring habits, traits, appearances, histories, past actions, familial associations, relationships, and whatnot across the dead time that composes the interval between episodes; in this way, the sitcom may be a form that embalms its own past. Likewise, guests and minor characters occupy less screen time than their recurrent counterparts and are frequently consigned to playing for type, condensing a lived past into a panoply of signifying data, whether through appearance, costuming, gesture, or dialogue. Here we are in the realm of stereotypes, where brevity, instantaneous recognition, caricature, shorthand, innuendo, and the like must interact with more fully developed or familiar characters in the funny rhythms that the genre promises. I am not trying to shoehorn Doane's tripartite and careful distinctions into a description of the sitcom. Rather, because I attend more deeply to the sitcom's particular rhythms in what follows, I am merely appreciating, thanks to her, that multiple temporalities already permeate televisual forms (in the plural). One of the consequences of so apprehending forms other than the event (seen as nonfiction and news) is that we can understand the broader crisis of temporality that television seeks to manage as attaching to degraded or trivialized images.[7]

I seize on insights from Adorno that betray some similarity to Doane's recognition of the structure of the event: for him, there is a crisis of living even, or perhaps especially, in brief comedies about alienated schoolteachers and their cats. ("Gets me where I live," I can't help but respond, schoolteacher of a sort that I am, and with cats of course! But this is precisely the point.) His work has been too coolly assigned to the realm of an unceasing and undifferentiated critique. As Robert Miklitsch puts it, in his inventive reading of Adorno in *Roll over Adorno*, a dismissive tone in scholarly criticism renders Adorno either outmoded or frozen in the past: "Adorno and Co., with their programmatic, for some unremitting, stress on the dire machinations of the culture industry, seem absurdly out of touch with the times, imprisoned like so many Madame Tussauds wax figures in the now outdated critical dress of the period, but without the endless trivial pursuit possibilities of retro or kitch appropriation."[8] Arguing as strenuously as I can to the contrary, I think that Adorno may represent a figure who can mine the real and persistent dislocations of modern life, who may be more prescient than we have believed.

In this regard, I value David Jennemann's contention, following the late Edward Said, that Adorno indeed gestures "toward a future where everyone is brought together by their alienation."[9] Jennemann, in his study *Adorno in America*, recognizes how intimately Adorno interacted with popular culture during his time, almost a decade, in exile in America: "To dismiss Adorno as politically and socially detached is also to misunderstand how thoroughly he immersed himself in America's myriad forms of entertainment and communication."[10] The work of this chapter is to begin the process of bringing the wax figures, as it were, to life, noticing how attuned Adorno's antenna was to gendered and sexual life on TV and how that awareness alerts us to the specific transmissions between television and queer life in the 1950s.

TUNING IN

Measuring the distance between Adorno's moment and our own is a project made difficult by the domestication, institutionalization, and demonization of Adorno's writings on culture. I seek neither to rescue nor to condemn his writings but instead to understand them within the context of present political struggles over representation; I take heart in Jennemann's similar desire to rediscover Adorno's actual inter-action with the products and practices of American popular culture as a means of calculating his continuing significance. Emphatically, I do not see Adorno as a kind of extreme theorist, outmoded and inatten-tive to cherished chunks of mass culture (as he was frequently alleged to be by those who seek to defend particular programs he is seen to dismiss). I am against reductions of Adorno's conceptions of the cul-ture industry, and I hope to open routes for further analysis of tele-vision throughout the past sixty years in subsequent chapters.[11] With this chapter's title, particularly by invoking the antenna that received ethereal signals during the era of broadcast network television, I mean to capture a first sense of differentiation in the form of historically situ-ating Adorno's article. I do this with the conviction that historicizing is in this case a necessary but by no means sufficient methodological step. Fredric Jameson suggests as much, presuming, however, the change I seek to explain:

> The Archimedean point of view of some "genuinely aesthetic experi-ence" from whose standpoint the structures of commercial art are critically unmasked has thus disappeared; what has not disappeared, however, is still the ancient philosophical problem of true and false

happiness (from Plato to Marcuse) and whether watching thirty-five hours a week of technically expert and elegant television can be argued to be more deeply gratifying than watching thirty-five hours a week of 1950s-type "Culture Industry" programming.[12]

While Jameson here underscores the shift from a modernist capacity to distinguish autonomous from commercial art to a postmodern immersion in simulation and spectacle, there are other ways to mark the movement from Adorno's moment to this one: in terms of the location of critical theory in the postwar context and in terms of television itself. A word about the former is crucial: Adorno's time in the United States, from 1938 to 1949, was experienced by him as a period of traumatic exile and alienation. (Let me note that Adorno composed "How to Look at Television" during the period from 1952 to 1953, when he returned to California to serve as research director for an institute run by the psychologist William Hacker.[13]) In California both during the initial period of his exile and upon his return for a year, he found himself sunk in a community and society dominated by mass media and its institutions, Hollywood foremost among them. His view that modern mass society tends toward totalitarianism and authoritarianism strengthened as he witnessed the almost seamless integration of high culture with mass entertainment, specifically film and television.

In this first section, I mean to distinguish between the kind of television that Adorno was watching and trying to understand when he wrote "How to Look at Television," broadcast television of the mid-century (centralized, limited to network channels, picked up through the ether via an antenna on a home set) and the digital spectrum on offer in the household and in public spaces through the five-hundred-channel world, perhaps on a plasma, liquid crystal display (LCD), or light-emitting diode (LED) screen, of the current moment.[14] Just as it is true, by way of a qualification, that not every household in the United States currently subscribes to satellite delivery or digital-cable services, it is also true that variability between receivers or television sets in the 1950s led to significant differences in the experience of television reception. It is not an easy task, in other words, to characterize using Jameson's very general terms, the distance between that "culture industry" programming and the ostensibly elegant flow of today's television, since the phenomenon of television, its physiognomy (to use one of Adorno's terms), is itself varied. Yet, despite significant historical, phenomenological, and cultural similarities between the television of then and now, there nevertheless remain a number of equally significant differences between midcentury television and early twenty-first-century technologies that particularly influence Adorno's take on television in his article.

I emphasize those differences because our cumulative historical knowledge of television—understood, as Raymond Williams again puts it in order to stress the multidimensional nature of an apparently simple noun, as "technology and cultural form"—tends to obscure them.[15] In left-sympathetic cultural histories of television, the narrative of evolution emphasizes television's commercial nature throughout its brief history. Adorno was palpably aware of how the domestic space of the home and the family was becoming a site for immense productive capitalist labor. These effects were keenly felt in the 1950s, the decade of television's most spectacular growth and consolidation in the United States, particularly the period from 1953 to 1955, when Adorno's study of television programming was published in what was then called the *Quarterly Review of Film, Radio and Television*.[16] In those years, by way of a summary from Erik Barnouw, "stations made their debuts and were joined by coaxial cable and radio relay. National networks took shape. Sponsors made their moves. Schedules expanded. Important stars made the plunge. Sets sold rapidly. Euphoria ruled in executive offices."[17] In addition, by way of further contextual reminders: news became increasingly marginal to the prime-time schedule, the Army-McCarthy hearings were broadcast, the anthology form peaked, the U.S. media expanded its worldwide broadcasts, and the ACNielsen company secured its monopoly on ratings. Three overarching developments in the history of television further structure its form of appearance in the early 1950s, and they ask for some elaboration.

First, as Lynn Spigel and others have shown, television, specifically during the 1950s, was conceived almost without exception as a domestic technology, based on ideal images of the female viewer and rooted in a gendered division of labor in the imagined typical American household.[18] Daytime programming, which began in 1949 in order to expand available advertising time, allowed viewers to perform practical or functional household labors while watching television, in effect conjoining or doubling two labor times: the capacity to pay attention to television, whether sustained or not, was one commodified time sold to advertisers, and the time of domestic chores was superimposed upon that attentive work. The former productive time, sheathed in the allure of pleasure, indeed becomes a lure to further, or more extensive, or more intensive, labors of the second sort. Spatial relations between work and viewing condensed. The antenna's location mattered. Moreover, and I wish to emphasize this strongly, televisual strategies of segmentation, seriality, variety or magazine programming (segmentation based on the model of women's magazines), the marketing of consumer fantasies, and the like all derive from the assumption of a female viewer, steeped in domestic labor and in the worldview proffered through women's media. While Adorno acknowledges the gendered nature of the programming that he analyzes in the fragmented examples he alleges to be random, he tends to perform extremely careful textual analyses, without too much concern given to time slot, advertising, or contextual determinations on those readings, but he does align himself very explicitly with a female viewer. Contrary to Williams and the cultural-studies tradition of television studies, this theorist who has been most associated with understanding the so-called holistic industry actually tends to read programming closely and with a very accurate sense of audience. These deeply gendered contexts matter: in terms of what one constitutes as an object ("television") and in terms of the semantic and rhetorical force one ascribes or brings to the object.

Second, the relative paucity during the period in question of broadcasts in a synchronic slice (that is, the few programs on at one time) tends to produce a strong sense of television's conformity, uniformity, or univocality. In an environment in which three or four alternatives aired at a given moment during the broadcast day, the idea of forced choice or the insistence on a certain generic consistency seems more reasonable than in the current milieu. Jameson's remark can be understood to emphasize this univocality. As opposed to the immense grid that currently scrolls before subscribers to digital-cable or satellite services, the grid for prime time in 1954 included only four channels (ABC, CBS, DuMont, and NBC), combining variety and magazine shows, anthology dramas, sports (boxing), quiz shows, sitcoms, and the news. To take an example, a Thursday prime-time schedule would look like table 1.1. The time slot, as short in duration as fifteen minutes, organizes the evening's programming.[19] Although Adorno refrains from naming the various episodes and programs he examines as examples in his article, for reasons that are not entirely clear to me, a bit of reconstructive labor suggests that his main preoccupations were serial comedies (*Our Miss Brooks*) and anthology dramas, perhaps particularly appealing for their claims to realism. Against his examples, one might proffer other counterexamples in order to argue with Adorno's readings, yet it is important to note that his comparisons were limited to what was on hand, at the moment, in small quantity. One could not yet imagine an archive, much less a queer one, encompassing the stunning generic variation displayed in the list I generated for fun in the introduction; only recording makes such an archive even imaginable. In addition, scholars now have access to the diachronic archive via compilations or curatorial assemblages of recordings, the accumulation of what video retailers call "golden age" television as a whole, or at least as a larger set. For Adorno, haphazardly tuning in (or, later, relying on program listings such as *TV Guide*, which debuted in 1953) and reading scripts, these programs likely offered themselves as that homogeneous flow noted by Williams.

A third difference follows: only with the advent of video recording for the home consumer did it become possible to record, or time shift, one's viewing. Adorno's notes on programs, apparently based on script analysis but undoubtedly also viewed during real-time broadcasts, necessarily pale when compared to the shot-by-shot analyses possible in recent cultural criticism, which are attentive to the nuances of television language and able to capture the overwhelming volume of information on display on television at any given time. When my students perform a "strip analysis" (a close reading of every detail) of one to two minutes of prime-time network television, they invariably respond to that volume: in terms of the density of edited sound, the visual information on-screen (banners, logos, weather information, and so on), the speed of editing during commercial blocks, the complexity of bumpers and transitions, and the like.[20] Compared to the broadcasts of 1954, current television allows for, perhaps demands, a much more mobile form of spectatorship and meaning making, even if the semantic content might present itself as similar. I find this last difference helpful for thinking

TABLE 1.1   Prime-Time Schedule in 1954

	ABC	CBS	DuMont	NBC
7:00	*Kukla, Fran & Ollie*		*Captain Video*	
7:15	News		News	
7:30	*The Lone Ranger*	News		*The Dinah Shore Show*
7:45		*The Jane Froman Show*		News
8:00	*Mail Story*	*Ray Milland Show*	*They Stand Accused*	*You Bet Your Life*
8:30	*Treasury Men in Action*	*Climax*		*Justice*
9:00	*So You Want to Lead a Band*		*What's the Story*	*Dragnet*
9:30	*Kraft Television Theatre*	*Four Star Playhouse*		*Ford Theatre*
10:00		*Public Defender*		*Lux Video Theatre*

Source: TV *Guide*, www.tvguide.com, archives for the fiftieth anniversary of TV *Guide*, accessed October 14, 2002.

about how Adorno's remarks on television might be similar—in the sense of how he responds to the text of mass culture—to his study of radio for the Princeton Radio Research Project in *The Psychological Technique of Martin Luther Thomas' Radio Addresses*. This empirical study of radio broadcasts, funded by the Rockefeller Foundation, began in 1937 and was headquartered at Princeton, in its School of Public and International Affairs. Under the leadership of Paul Lazarsfeld, a team of researchers began some of the first work on the effects of mass media, particularly radio, on society. Adorno left in 1941 due to significant methodological objections to Lazarsfeld's work. In fact, Susan Buck-Morss reminds her readers that nothing had prepared Adorno for his job with the project, and part of its charter expressly required the researchers not to question the commercial constraints of broadcasting, something Adorno could not contort himself to do.[21] Adorno is a good close reader, as his analysis of high culture and his reproductions and readings of newspaper astrology columns demonstrate, for example, in *The Stars Down to Earth and Other Essays on the Irrational in Culture*.[22] He is a less agile reader when he lacks a text in front of him, as previous commentators have noticed, despite his stunning ability to show how both radio and television tend to reproduce the existing socioeconomic structure by recycling its characteristics as psychological traits in dramatic or other narratives, thereby reproducing complacency in those who might otherwise have challenged the status quo.[23] I examine further the consequences of Adorno's textual models in my reading of "How to Look at Television."

The gendered audience, the restricted programming flow, and the limits of textual analysis thus form a triad of important historical determinations on Adorno's sense of how to look at television as an apparatus or phenomenon; it is significant that the article is not devoted to how to *watch* programs. (Samuel Weber belabors the question of the verb in his chapter "Television: Set and Screen."[24]) Scholars frequently fling other criticisms at Adorno in retrospect, from the vantage point of a half century's distance from his writings in America on mass culture: that his work is saturated with political and historical despair, or that he ultimately recycles the kind of "reflection theory" proposed by György Lukács. Among several other criticisms that Paul Bové mentions in his assessment of Adorno's impact on twentieth-century Marxist thought is the sense that Adorno undermines the legitimacy of his analysis with the foregone conclusion that there is no possible opposition to authoritarianism, or that Adorno ignores the "oppositional impact of certain everyday modes of resistance to the state as well as certain contradictions within mass society."[25] Others, including J.M. Bernstein in his introduction to the *Culture Industry* volume in which the television article was reprinted, emphasize that some see Adorno's works, when understood as inherently or expressively modernist, as superseded by postmodernism.[26] Such has been the case in the arena of popular culture studies, most notably in the work of Jim Collins.[27] Both Bové and Bernstein, just to take these two examples, nevertheless see in Adorno's thought (and the thought of the Frankfurt School, if taken more generally) an invaluable and even brilliant corrective to certain tendencies in cultural criticism: Adorno remained insistent on negation.

One final note before turning to Adorno's article: I am not alleging that Adorno was gay, but I am arguing for his importance to queer theory. An intriguing window into Adorno's homoerotic life, however, has recently been opened by Johannes von Moltke's translation of and introduction to several letters exchanged between Adorno ("Teddie") and Siegfried Kracauer ("Friedl"), whose plainly erotic friendship reveals Adorno's everyday awareness of queer attractions and exchanges.[28]

ADORNO AND MASS CULTURE

The first several pages of "How to Look at Television" reveal in Adorno neither a man blindly critical of mass culture nor an intellectual committed to autonomous art, as his detractors frequently allege him to be. His interest in the effects of television stems from his suspicion that television may have nefarious effects on its spectators, and one needs only to critically expose, in a somewhat mechanistic fashion, the apparatus through which those effects are produced. He phrases the goal of the article in this way: "By exposing the socio-psychological implications and mechanisms of television, often operating under the guise of fake realism, not only may the shows be improved, but, more important possibly, the public at large may be sensitized to the nefarious effect of some of these mechanisms."[29]

Putting aside for just a moment the monumental question of the "socio-psychological," I want to call attention to the phrase *fake realism*, for it will become central to Adorno's concerns in the article. In this first mention, in the first paragraph of the article, it's not entirely clear what Adorno means to communicate, even if one brings to the article ample and retrospective knowledge of Adorno's significant contributions to aesthetic theory around that very term. Realism, let alone a false version of it, has traveled a long road, if one is to take seriously Adorno's mention of Daniel Defoe and Samuel Richardson, not to mention Ian Watt's study of them which would become *The Rise of the Novel*,[30] as historical markers, yet Adorno doesn't specifically reference here the rise of the bourgeois novel or the effects of individuation, the treatment of everyday life, or the specification of locale and detail that one generally associates with the two-century rise of realist literature and its kin. Later, Adorno would use the phrase *posing as realistic*, and later still, *pseudo-realism* to denote what is the same phenomenon: the fusion of mass art and empirical reality, the liquidation of art's opposition to, as he puts it elsewhere, "the reality out there."[31] In "How to Look at Television," realism in a narrow sense thus comes to mean loosely anything from a representation being up-to-date (realistic in detail) to a sentiment of defeat, encouraging conformity to the status quo, as Tobias Wolff remarks in the passage I excerpt in the chapter's epigraph ("be realistic").[32] In some larger sense, however, fake realism also means that televisual representations fail precisely to mark the difference between actually repressive social conditions and psychological conformity to them by those who might otherwise challenge those conditions. Television, insofar as its social function is precisely to promote adjustment to humiliating conditions, necessarily operates under a system of fake, false, or pseudorealism. I will return to this point in Adorno's text soon, but note here how the merging between spectator and temporal object would be seen by Adorno to have a repressive function by definition.

The distinction between understandings of realism is worth making at the outset of a reading that seeks to link critical theory with queer theory, especially because realism remains the single most powerful operator of a commonsense version of queer visibility. Drained of any political complexity, however, the term has become vacuous. From a Gay and Lesbian Alliance Against Defamation (GLAAD) press release: "media coverage of gay and lesbian issues (and increasingly, bisexual

and transgender issues) has moved beyond simplistic political dichoto-
mies and toward more fully realized representations not only of the
diversity of our community, but also of our lives, our families, and our
fundamental inclusion in the fabric of American society."[33] Examples
could be multiplied from a gay and lesbian press obviously disappointed
with the declining number of gay and lesbian characters on prime-time
television (up, in 2012, to a whopping 4.4%[34]), and a number of scholars
of queer media tend to bolster the commonsense position with sound
bites.[35] In these texts, realism denotes a nagging demand for representational justice: as Stephen Tropiano asks in *The Advocate*, "If you do a
show about three couples, why can't one be gay?"[36] The demand pre-
sumes at least three discrete things, to parse them again: (1) that the
inclusion of gay, lesbian, bisexual, and transgender lives and stories is
the responsibility of mass culture; (2) that the "accurate" or "positive"
representation of such stories and characters will have political effects
and will combat homophobia, fear, and violence among television spectators; and (3) that such sustained, complex, multicultural, multiracial,
and multiethnic and rich representations will have political effects beyond the sphere of television. In this single article, Adorno provides
powerful rejoinders to all three components. He does this first by suggesting that television's structural function, its pseudorealism, is to promote accommodation to the effects of capitalist subsumption: alienation and humiliation. Nothing more, at least at this structural level.

Unlike the mainstream queer media's interest in the particulars of
programming (gay characters or story arcs), Adorno's focus on television is structural: he finds himself initially interested not in any particular show or program but in the nature of television as an apparatus
and as an image-making machine. Despite that structural interest, however, he hesitates to propose a method that is too abstract: "The findings
should be so close to the material, should rest on such a solid foundation of experience, that they can be translated into precise recommen-
dations and be made convincingly clear to large audiences" (213), hence
the use of a number of clarifying examples. And his approach resists an
artistic or aesthetic prescription for television's ills; indeed, he insists
that one not "naively take for granted the dichotomy between autonomous art and mass media" (214). The division, he remarks, is itself a
function of commercialization, and Adorno refuses a romantic concep-

tion of "pure art" by noticing the interaction between the artifact and its spectators, or the audience reaction. That interface becomes the domain of the sociopsychological.

The weakest section of Adorno's article, in my own reading of it, obstructs the otherwise powerful movement of his immanent criticism from the thesis of television's mechanisms to an understanding of its multilayered structure through these sociopsychological terms. In the section "Older and Recent Popular Culture," Adorno introduces some of his thinking about the culture industry's evolution into a unified and increasingly strong system, capable of assimilating serious art, and he cursorily traces the evolution of the audience's structure from the eighteenth century to the middle of the twentieth. While Adorno acknowledges the sketchy nature of his historical outline, he tends in this section toward the kind of reductionism and pop psychology that provoke the ire of his critics, stressing the capacity of mass culture's ubiquity and repetitiveness to produce "automatized" reactions, or diagnosing the spectator's "infantile" need for protection, and giving spectators a sense of "feeling on safe ground" as the reason for strong closure in most television programs (216). Alleging that hidden messages of adjustment and unreflecting obedience emanate from a monolithic culture industry, Adorno proposes a reductive and juvenile model of interpretation for mass-cultural texts, one I like to call the "secret decoder ring" theory of media (whereby a message is hidden in a given text, and it wends its way nefariously toward an unwitting receiver; the astute cultural critic knows better, decodes the hidden message, and exposes the lurking evil). Amid these weaknesses, however, Adorno begins a commitment to the figuration of gender roles in this section that invites further reflection.

Insistent on the increasing degree of psychological control exerted by the modern culture industry, Adorno coughs up an occasional counterexample, only to deem it a trivial challenge to his continuist account: "Certainly, there are many typical changes within today's pattern; e.g., men were formerly presented as erotically aggressive and women on the defensive, whereas this has largely been reversed in modern mass culture, as pointed out particularly by Wolfenstein and Leites" (215–216). And a bit later, similarly keen to confirm continuity within patterns of culture, Adorno wonders whether differences inhere in the movement from religious to secular derivations of shared values. Again, he turns to a particular case: "For example, the concept of the 'purity' of women is one of the invariables of popular culture. In the earlier phase this concept is treated in terms of an inner conflict between concupiscence and the internalized Christian ideal of chastity, whereas in today's popular culture it is dogmatically posited as a value per se" (219). The final example Adorno summons to illustrate social control ("society is always the winner, and the individual is only a puppet manipulated through social rules") involves gender conflict: where nineteenth-century literature presented gendered social conflicts such as "women running away from their husbands, the drabness of provincial life, and daily chores," twentieth-century media decide "in favour of the very same conditions from which these women want to break away" (220).

Adorno uses these three examples, all hinged on women's relationship to power, to explain the mechanism of televisual realism: a reversal in which women become erotic aggressors, a transmutation in the calculation of the value of women's purity, and a trap wherein women's resistance to patriarchy and domestic labor is presented back to women as their likeness. His decision to use these examples is interesting but perhaps not surprising given television's social role and domestic address to women viewers. But as one can see immediately, these examples operate on very different registers. In the first case, an actual shift has taken place in the possibilities and language of representation of gendered desire, so that, for example, in the cinema, one can observe this reversal as effect or as symptom of a deeper tendency in the national psychosocial landscape (as suggested by a book cited by Adorno, Martha Wolfenstein and Nathan Leites's *Movies: A Psychological Study*).[37] If not read symptomatically, there would simply be no explanation for the reversal. In the second case, however, while the gendered ideological construct (women's purity) remains constant, its inflection has changed. Where in a religious context the idea of purity referenced a struggle between desire and an ideal of chastity, now in the modern, secular context the tension gives way to a more reductive, prescriptive command: be pure. What is significant is the constancy of the ideal of purity, and no historical current strong enough to wash it away can be detected in the period under scrutiny. In the first case, Adorno appeals—even if in a secondhand reference—to a symptomatic reading, where the representation of women's erotic aggression is an effect of a prior shift recorded in the psychosocial field. Television is here understood to be more like a VCR or DVR: taking the image of a prior broadcast as its own. In the second case, Adorno seems to appeal to a timeless construct (not a timeless nature), the representation of which bends according to the determinations on the popular imaginary (religious versus secular) in a given moment. Presumably, one could explain the very timelessness of the construct through the same reasoning as that which operates in the first example: a significant shift in the psychosocial landscape might have the power to effect an alteration or reversal, yet that shift cannot yet be imagined. In this second case, television is the same as its nineteenth-century precursors; it is the same thing as a novel, a play.

In both of these first two examples, television is not really television at all. In the first example television records something else given as prior (as many sociological studies of television allege it to do, i.e., TV reflects a prior reality), and in the second example, it is no different from any other form of cultural production, such as literature or theater (as many textual critics of television would insist as well, i.e., good TV is just as good as nineteenth-century literature). Television only really comes into its own, it only really describes itself or presents itself, in the third example, and it only really documents what it is in relation to gender roles in this example. To repeat the example: where literature of the nineteenth century offered images of women breaking free from tripartite constraints (husbands, provincial life, chores), television promotes these as the very solution to women's ills, it decides, to repeat his phrase, in "favour of the very same conditions from which these women want to break away" (220). In appealing to women (as spectators), television reflects back to women their own imprisonment: women become doubled as their own guards or keepers. More than that, television makes a choice for the values of the prison when it could instead make a bid for freedom.[38]

Lawrence Rickels, in his fabulous experimental study, titled *The Case of California* because of the place that the idea of California holds in psychoanalytic and critical thought, describes the reflecting structure I have just noted in this way:

Within the primal one-on-one of consumerism—in front of the tube—dreams of omnipotence turn around, Adorno advises, into realized impotence: although utopias appear to tune in on the tube, the TV screen's sadomasochistic and miniaturist share in the funnies realizes utopias only by aborting any genuine and full-scale utopia in fact cherished by the viewers who have been bonded that much more closely to the curse of the status quo. In short, there can be no illusion of the "life-size" on TV.[39]

As much as there can be no illusion of the life-size, there can be no adequate double of us at all on television. Insofar as on television "we watch ourselves trying to conform[,] . . . assimilation renders us 'like,' 'similar,' or indeed, the double we already are from the point of view of the one who controls us."[40] Rickels explores the psychoanalytic consequences of that doubling relation through the challenges that the "live" nature of television broadcast poses to Freudian and Lacanian models of transference (ultimately aligning that liveness with both perversion and psychosis). I similarly seek to understand television's crucial role in constituting its spectators spatiotemporally as social subjects through psycho-dynamics, looking particularly at television as an apparatus that participates, as Peter Hohendahl puts it, in the "material processes of social integration," where psychoanalysis or the analysis of what Adorno describes in the article as social-psychological dynamics can therefore serve as an "immanent critique of social deformation."[41]

If television structurally reproduces its viewers as their inadequate, pseudo, or false doubles, and if television primarily reflects women (or queers, as I will come to shortly) back to themselves from the point of view of the one who controls them, and if the material of television (its semantic content or its meaning, insofar as one can oppose that to its structures of reflection) is as gendered as Adorno makes it out to be, then television in itself and in what it means is gender identification, and by extension sexual being. To clarify: I don't mean, or I don't just mean, that television contributes to our process of gendering: that Barbie commercials interpellate little girls. I mean that, in Adorno's terms, television, insofar as it is a structured process of identification (doubling) and insofar as that doubling cedes to the regulative binary of gender, and to sexual dimorphism, and to compulsory heterosexuality,

is both the apparatus or mechanism and the content of gender identification. But only, and this is a big only, insofar as television is realist.

TELEVISUAL INCORPORATION

Adorno says that television produces or reproduces (he is not sure)
our egos: he is interested, above all, in the *integration* achieved by mass
media (220). Why, he asks, does the middle class conform to authoritarianism even when its culture has replaced top-down models of authority with peer-group conceptions of shared or "other-directed" influence? In other words, given a profound shift in the middle-class
ideology from Puritan or religious ideas to the more recent emphasis
on group or democratic value coding, why does the middle class adhere
to outmoded conceptions of power? Because somehow something has
been internalized through historical processes, preserved even though
the objective conditions have shifted. The middle classes obey a code
that no longer corresponds to their historical mise-en-scène, and that
code therefore, and paradoxically, acts on them all the more strongly:
"The middle-class 'ontology' is preserved in an almost fossilized way,
but is severed from the mentality of the middle classes. By being superimposed on people with whose living conditions and mental makeup it
is no longer in accord, this middle-class 'ontology' assumes an increasingly authoritarian and at the same time hollow character" (218). Sound
like (Freudian) melancholia? Something lodged within, controlling yet
hollow, authoritarian and yet strangely disconnected from the actual
conditions of one's immediate life circumstances?

Melancholia, I am generalizing here in Adorno's text to a class as
some have tried to extend it to queers as a group, has proven to be a
critically useful way to describe the effect of an overidentification, the
refusal to cede a loss in the form of an incorporation. Cherishing and
preserving that loss, the melancholic builds her or his ego on that incorporated ideal; as a process of ego construction, melancholia has
provided, instead of a pathological response to loss as opposed to the
"healthy" process of mourning, a model of how identification functions
in general. Identification is a process founded on loss: it is, as Diana
Fuss suggests (and I follow her elegant introduction to *Identification
Papers* here very quickly), an "embarrassingly ordinary process, a rou-

tine, habitual compensation for the everyday loss of our love-objects."[42] Fuss follows Freud, "If one has lost a love-object, the most obvious reaction is to identify oneself with it, to replace it from within, as it were, by identification."[43] Ordinary though it is, the process of identification is also a strange one, a defamiliarizing affair, since the process of compensation involves fantasy, representation, surrogates: we replace that "it," that "object" with what we imagine the loved one to have been. We replace "it" with a likeness or an image, a specter of a past love, a phantom. Identifications are therefore all of the following: surprising and predictable, pleasurable and disturbing, grounding and destabilizing, familiar and haunting.

This understanding is not, however, to relegate identification entirely to the realm of the unconscious, the private, the individual, for the accumulated processes of identification in fact make identity: they make the self coherent and recognizable as a self and make the self identifiable. But if identifications order and organize the self, they also disturb its coherence; they put into play the very relation that establishes the self and its precarious contours, that is, they establish the self in relation to an Other, subject to object, inside to outside. Identity is then one way to mark the relation of the self to the self (a process of self-recognition) that allows us to posit the self as other, to set ourselves in relation to the Other.

It would not be a surprise to take visual culture within this model as central to the elaboration of identity through identifications. In commonsense terms, culture frequently provides the materials with which we make sense of ourselves and through which we encounter other experiences, other sensibilities, other sexualities, other communities. Like identifications themselves, culture can be understood, again with common sense, to offer imaginative, unsettling, aesthetically rich, intellectually challenging, disturbing, pleasurable, and haunting facsimiles and representations. Visual culture (in the form of films, television, digital media, and installations, to name a few) can spark engagement, contemplation, action, erotic response, questions, horror, fantasy. For some time, television in particular has been the object of a sociological frenzy involving precisely these processes or mechanisms of identification and identity formation as they work on television's primary viewers, women and children.

Adorno's article, by adopting the model if not the language of melancholic internalization that is surprisingly close to that which Fuss and others have developed to describe queer identifications, powerfully refuses this commonsense model of visual culture in which television has an exterior reality or where it can offer images of others. This is the heart of the contribution that I think his article offers to those of us thinking about what critical theory and queer theory have to say to one another on the terrain of culture. In still other words, Adorno contests—through his very model of how television realism works—a view of television as a buffet of identificatory possibilities, a range of couples, to return to Tropiano's question in *The Advocate*, one of which might be gay. If we take Adorno's view regarding the structure of authoritarianism in the middle class, there is in relation to television something preserved, fossilized in the mentality of that group, that acts against its own historical conditions and interests. Of this embalmed core, this mummified ontology, there are further questions to be posed: What relation does this ontology have to the ontology of realism (the *real* in realism)? And, assuming that this thing preserved cannot *not* obey the regulative matrix of gender and sexual identifications to which Adorno has seemed to subscribe in his examples, might this ontology serve as a spectral excess, a further challenge to self-presence? I take these two in order, continuing to read Adorno's article through its final three sections.

THE ONTOLOGY OF REALISM

Adorno contends that mass media are structured in complicated, multi-layered ways. As I have already suggested, his "secret decoder ring" model of mass communication reduces the apparatus to processes of encoding and decoding, a model much discussed and elaborated in subsequent research and theory, and a model seen, for example by Stuart Hall, to require much further analysis with regard to struggles over signification.[44] Despite the reduction, however, Adorno insists that the idea of the message is not transparent, and that mass media have taken for themselves the idea of "polymorphic meaning," which previously inhered only in complex works of high art, with the result that the irrational and unconscious motivations of a given text may seep or "sink into the spectator's mind" all the more deeply (141). How this happens, he does not know. One has the sense, in the section of Adorno's article called "Multi-layered Structure," that he is making most of this stuff up on the spot. "Probably," he says, hedging his bets, "all the various levels in mass media involve *all* the mechanisms of consciousness and unconsciousness stressed by psychoanalysis" (221). Throughout the section, he qualifies: "probably" (221), "the suspicion widely shared, though hard to corroborate by exact data" (222), "the implication is that somehow . . ." (223). "Somehow" some shows elicit mature, adult responses; "somehow" others enforce pseudorealistic attitudes.

One possibility for these mechanisms of pseudorealist identifications comes in the idea, borrowed for the duration of a paragraph, from Leo Lowenthal, of "psychoanalysis in reverse" (223). Much as with "polymorphic meaning," the psychoanalytic concept is the "multilayered personality," which is "somehow" taken up by the culture industry, deployed in a given text to "ensnare" him or her (the television spectator) as completely as possible by engaging him or her "psychodynamically in the service of premeditated effects" (223). Such a model will prove useful, albeit only loosely, for Adorno's reading of two examples, both taken from *Our Miss Brooks*—the comedy series begun on radio and extended to television and featuring Eve Arden as the saucy and spirited schoolteacher Connie Brooks—without his saying so (see figure 1.1). Both episodes could also be understood to be queer, insofar as Adorno reads the Arden character as a modern-day Joan Rivière (intellectually superior and punished for it) and insofar as the second example involves a cranky woman and her cat, a nonnormative couple whose significations often slide into "lesbian." Patricia White has in fact convincingly suggested that the type represented by Arden, the sidekick, could find an appropriate home on television during the 1950s and that Arden's social type frequently stood in for lesbian (a sidekick role further explored by Judith Roof and discussed later).[45] I, however, am less interested for the moment in that connotative force of Arden's appearance than in how strongly Adorno stresses the dynamics of identification as a structural element of these episodes' "reverse psychoanalysis" or mechanism for "ensnaring" the spectator.

As I did with Adorno's earlier examples, let me take these one at a time. In the first episode, our Miss Brooks is the underpaid school-

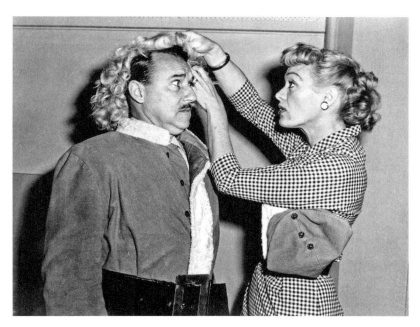

1.1. *Our Miss Brooks* (CBS, radio program, 1948–52). Shown, from left: Gale Gorden and Eve Arden. Courtesy Photofest.

teacher who is, to add insult to injury, fined a number of times by her "pompous and authoritarian" school principal (223). The "situation" of the sitcom (and it's not very comedic) is that she has no money, is actually starving, and tries in vain over and again to hustle a meal. Adorno finds it an index of repression that food or the mere mention of eating can provoke laughter; the humor of the episode derives from representing the character's painful struggles toward gratification. (With a proto-feminist inclination, Adorno is interested in the politics of food and their relationship to incorporation and embodiment.) In Adorno's view, then, the hidden meaning simply accompanies the episode's construction of a worldview, which in turn is accomplished by ensuring the audience's identification particularly with Eve Arden's character, a compromise between scorn for intellectuals and a conventional respect for culture. "The heroine shows such an intellectual superiority and high-spiritedness that identification with her is invited, and compensation is offered for the inferiority of her position and that of her ilk in the social set-up," Adorno concludes (224). Through identification—through the incorporation of what is best and noble in the character (her humor, good nature, quick wit, and charm)—the episode manages to promote adjustment to objectively humiliating conditions, indeed to produce us as and through doubles of our oppression.

In the second example, the opposite mechanism of identification is at work: identification teaches us a lesson. Adorno invokes another episode of *Our Miss Brooks* that involves a cranky old woman and her cat, named Mr. Casey (and in this example Adorno incidentally reveals that he is a habitual viewer and knows the distinction between members of the permanent cast and episodic visitors). The old woman, then, sets up the will of Mr. Casey and makes some of the recurrent characters heirs: "Later, the actual inheritance is found to consist of the cat's valueless toys. The plot is so constructed that each heir, at the reading of the will, is tempted to act as if he had known this person (Mr. Casey). The ultimate point is that the cat's owner had placed a hundred-dollar bill inside each of the toys; and the heirs run to the incinerator to recover their inheritance" (224–225). The message in this case involves punishment for identification: "Don't daydream," the episode tells its viewers, "don't expect the unexpected." Be realistic: "Those who dare daydream, who expect that money will fall to them from heaven, and who forget any caution about accepting an absurd will are at the same time those whom you might expect to be capable of cheating" (225).

Those whom we might expect to be capable of cheating? What's this? In this second example, it seems as though the lesson, "be realistic," has now spilled into its more general sense as realism. The episode has blurred the line between a world of anthropomorphized cats and their (perhaps lesbian) owners and the world "out there," in which someone might be capable of cheating. Television, realism, thus has at its core the refusal of such boundaries. Such a refusal is built on the incorporation of *something* from television, whether in the form of an identification with an ego ideal, as in the first example, or in the form of a lesson or punishment following an improper identification, as in the second. In either case, Adorno hopes to have shown how empirical life becomes infused with a kind of meaning through television, where we become, as it were, TV.

The problematic of realism is thus a question of that becoming, of the relation between being and the apparatus. What is television? But also, are we television, and how? André Bazin famously posed the question, "what is cinema?" at roughly the same moment when Adorno's article puzzled over television, and while a sustained comparison between the two is impossible here, Bazin's comments particularly on surrealism toward the end of his essay complement Adorno's position in remarkable ways. Bazin's partial answer to what cinema is, or that part of his answer in which he defines the ontology of the photographic image, which he then extends to the cinema, emphasizes realism in this way:

> The film is no longer content to preserve the object, enshrouded as it were in an instant, as the bodies of insects are preserved intact, out of the distant past, in amber. The film delivers baroque art from its convulsive catalepsy. Now, for the first time, the image of things is likewise the image of their duration, change mummified, as it were. Those categories of *resemblance* which determine the species *photographic* image likewise, then, determine the character of its aesthetic as distinct from that of painting.[46]

Like Walter Benjamin's more notorious reflections on the artwork, Bazin's essay traces the conflict—produced retrospectively with the invention of photography—between style and likeness in the history of Western art, between a quasi-universal, human need for illusion and the ambition to duplicate the world outside. For Bazin, the term *pseudorealism* designates a false realism, a deception "aimed at fooling the eye" (12). In particular, he sees Western painting as liberated from the struggle between these two tendencies by photography, which alone satisfies "our appetite for illusion by a mechanical reproduction in the making of which man plays no part" (12). Photography's privilege comes from the "transference of reality from the thing to its reproduction," and photography alone can thus bear the burden of that human desire for eternal life that drives the quest for reproduction: "it embalms time" (14). Toward the end of Bazin's short essay, photography acquires a more powerful capacity, recognized by the surrealists, to contribute to the material world rather than only to reproduce it: "The logical distinction between what is imaginary and what is real tends to disappear. Every image is to be seen as object and every object as an image" (15–16). Adorno's model converts what Bazin pinpoints as an element of the medium for the spectator to the psycho-dynamic processes between medium and spectator: in the spectator is embalmed the mechanism of television. Since this reading of an affinity between Bazin and Adorno is obviously dependent on Philip Rosen's careful and patient reading of Bazin in *Change Mummified*, a brief further word about the philosophical and conceptual issues that make Bazin and Adorno odd bedfellows is in order.

From Rosen, I take first the stress in Bazin's work on the activity of the subject, and next the elusive nature of the real (or realism as a limit) as key contributions. Conjoining the two, in one of many such observations, Rosen writes that "the world can never present itself or write itself apart from the abstracting drive of the subject to find meaning; the pure, brute concrete real in its totality and apart from the intentionality of a subject is simply unavailable as such to humans."[47] The oft-quoted idea of realism as asymptotic similarly figures the idea of a limit never attained. But Rosen pushes further from these two observations in order to displace readings of Bazin that attribute to photography and cinema the capacity to produce an ostensibly unmediated record of the real: it is not this aspect of automatically produced images that lends them a special credibility but rather "markers of indexicality itself, which signify the presence of the referent at some point in the sign production" (20). Rosen calls these markers "indexical traces" (20), testifying to an essential gap between referent and signifier that is itself both troubling and enabling for the subject's preservative obsession, his or her desire to maintain the body against decay and death, his or her desire to embalm time.

As Rosen notes, Bazin's theory of cinema is "an explicitly phenomenological one" (137), the grounds of which Adorno also explicitly attacks as providing a false sense of epistemological security. In the passage that Rosen cites (he chooses all the best ones), Adorno wittily historicizes this drive for security, evidenced as much in Bazin as in Edmund Husserl and Martin Heidegger, who are Adorno's targets, as a capitalist symptom:

> Dread [*angst*] stamps the ideal of Husserlian philosophy as one of absolute security, on the model of private property. Its reductions aim at the secure: viz. the immanence to consciousness of lived experiences whose title deeds that the philosophical self-consciousness

to which they "belong" should possess securely from the grasp of any force; and essences which, free from all factical existence, defy vexation from factical existence.

The two postulates contradict each other. The world of lived experiences is, according to Husserl, changeable and nothing but a "stream." But the transcendence of essences can itself never become lived experience. Husserl's development may be understood in the tendency to unite the two postulates of security in a final one which identifies essence and stream of consciousness.

His [Husserl's] drive to security is so great that he mistakes with the beguiled naivete of all propertied belief [*Besitzglauben*]: how compulsively the idea of absolute security drives to its own destruction; how the reduction of essences to the world of consciousness makes them dependent on the factical and the past; how, on the other hand, the essentiality of consciousness robs it of all specific content and sacrifices to chance everything that should be secured.

Security is left as an ultimate and lonely fetish like the number, one million, on a long deflated bank note. (cited in Rosen, 138, brackets in the original)

If phenomenology is to be revised, it is by locating it within the specific terms of capitalist modernity and to understand its subject, defensive in the face of temporality, as Rosen notes, as "socio-historically determined" (138). For Adorno's television spectator, a similar historicizing gesture is therefore necessary. For him, television lodges itself in the spectator, confusing the distinction between what is imaginary and what is real; identification is a process that, strictly speaking, happens with television, not with its contents, yet who can tell the one from the other? Adorno's final remarks, in which explicitly he turns to historically produced stereotypes of gay men, confirm the overwhelming effects of pseudorealist confusion.

THE STEREOTYPE

Adorno's final two sections, on "presumptuousness" and "stereotyping," explain how genres and stereotypes produce generic and constrained readings of the world. The phenomenon of the psychic carryover, in which the worldview encouraged in the episode of *Our Miss Brooks* with the cranky woman and her cat spills into the world at large, prompts Adorno to meditate on the power of television to shape conceptions of the world and specifically on the psychological backdrops, the "halo effects of previous experiences" (such as pseudorealism) necessary for television's stereotypes and clichés to become intelligible (226).

Adorno objects not to stereotypes per se but to a functional change in which they have become rigid and reified. Stereotypes keep chaos at bay; they are "an indispensible element in the organization and anticipation of experience" (229). Instead, Adorno worries about the culture industry's reliance on those unyielding worldviews, materialized in stereotypes and clichés, "which seem to bring some order into the otherwise ununderstandable" (230). In meeting real needs, such stereotypes may nonetheless lead people to "not only lose true insight into reality, but ultimately their very capacity for life experience may be dulled by the constant wearing of blue and pink spectacles" (230). It would require a certain amount of contortion to make Adorno's understanding of the stereotype congruent with a more pliant and less mechanistic understanding of common sense (such as Antonio Gramsci's), but it is worth remarking that Adorno is aware of how television—not simply as an ideological vehicle but as an apparatus—is particularly reliant on rigid typing for two reasons: (1) the relatively short period of time available for production (this was particularly true for anthology dramas); and (2) the relatively brief duration of the time slots for serial comedies (fifteen to thirty minutes).

According to Adorno, stereotypes, like melodrama, threaten to displace social relations into personal psychobiography, as he shows by reading an anthology teleplay about a fascist dictator, and they distract from social antagonisms by relying on abstractions and typology and Manichean divisions and timeless generalizations. Adorno's assessment seeks balance: "Certainly, no artistic production can deal with ideas or political creeds *in abstracto* but has to present them in terms of their concrete impact upon human beings; yet it would be utterly futile to present individuals as mere specimens of an abstraction, as puppets expressive of an idea" (231). Erring on the side of concrete impact leads to "pseudo-personalization" (231), a pressing issue that is nonetheless beyond the scope of Adorno's remarks. Erring on the side of abstract ideas leads to overemphasis on social prescriptions and taboos and positive and negative messages (now seen by Adorno in a pejorative sense) that ignore what happens "in real life" (232).

His example of the latter reinforces his preoccupation with normative gender roles and with a Freudian conception of sexual development (Adorno indeed preserves, or embalms, Freud's ideas), and this example sets the stage for the final case of his essay, the gay artist. Here Adorno concerns himself with the fact that "many television plays could be characterized by the soubriquet 'a pretty girl can do no wrong'" (232). Borrowing a term from George (Gershon) Legman, Adorno jarringly dubs this type of heroine the "bitch heroine," aggressive and cruel, particularly toward the father, but rarely punished. She confirms the requirement that the pretty girl be preserved, that nice makes right, that the pretty girl "must be what she appears to be" (232). In so doing, she tends "to confirm exploitative, demanding, and aggressive attitudes on the part of young girls" (232). In this example, what is significant is that television exalts the very syndrome that psychoanalysis seeks to treat. Television structures an identification that is ultimately poisonous, engaging in what Adorno calls a "psychoanalysis in reverse" (233). Television secures regression to infantile developmental phases, particularly for female viewers, lodging them within the confines of the oral without the tools to dissolve the reversion that psychoanalysis would provide.

Brief though it is, this passage on psychoanalysis in reverse is enormously suggestive. Adorno enthuses in an aside: "Incidentally, it is amazing to what degree television material even on superficial examination brings to mind psychoanalytic concepts with the qualification of being a psychoanalysis in reverse" (233). The passage suggests, by way of summary, that television's pseudorealism enlists its spectators in a series of identifications. Those identifications with a pedantically maintained realism can be infantile, regressive, restrictive, melancholic, or otherwise, all with the consequence of incorporating a hollow and nonetheless powerful kernel that directs subsequent sense perception and meaning making, and are powerfully gendered and sexualized, as are those identifications that bleed into the relation between the self and the world. Let me give an example of my own choosing from the same series by way of illustration.

One final example drawn from the series *Our Miss Brooks* offers a chance to read more closely these gendered and sexualized machinations of stereotypical representation of the 1950s in staccato bursts. It's the Christmas show from the first season, made available for me on VHS tape thanks to fan nostalgia for "golden age television" and converted by me to DVD for stilling; note that my capacity to cite dialogue is much greater than Adorno's was, and it allows me to privilege it in my analysis over quick plot summary. Like the episodes that Adorno describes, this episode makes comedy out of need or necessity, taking as its premise the fact that Connie Brooks, the schoolteacher, has no money to buy gifts for her friends and colleagues at Christmastime. It is a stunning twenty-two minute meditation on theories of the gift and exchange value, consumer culture, gender, and sexuality.

One further comment, before delving into this meditation, on the nature of hindsight in the age of digital reproduction: it is possible from a critical-media-studies position now, more than a half century after the serial aired, authoritatively to condense its achievements, place its breakthroughs, highlight particular episodes, and assess its contributions to gendered and sexual becomings. To watch episodes now on DVD is to recognize, of course, the demands for conformity in the 1950s and the pathos and thrill of the saucy, ironic, and feisty response to that conformity represented by the schoolteacher–Eve Arden composite who is Miss Brooks. In one sense, it is impossible to supply something like adequate information about what it meant to live in or as Miss Brooks, or, to be more academically fancy, "discursive context" that would allow readers who don't know much about the 1950s, or 1950s television, or this 1940s and 1950s program to get it sufficiently.[48] I have a certain faith in making explicit how a given response, an auto- or otobiography is of course implicated in understanding. There are moments in this book when autobiography imperfectly grasps moments and contexts and impulses.[49] In another sense, however, it is now possible for my students, via YouTube and the Internet, to have almost instantaneous access to these texts that appear from other times and to find their own routes into understanding—intellectually, experientially, and personally—such that this episode may lodge itself into different lives and new contexts.[50]

To return to the specifics, much of the humor centers on the gift-exchange office of the local department store, staffed by a character who turns out only in the final moment to be named Mrs. Carney. Mrs. Conklin, the wife of the school's principal, the gruff Osgood Conklin who is Miss Brooks's chief nemesis, mentions a Mrs. Carney in the context of her volunteer group, Helping Hands Society, but we learn only in the episode's final scene that she is the same shop employee. I am undone by the fact that even the attribution of a name can be withheld for the queer character until the episode's closure. The role is also uncredited, doubling the absence of a name, but is played by Florence Bates, a familiar cinema and television character actor and bit player— she played bossy Mrs. Edythe Van Hopper in Hitchcock's *Rebecca*—from the 1930s through her death in 1954, just two years after this episode aired. In her bodily demeanor, line delivery, costuming, and makeup, this Mrs. Carney activates gender and sexual trouble; she is butch (in tortoise-shell glasses and a tailored suit jacket, barking her lines like a linebacker coach), but she also pushes buttons that set off Eve Arden's own queer significations (see figure 1.2). The office's name suggests that the two terms, *gift* and *exchange*, cannot be as theoretically separated as someone such as the anthropologist Marcel Mauss would like. It also invokes the commonsense truism that "we never get what we want." Especially, it would seem, when we need things.

The dialogue in the initial setup in the office follows a classical sitcom shot reverse shot that emphasizes the recognition of queer stereotypes. Arden's character enters, asks whether she can exchange perfume, and Mrs. Carney delivers a bureaucratic line to the effect that the store accepts exchanges "cheerfully." Straight-faced and rigid, Bates all but blasts the word across the table, and Arden reacts with a double take and mug that catalyzes the following exchange:

MRS. CARNEY: Now then. It's a lovely scent. What's the matter? Too *feminine* for you?

MISS BROOKS: Too feminine?

MRS. CARNEY: Well, you look like the *self-reliant* type. Maybe you want something a little more *rugged?*

1.2. *Our Miss Brooks*, "Christmas Show 1952." Shown, from left: Florence Bates as Mrs. Carney and Eve Arden as Connie Brooks.

> MISS BROOKS: I do not. I want to exchange that perfume for a briar pipe.
>
> MRS. CARNEY: A *pipe?* You want a pipe?
>
> MISS BROOKS: Doctor's orders. He told me to cut down on cigars.[51]

Dialogue is, of course, a form of exchange in itself. Here both women traffic in innuendo, each one-upping the stakes of naming queerness at each turn. Innuendo is umbilically linked to the stereotype, and it did not bypass Adorno's attention: "Innuendo is a psychological means of making people feel that they already are members of that closed group which strives to catch them. The assumption that one understands something which is not plainly said, a winking of the eye, as it were, presupposes a kind of esoteric 'intelligence' which tends to make accomplices of speaker and listener. The overtone of this 'intelligence' is invariably a threatening one."[52] Innuendo presupposes that one is not given or cannot take the time to speak out of fear. Mrs. Carney's initial presupposition that the perfume's scent is too feminine for Miss Brooks (a word she spits with the force of the previous "cheerfully") casts suspicion on Arden's character as a form of projection and seduction. The butch saleswoman dangles the possibility of queer gender before a potential comrade, then renames the terms of that gender stereotype of lesbians as "self-reliant" and "rugged." If the humor of the scene derives from Miss Brooks embracing the stereotype only to redeploy it (explaining her desire for the pipe as a replacement for the butchest and most phallic cigar), we may want to ask further about what such an exchange reveals about the exchanges that are its subject. That is, how does this dialogue, the staple of sitcom humor, partake of the logic of exchange that is this episode's subject? How does the form become a transmission of its content and its spectators?[53]

The broader argument of the episode, much like Jacques Derrida's thesis, is that "the gift" may not exist. The gift here, if there is one, is always enveloped back into a relation of exchange, further revealed to be (equivalent to) affective extortion, always gendered and sexualized. When Osgood Conklin, the principal, presents gifts to Miss Brooks and Mr. Boynton (another teacher and Miss Brooks's comic love interest), he warns that he'll soon be leaving on a trip that pushes up the deadline for the countergift; when the screechy-voiced teenage student Walter (played by a twenty-something Richard Crenna) presents Miss Brooks with a microflask of perfume, he cannot help but convey his wish for a sweatshirt. Both of these exchanges of so-called gifts alert spectators to the everyday necessity of reciprocation even when social roles are unequal, nonreciprocal. But they also call attention to the inherently gendered dynamics of such exchanges, both in terms of the participants and in terms of the objects exchanged. The perfume and the pipe occasion the *pas de deux* with Mrs. Carney that I've transcribed. The pursuit of the sweatshirt causes Miss Brooks to return to the gift-exchange office for another round with Mrs. Carney:

> MISS BROOKS: I'd like to exchange this bottle of perfume.
> MRS. CARNEY: I thought I'd seen the last of you.
> MISS BROOKS: Not quite. Do you mind if I sit down?
> MRS. CARNEY: No, but if you plan on making this your home, I'll take that chair out and put in a daybed.

MISS BROOKS: I'd only exchange it for a loveseat. Don't bother.
MRS. CARNEY: Now, what do you want for the perfume?
MISS BROOKS: A sweatshirt.
MRS. CARNEY: [Beat] Naturally.

As Miss Brooks exits the office, she mistakenly takes Mrs. Carney's handbag, which is roughly identical to her own. With a final flourish, she returns to exchange "yours" for "mine."

As is immediately clear, this sequence transcodes the exchange of commodities *into* the exchange that is not *of* but *between* women read as queer. In the banter about the chair becoming a daybed becoming a loveseat, we chart a tongue-in-cheek itinerary of a lesbian relationship, both in terms of the stereotypical quickness of becoming coupled (as the joke goes, the second date is with U-Haul) and in terms of a seduction that confirms the rightness of queer gender as much for Miss Brooks ("naturally") as for Mrs. Carney, about whom "we knew it all along." As if to seal the deal, the handbag switch remakes desire into identification. Somehow Miss Brooks *is* Mrs. Carney, which is to say that they are both stereotypically encircled as queer.

In terms of the circulation of those identifications with spectators, we are enfolded into a kind of recognition that Roof beautifully pinpoints in her discussion of minor characters. I cite it at length appreciatively:

> With secondary characters, our recognition tends to be subliminal; familiarity might be invoked by their name, but it is more likely to be elicited by their first appearance in the film because our experience of them as actresses or as types brings us the small glow that comes from recognizing someone whose reappearances seem more day-to-day. There is the sense that we know who they are, if only we only knew who they were. I can't emphasize this feeling of incipient recognition and mastery enough; it functions from film to film and within film culture in the same way female comic seconds function in individual films, providing us with a safe repetition, reliability, and a haven of comfortable familiarity.[54]

Arden is, of course, one of the comic seconds on whom Roof focuses. While she is describing the tinge that reappearance involves, her emphasis on repetition and its sense of containment is germane to the situation comedy's tactics as well, not surprisingly as film actresses migrated to the form in the 1950s, as Christine Becker shows.[55]

Aside from seeing traffic in recognition and innuendo in these exchanges that might solidify an understanding of the lesbian resonance of her character, it is also crucial to see how Arden's choices as an actor shape our response to her character, choices I would put more firmly on the side of what's queer here. Although there seems to be no more divisive debate in acting instruction than comic timing being taught versus comic timing being innate, I am sidestepping that tension deliberately to focus on Arden's comedic *detachment*, signaled by her eyes widening (though not quite mugging) and elevated recognition of other characters' dialogue. Reminiscent of a dandy figure, a kind of free-floating presence or wordless epigrammatic mode, Arden hovers over the action, appreciating its dynamism and her capacity to register its mobility.[56] In part, Arden showcases her mastery of scripted material, cultivated through the period of the radio version of *Our Miss Brooks* (from 1948 to 1957), during which the entire episode had to be enacted twice, one for East Coast stations and again for West Coast stations, the repeat performance alone demanding a kind of virtuosity. Audiences appreciated Arden's talents as a comedienne as she and the series moved to television, whose early three-camera setups and recordings in front of live audiences allowed her to convert those talents for the specific apparatus of 1950s television. As with Lucille Ball, in whose studios *Our Miss Brooks* was shot (and with the same crew), Arden had to hone her television comedy within the relentless constraints of the production schedule: one day for setup, one day to shoot. Her control, manifesting a surrogacy for the audience, came in this strength in acting *above*. If the traffic in stereotypes allows one form of belonging, this queer detachment, I think, offers another, routed through the apparatus itself.

Adorno also alerts us to the ways that stereotypes become vehicles for social participation, exchange, and recognition, even if they retreat into the abstractions he criticizes in the passage I cited earlier in which he worries about individuals simply becoming specimens of a larger generalization or abstraction. What is striking in his article and about this episode is not so much the presence of these shorthand views of the world, for the form depends on them, but how decidedly queerness permeates this view as and through its form. In addition to the dialogue exchanges I've cited, I could add the line that Miss Brooks delivers to Mr. Boynton, whom she desires but by whom she is also denied reciprocation, about hanging the mistletoe in the closet. When he asks where she'll be at her Christmas party, she retorts: "I'll be in the closet."[57] Or the final scene of Miss Brooks's Christmas party, where, in order to avoid recognition (as the irritating shop clients) by the surprise guest Mrs. Carney, all three central characters (Miss Brooks, Mr. Conklin, and Mr. Boynton) in succession don Santa's beard as disguise. That is, they become beards. By the episode's end, the beard (a figure for a woman companion who covers over her male companion's homosexuality) is but one link in a chain of queer significations and mechanisms that extends to the closet, the gift, the wrapped Christmas present (prodded, poked, partially unwrapped, prematurely glimpsed), banter, innuendo, double entendre, slang, and, finally, stereotypes.

Adorno encapsulates them all in his contradictory model of 1950s television, which, in seeking to address real needs to make the world understandable, nonetheless enchains us. I think it's a complicated model, one that refutes a commonly held sense of Adorno's writings as presuming a monolithic mass duped by a centralized, rationalized culture industry. It's also a model that challenges the simple demands for representational justice in the form of gay characters on television. The final element of differentiation that Adorno brings to his understanding of how to look at television is sexual: he wonders whether "something similar [to the bitch heroine] applies to the same types of male heroes" (233). Of course, it does: "the modern synthetic folklore tends to identify the artist with the homosexual and to respect only the 'man of action' as a real, strong man" (233–234). Adorno again worries about a reversal, where in a comedy he describes only briefly a shy, retiring poet who cedes to the aggressions and "woman-handling" of his girlfriend (234). Innuendoes of homosexuality surround the artist character "of which one may be quoted: the heroine tells her boy-friend that another boy is in love with someone, and the boy-friend asks, 'What's he in love with?' She answers, 'A girl, of course,' and her boy-friend replies, 'Why, of course? Once before it was a neighbor's turtle, and what's more its name was Sam'" (234). While Adorno's concern appears to reside in the interpretation of the artist (as socially incompetent, as passive, and as queer), he also concludes by worrying that critics and social theorists might simply respond to this abjection of queers—the rendering of the queer character as "social outcast (by the innuendo of sexual perversion)" (234)—as obvious: "But we all know this!" The queer character sends an alarm about the tyranny of these identifications, the false powers of the normative. Adorno cautions, in his closing paragraph, that we not defend ourselves from uncomfortable truths and insights that "make life more difficult for us than it already is" (235).

Truth seeking is of a moral nature, in Adorno's view: "knowingly to face psychological mechanisms operating on various levels in order not to become blind and passive victims" (235). This intellectual resistance is Adorno's moment of negative utopia: the belief that vigilant thought can bring us closer to justice without the necessary accompanying idea of a material utopia. I have sought to make available some paths toward greater understanding not only of Adorno's writings (which I see as inviting and worthy of much further scrutiny by queer readers in response to my initial forays) but also of the apparatus of television in the 1950s, as it produces and reproduces our likenesses, miniatures, and masters. That we not become blind and passive victims, that we "take seriously notions dimly familiar to most of us" (235) and put them to the test: Adorno's antenna, it turns out, sends and receives, and its signal sends a strong mandate to take television's time as our own. In leaping ahead to the invention of new television temporalities in chapter 3, focusing more tightly on the transmission of the family and *An American Family* on public television, I don't quite depart from Adorno as I return to his fundamental questions about freedom and simulation such as they are styled by Lance Loud.

CHAPTER 2

Excursus on Media and Temporality

Let me begin with a glimpse at a moment that founded the model of broadcasting to which this study is devoted, a little playful historicism from Bernard Stiegler entwining technical invention and Continental philosophy:

> In 1926, civil broadcasting by radio had only existed for a few years—fewer than five. Hertz had discovered electro-magnetic waves in 1888, eleven years after Edison's invention of the phonograph and thee years before the appearance of Husserl's *Philosophy of Arithmetic*. In 1895, Marconi made use of Hertz's discovery and invented the defining principles of radio diffusion, five years after Marey's invention of chrono-photography, one year after the Lumière brothers' cinematic camera (which was also a projecting machine), and six years before the publication of Husserl's *Logical Investigations*. Lee de Forest created the triode in the United States in 1912, the same year as Husserl's courses on the temporal object and one year before the publication of *Ideas Pertaining to a Pure Phenomenology*. Electron tube amplifiers were developed during the First World War while Heidegger was editing his *Habilitationsshrift*, "The Categories and Theory of Meaning of Duns Scotus," and Husserl was working through his investigations on time. The first radio "stations" began their emissions in 1923, a year before the conference entitled *Concept of Time*.[1]

Enmeshed in thought about temporal objects such as music and radio broadcasts, Edmund Husserl and Martin Heidegger each contributed to a philosophy that engages technology. To put it more finely, they develop an existential phenomenology that can at least begin to hear these new technologies, that is, can tune in to the problematic that the technologies generate for time-consciousness, just as Adorno seemed poised to be able really to look at television. I want to think less about a general problematic of time-consciousness such as that elaborated by Husserl in *On the Phenomenology of the Consciousness of Internal Time* and more about the specific qualities of duration across forms of art and media.[2] The chapter is in three sections, in order to differentiate ever more carefully the experience of television time from these other prevalent forms with which it is frequently compared. In the first section, I examine synchronization and endurance in theater and installation art. In the second, I lay out some prevailing models for thinking about cinematic time. And in the third, I propose that we think about televisual time, complicating Stiegler, more directly through the apparatus that it has been, that is, through its own rhythms. In this sense, I reframe the chapters to come with what Daniel Bensaid called, in reference to Walter Benjamin's *The Arcades Project*, a "rhythmology," here of television.[3]

GATZ AND THE CLOCK

A number of art pieces in the past few years have directly engaged the issue of endurance, or at least much of the commentary surrounding them focuses on the extreme temporal experience of audiences and spectators. My first example is the play called *Gatz* (not *Cats!*) a six-and-a-half-hour production by the Elevator Repair Service that involves a reading of the entire F. Scott Fitzgerald novel *The Great Gatsby*. An imaginatively and visually rich production, *Gatz* fuses the reading of the novel with its enactment, in a time and space not quite identical to the one of the performance in 2012 but only about a decade in the past in a dreary office, a distance signaled largely through obsolete technology (computers with monochrome screens, or impossibly large cordless phones with antennae). Nick, as in Nick Carraway, moves in and out of his role as protagonist and as narrator, bridging at least three worlds:

that of the novel, that of the novel's enactment, and that of the performance (as when, before the first intermission, the actor, Scott Shepherd, addresses the audience directly).

The running time is arduous only by the narrowest standards of American audiences for commercial theater. For me, at the Public Theater in New York, it never felt burdensome. What is most notable about *Gatz* has less to do with the demands thought to be borne by audiences than those imposed on, or rather showcased by, its actors, to which the audience in turn responds. The conceit here is that Shepherd knows the entire text of *The Great Gatsby* by heart: open the book at any point, and he can take it from there. To read the book aloud each night is a feat of the body, especially the throat; to recite it on demand is a parlor trick of a most impressive order (and in fact is a trick that Elevator Repair Service trots out at fundraisers). The audience gets only a slight glimpse of this capacity, when, in the final segment, Shepherd puts the book down and recites its final pages, including its famous ending, itself about time's passing: "So we beat on, boats against the current, borne back ceaselessly into the past." But the audience is nevertheless conscious of the labors and skills, the endurance, necessary to sustain six and a half hours of exhilarating theater.

What *Gatz* stages, when we think about it phenomenologically, is the encounter between an embodied man and his book; it is, as the critical press was quick to notice, a love affair: "Boy meets book. Boy *gets* book. Boy gets lost in book."[4] As Shepherd finds his voice melded with Fitzgerald's texts, he, and we, discover its rhythms, and the embodied worlds of the theater fuse with those of the novel in ways that are simply extraordinary, never merely translating prose into performance or vice versa but performing the enigma and richness of the word in the real time of the theater. As Ben Brantley notes in the *New York Times*, it is slightly disingenuous to refer to that "real time," since there is a clock onstage that Shepherd regularly consults, one suspects in order to pace the performance and its intermissions. As it turns out though, the clock doesn't move; it always reads 9:38.[5]

This theatrical time of embodied encounter confirms Peggy Phelan's important claim about theatrical liveness, a claim that has been misunderstood in light of various horrible readings of it. Her ontology of performance, that "performance's only life is in the present,"[6] sought to clarify how fundamental ephemerality is to the experience of embodiment in the mutual presence of actors and audience. She sought, as she later put it, "to move the field away from a constant preoccupation with the content of performance, a descriptive fixation on what performance enacted, and toward a consideration of performance as that which disappears."[7] Not only did such an ontology distinguish performance from the photographic and recording arts and media, but it also valorized the power of ephemerality to say no to preserving everything, purchasing everything, to commodification. I admire her insistence on the possibilities of mutual transformation in the theater, both aesthetic and ethical, and I think that her claims are strengthened rather than diminished by the copresence of cast and audience over a relatively longer period of time, at least in the experience of this production, in which the elongated time brings with it a particularly empathetic admiration for the embodied actor. In short, I would want to accept that recorded media mediate differently. How?

Christian Marclay's installation *The Clock*, my second example of long-form artwork, was on a global tour of museums and digital-art spaces also in 2012, the year I saw *Gatz*. A twenty-four-hour single-channel video installation, *The Clock* is a found-footage compilation of roughly ten thousand clips from the history of cinema and television, in which segments containing literal images of time (clocks, watches, detonators, and so on) are synchronized exactly with the time of projection: if a character on-screen looks at her watch that reads 4:25, it really is 4:25 when you're seeing it. At various museums in which it has been housed, including the National Gallery of Canada in Ottawa where I saw it, *The Clock* has primarily run during regular museum hours, so most people saw some or all of the material running from, say, eight or ten in the morning until five in the afternoon or later in the evening. Rare twenty-four-hour projections allow a few audiences to see the entire work. (These are not screenings, strictly speaking, because the platform of *The Clock* is actually a computer program that, when booted, synchronizes the projection to the exact time of the computer.)

Daniel Zalewski calls Marclay "the most exciting collagist since Robert Rauschenberg" and catalogues in the *New Yorker* the micro-stories, rhythms, and juxtapositions produced through Marclay's magisterial editing. Helped by a team of researchers (read: graduate students) who have signed nondisclosure agreements, Marclay did not assemble the footage himself, but it is fair to say that he is the overall mind behind the project. Marclay is indeed a knowing artist and understands the history of cinematic thought, including precedents in compilation (such as Bruce Conner's *A MOVIE*), precedents in elongated time (such as Douglas Gordon's *24 Hour Psycho*), and precedents in long duration (such as Andy Warhol's *Empire*). For Zalewski, "there were darker resonances, too." He says, "People went to the movies to lose track of time; this video would pound viewers with an awareness of how long they'd been languishing in the dark. It would evoke the laziest of modern pleasures—channel surfing—except that the time wasted would be painfully underlined."[8]

Through the reflexive artwork, time's passing, via this orderly and synchronized metaclock, is somehow understood to be rendered palpable or felt as suffering, whereas watching television is figured as effortlessly pleasurable. It's true that *The Clock* explicitly stirs up philosophical soup, offering startling provocations of being toward death in the images of actors aging as we watch (Catherine Deneuve, Jack Nicholson) or many, many actors who are now dead: Ronald Reagan got an uncomfortable laugh from the audience of which I was a part. In a wonderful 2011 article on *The Clock* for the *New York Review of Books* (titled "Killing Orson Welles at Midnight"), Zadie Smith glosses Marclay's use of sound within this philosophical richness:

> As far as the philosophy of time goes, Marclay's with Heraclitus rather than Parmenides: the present reaches into the future, the past decays in the present. It's all about the sound. The more frequently you visit *The Clock* the more tempted you are to watch it with your eyes closed. Is that the Sex Pistols leaking into the can-can? Nostalgia is continually aroused and teased; you miss clips the moment they're gone, and cling to the aural afterglow of what has passed even as you focus on what is coming, what keeps coming.

For the most part Marclay withholds narrative causality and closure, and he subjects spectators to an endless game of engagement with no consistent rules for its work of memory as citation: we either try to assemble sequences (dialogue, music, visual tempo, and patterns) or we lose ourselves in the images as they pass by. One may want to argue that watching *The Clock* demands our labors of attention and activity in a way that television does not. But I think there is a fundamental set of assumptions that want to hold out the artwork, once again, at arm's length from television by declaring it (1) more arduous to engage; (2) more complex in its thinking, so much so that Smith calls it "sublime"; and (3) formally distinct. For Americans who watch on average more than one hundred and fifty hours of television per month (about five hours per day), I suspect that watching *The Clock*, especially on the IKEA sofas that are required by Marclay for the installation, posed no great hardship, and I suspect that we could generate examples of complex thought on and through television.[9] But the crux here has to do with specifying the formal elements of the artwork with respect to duration: *The Clock* has the capacity to generate twenty-four hours of distinct footage, but very few spectators saw it in its "entirety." Fewer still will have seen it twice. It exceeds the current capacity of DVD storage, and its astronomical price of over a quarter million dollars for a copy of the program will guarantee that it remains a museum showpiece for some time. It exists as a sort of potential for various forms of engagement, some limited by its context of exhibition. It is one *program*, much more like a discrete film of all films, whose formal properties of montage may mimic those of channel surfing but whose real antecedents are in the world of the art film, to which one may or may not pay careful attention for its duration. A film may be long, but twelve hours is nothing compared with the seventy-two *years* of the soap opera *Guiding Light*. My point here is that *The Clock* remains a delineated, autonomous object, unfolding in real time in a way that mimics television's flow but that does not in any way capture the complexities of televisual time or its experience. Let me turn more explicitly now to conceptions of cinematic time to thicken the counterpoint.

CINEMATIC TIME

Bernard Stiegler's essay, "The Time of Cinema: On the 'New World' and 'Cultural Exception,'" attempts nothing less than to explain "how and why cinema and television—now industrial and global techniques— may satisfy the universal desire for fiction and thereby condition the becoming of humanity as a whole."[10] I read it here in hopes of arguing precisely against his conflation of the two, cinema and television. (Incidentally, in the book version of the claim I just cited, Stiegler writes: "how and why the cinema, *in becoming television*, combines the universal desire for fiction, and through it, conditions the entirety of humanity's evolution" [9], emphasizing even more dramatically the conflation I seek to challenge.)

Stiegler is not the only intellectual route to follow to generate the account of the apparatus's temporality that I'm seeking, and his arguments are not without their problems. "The universal desire for fiction" is one of them. But here is a beginning. Imagine a Sunday afternoon. It is rainy, or you are perhaps bored (you perhaps live in Ithaca, New York, as I do). You desire to lose yourself in a television program or in a film on DVD. (It does not yet matter whether we can distinguish between cinema and television.) "During the passing ninety minutes or so (fifty-two in the case of the tele-visual 'hour') of this *pastime*," Stiegler alleges, "the time of our consciousness will be totally passive within the thrall of those 'moving' images that are linked to one another by noise, sounds, words and voices. Ninety or fifty-two minutes of our life will have passed *outside* our 'real' life but *within* a life or in the lives of people and events, real or fictive, to which we will have conjoined our time, adopting their events as though they were happening to us as they happened to them" (10).

How to explain this strong sense of adoption, in which we merge with or become cinema or television and reinvigorate (inject new life into) ourselves? For Stiegler, it is important that cinema combines two basic principles. The first is the well-known ontology of the photographic image. Like Philip Rosen, in his book *Change Mummified*, Stiegler means to establish continuity between the photographic image and cinematographic recording, citing Roland Barthes, as Rosen does, on the *noema* of the photo, the "that-has-been."[11] Stiegler renames this reality effect as the first of two coincidences conjugated by cinema: the moment of capture coincides with the moment of what is captured (what Barthes, incidentally, calls a projection: "the thought of that instant, however brief, in which a real thing happened to be motionless in front of my eyes").[12] As Barthes and many of his readers, including D.N. Rodowick have noted, such a coincidence founds the possibility of a conjunction of past and reality.[13]

The second principle is that cinema, like a melody, is what Husserl—in *On the Phenomenology of the Consciousness of Internal Time*—would call a "temporal object."[14] It is essentially a flux, a flowing away. In Stiegler's words, "The coincidence between the film's flow and that of the film spectator's consciousness . . . initiates the mechanics of a complete adoption of the film's time with that of the spectator's consciousness—which, since it is itself a flux, is captured and 'channeled' by the flow of images" (66). A properly temporal object is not only in time but "it is *formed* temporally, woven in threads of time—as what appears in passing, what happens, what manifests itself in disappearing, as flux disappearing even as it appears" (14). This flux of the temporal object (both its visual and its aural elements) coincides with the flux of the spectator's consciousness of which it is, in turn, the phenomenal object. While Stiegler perhaps overemphasizes the incorporation of sound in the cinema in order to reflect comparatively on Husserl's example of music (the melody, in particular) as temporal object, Stiegler nonetheless distills the central phenomenological Husserlian task: "To account for the structure of the temporal object's flux is to account for the structure of the stream of consciousness of which it is the object" (14).

Stay with it, if you will, for a moment longer. For Husserl, the temporal object invites two forms of memory or retention. The first, primary retention, is the encounter with each now as it is perceived by the eye or the ear, held in a continuous and originary association between each now and the "just-past," connected into a flux as the perception of time (16). Secondary memory assembles what has passed of the temporal object to the moment of the now. Secondary retention allows one to understand the note of a composition as melody (a note in a succession) rather than as arbitrary sound or noise, since it furnishes criteria for the selection of primary retentions. Primary and secondary retention are both types of memory born of perception. They are necessarily selective, because all memory entails a process of forgetting. A third type of memory, tertiary retention, is what Stiegler notes that Husserl calls "consciousness of image" (20). This is an artificial memory of what was never perceived; his examples are a painting, or a sculptural bust. They retain something of what the artist perceived but do not present to the viewer an image produced through his or her own perceiving consciousness.

Now, for Stiegler, what has changed since Husserl thought about these temporal objects in the early moments of the twentieth century is, as you well know, *recording*. With recording, we can hear or see a temporal object, the *same* temporal object, over and over again. Our processes of primary and secondary retention are altered; they are affected by selection, anticipation, and expectation by previous retentions. But our perceptions of the audiovisual temporal object are also affected by consciousness of image, by a whole host of tertiary memories that are inherent in our recordings. This is true of cinema in general. To illustrate the point, however, Stiegler uses the specific example of Federico Fellini's film *Intervista*, in which Anita Ekberg watches herself in his previous film, *La Dolce Vita*, almost thirty years earlier. The cinema captures the catastrophe of death, of life passing, and offers it to us as concurrent with the flux of our own consciousness. According to Stiegler, "in *Intervista* the fact [is] that film is a temporal object in which the actor's body is conflated with the character's; where the film's passing is necessarily also the actor's past, the moments of life of a character are instantly moments of the actor's past. That life is merged, in its being filmed, with that of its characters" (23). He later continues, "By the very fact of this juxtaposition of the cinematographic temporal object as between the real life of actors and that of their fictional characters, the Hollywood star could only *become* a star through a play of hauntings in which reality and fiction, perception and imagination become confused together—, and along with them, primary, secondary, and tertiary memory" (25).

In summary, cinema proposes the impossibility of distinguishing not only between reality and fiction, perception and imagination, retentions and protentions (anticipations) but also between actor and character, now and then. In cinema these conflate, and along with them, primary, secondary, and tertiary memories. The *cinematographic* (preferring, as Stiegler does, the French term to *cinematic*) in general is for Stiegler that which operates by the editing of temporal objects, and consciousness would then be "this post-production center, this control room assembling the montage, the staging, the realization, and the direction of the flow of primary, secondary, and tertiary retentions" (28). As an editing process, consciousness works by the contraction, condensation, and abbreviation of time: memory is always a process of forgetting. Because the flux of consciousness is a contraction of time, according to Stiegler, "stream of consciousness *is* the contraction of time, whose initiation process occurs in a cinema in which my time, within the film's time, becomes the time of an other and an other time" (31). None of this is possible without the technical supports of recording that function as tertiary memory supports, which transform life even as they reproduce it.

A final, lyrical passage from Stiegler:

> As Bergson says, the conscious present is the contraction of the entire past: "the present" for consciousness *is* memory, and because time, which is primary retention, consists of selection via secondary retention that is the cinema in/of accelerated life, I see, I remember everything that has been repressed/archived: images, sounds, smells, touches, contacts, caresses; I remember everything I forget *and* remember, everything I have abridged *and* condensed. This results in situations with characters: the very people onto whom I project a new scene and its visual images. The other is not simply "others": I construct the documentary in specific—I can see the garden, the street, the mountain, the sea, the highway, the cars in front of me on the highway, those passing by, the crowds, the entire world of observation in which nothing happens to me but what happens to me holistically. (32)

This holistic or total consciousness is editing, montage. This consciousness is already cinema. And by the middle of the twentieth century, the time of cinema becomes that of *television*, or so Stiegler's argument will go in the final section, "Television," of this chapter on cinematic time.

Cinema, here, serves as both a metaphor and a real object. At the metaphoric level, Stiegler analogizes processes of cinematic construction (viewing rushes, editing by selection, joining disparate experiences via the Kuleshov effect) to the processes of consciousness, including the three kinds of retentions (primary, secondary, tertiary) or forms of memory and recollection and protention and anticipation. Slippery though the analogies may be, they function to foreground the technical nature of tertiary supports and make the strong claim—that "we" are originally "technical"—stick. To the degree that Stiegler is really talking about cinema, the very strong sense of "adoption" here means that we often require recognizable others—human characters—with whom to synchronize our consciousness, and the conventions of classical Hollywood cinema and its derivatives tend to encourage such synchronization, or even make its pursuit the core task or issue of individual films (those that we would tend to call reflexive). He allows, too, for a more documentary procedure that entails the recognition of a total cinema of accumulated detail. The bulk of film theory of the midcentury is devoted to giving an account of these processes. The problem will come, in my view, in extending this account to television.

Briefly, a second rich phenomenological account of the experience of cinema comes from Vivian Sobchack, who places an equal emphasis on time and historically evolving technical and perceptual revolutions (via Fredric Jameson) and on embodiment in her essay "The Scene of the Screen," an updated version of which is a chapter in her remarkable book *Carnal Thoughts: Embodiment and Moving Image Culture*. For Sobchack, "Neither abstract nor static, the cinematic brings the *existential activity* of vision into visibility in what is phenomenologically experienced as an *intentional stream* of moving images—its continuous and autonomous visual production and meaningful organization of these images testifying not only to the objective world but also, and more radically, to an anonymous, mobile, embodied and ethically invested *subject* of worldly space."[15] In Sobchack's reading, this process of subjective embodied vision in the cinema fulfills the more crucial moment of existential presence described by Maurice Merleau-Ponty: "As soon as we see other seers . . . henceforth, through other eyes we are for ourselves fully visible. . . . For the first time, the seeing that I am is for me really visible; for the first time I appear to myself completely turned inside out under my own eyes."[16] As a perceptive and expressive structure of subjective embodied experience, such seeing is a performative, objective, and visible phenomenological achievement: it inscribes and provokes existential presence; *it renders time as visibly heterogeneous*. Processes of retention and protention thicken the cinematic present and expand cinematic presence into a world and situation. Elegiac, mysterious, seductive, and fulfilling, the cinematic experience is for Sobchack the ideal embodied encounter with the screen. What, therefore, happens when these thinkers turn their gaze to television?

In short, the thinkers either love television or they hate it. For Stiegler, who generally sees in television an extension of the cinematic, television importantly involves further coincidences. To the two coincidences of cinema, that is, television adds two more. A crucial third one comes in the coincidence of the time of seizure by the camera with the time of reception by the viewer. This is liveness, or what he will call with Derrida a "live effect" of quite a different sort.[17] And, finally, television enables a mass public simultaneously to watch the same temporal object. Television ushers in worldwide calendarity, a general economy of social time. Television is, again, *the* implantation of social time of the twentieth century. These two television effects, according to Stiegler, "simultaneously transform the nature of the event itself and the most intimate life of the population: the programming industries have initiated a synchronization that suddenly contains all diachronies that now constitute *culture* and also *consciousness* (34). Arguing for the primacy of the economic level for diagramming television's system, Richard Dienst proposes that television engenders a value form of its very own: "socialized culture time."[18] The consequences of this synchronization are geopolitical. And in Stiegler's view, at least, digital television (or what he calls a numerical version of temporal audiovisual objects, [77]) marks a decisive turn in the conditions of possibility for human freedom, linked inextricably to a pedagogy of the moving image, caught as it is within the paradox of technological modernity. This is his optimistic side; the other direction of his thought finds in this synchronization the situation of a generalized malaise.

For Sobchack, the "electronic," a category that too quickly sidesteps seventy years of television in order to describe the online world that we currently occupy, is a dismal hum of diffuse embodiment, instant stimulation, and impatient desire. Electronic presence disperses being across surface networks, and what it ultimately presents is apocalyptic danger: "Its lack of specific and explicit interest and grounded investment in the human body and enworlded action, its free-floating leveling of value, and its saturation with the present instant could well cost us all a future."[19]

New possibilities for human freedom or the end of the world?

My I-hope-uncontroversial contention, while recognizing the long-standing tension, is that if we spend some time—as I do in the following chapters—trying to apprehend actual television time, we will find ourselves not only somewhere in between but also more grounded in the apparatus itself. We need to understand precisely what kinds of embodiment and worlding television enfolds, and how its industrial form changes over the course of the medium's history. Take, for starters, the possibility of distinguishing between television and cinema as a historical problem alongside, as I will address shortly in returning to Stiegler, the problem of their ontological distinction's haunting as a conceptual issue. In Barbara Klinger's important work on domestic screens in the early part of the twenty-first century, for example, we see evidence of how viewing dynamics "commonly linked to the motion picture theatre—that is, attentive watching from beginning to end without interruption—have also affected domestic spectatorship."[20] In arguing that the theater and the home are not radically discontinuous spaces of exhibition but rather interdependent entities in terms of industry, aesthetics, and technology, Klinger helps us understand how discourses of value attributed to "high tech" attach to television, supplanting its "associations with the plebian" and surmounting the long-standing feminization of domestic technology.[21] While Klinger's work largely focuses on digital technologies (such as DVD players and the influence of gaming), movies and television intertwine in previous technological formations as well. Prescient in her understanding of how viewers transform domestic spaces into home theaters that mimic ideal conditions for attentive viewing in the now-ancient era of the VCR, Uma Dinsmore-Tuli contests the widespread assumption that remote-control viewing necessarily unseats models of theatrical viewing. Through a limited but thoughtful qualitative research project, she reveals that the presumed fragmentation, segmentation, and anticinematic textuality assumed to be produced via home recording is largely a figment of the imagination of a media studies keen to fix television and cinema in separate spheres.[22] If, reaching further backward from the VCR to the early decades of the medium, television programming has included feature films, we must be pushed to reconsider their imbrication and the forms of attention that such programming commands.

If cinema and television are intertwined historically in different ways, we must return to their conceptual distinction to see what kinds of claims hold. For many (and here Stiegler exemplifies a broader trend of thinking about television as merely a "live" and mass extension of cinematic technologies), the model is an additive one: cinema becomes television as the live effect is added to it, and both combine as the hypothetical structure of consciousness in general. Call it "cinematographic." Call it "tele-vision" or "tele-action." In any case, it is a "cinematic" model for the synchronization of consciousness that has the additional capacity for mass calendarity and the implantation of social time. In this way of thinking, broadcasting or mass communication becomes an important focal point: technology evolves from the sound recordings of Thomas Edison (and Charles Cros, to whom Stiegler pays homage) to cinema to television to the *Kulturindustrie* in general in its capacity to exteriorize and reify the imagination.

Stiegler's reluctance to elaborate medium specificity comes out of the need to make a broader philosophical point regarding the importance of tertiary retentions as originarily technical, a point I take as fundamental. If, as he says, there is an "industrial schematism," which Horkheimer and Theodor Adorno recognize in *The Dialectic of Enlightenment* but take as unproblematic, it is precisely because the *schematics are industrializable*: "They are functions of tertiary retention; that is, of technics, technology, and, today, industry."[23] In Stiegler's model of consciousness, tertiary retentions construct both the world in which I live and the world that I construct and adopt, providing me with a collective past that I never lived and with a stream of existential lives or lifestyles I access through technical prostheses. Tertiary retentions, as he says, allow for "transplantings, migrations, assimilations, and fusions that . . . can also constitute the *We* of an identificatory cinema."[24]

What I have been trying to suggest about the distinct ways in which we experience time across media, and I will argue further, is that the very mechanisms of adoption differ, *according to the organization of the temporal and formal structure of adoption*. On television, as Adorno quickly understood, our existential surrogates arrive on the tubes of the midcentury as miniatures, difficult to distinguish even as human. When revealed as doubles of ourselves, they imprison us rather than afford us reflective surfaces of freedom. To a measurable degree, television spectators in mid-1950s America, such as Adorno, were strained to adopt these flickering, fleeting images as indicatively part of a nameable "we." In the stereotypes that Adorno confronted of women, teachers, and gay artists, he found this adoption a difficult task. If in his macrologic Adorno believed in the overwhelming force of an administered society, he devoted himself to a micrologic of hope, putting into place a reading practice fanatically committed to small, heuristic maneuvers of possibility in the cultural sphere.[25] These maneuvers are finely tuned to the staccato bursts of the sitcom and its rhythms, and they are as powerful, and also more nuanced, than Stiegler's more general claims about the time of adoption in Fellini. Synchronization is never total, and access to prosthetic lifeworlds involves *particular* engagements that aren't always identificatory.

Industrializable in the sphere of television invariably means "domestic." Processes of recognition, expectation, remembrance, anticipation, repetition, assimilation—in short, the very processes of adoption— take place in families and through kinship networks established on and with television as family time.[26] In chapter 3 I turn to more extended sitcom rhythms, distinguishing between series regulars and the extended families that accumulate around them, fringes where queers come to be found in the 1970s. We are also found in the other stream of television time born in the 1970s: PBS, and the elongated, elegiac time of the Loud family, with whom we synchronized a new politics of visibility, of coming out.

CHAPTER 3

"Television Ate My Family"

Lance Loud on TV

From the early years of broadcast television through to the present day, television, as Jane Feuer puts, "brings families together and keeps them together."[1] The mode or ideology of liveness is not a necessary condition for this task; highly mediated and structured forms exemplify television's conceptions of relationality, generation, affiliation, kinship, reproduction, custody, and pedagogy. The situation comedy (or its animated offshoot) has been the generic home for the majority of television's families, presumptively nuclear and almost entirely white. The exception from the 1970s is, of course, *Roots*, subtitled *The Saga of an American Family*. Its images of captivity, of the brutality of American chattel slavery, and of uprising and emancipation helped my television generation viscerally to understand how deeply gendered and racialized are television's portraits of American families, how naturalized sitcom whiteness had become. *Roots* became remarkable for the subsequent litigation over its sources and accuracy, but it was for its broadcast moment remarkable for highlighting the whiteness of our television families through its melodramatic genealogical "saga." Linked to a much broader genealogy movement among American immigrants (that is, most Americans), *Roots* extended an inquiry into whiteness and a vision of ethnic solidarity that had been sanctioned by Congress a few years earlier, in the Ethnic Heritage Studies Program Act of 1974. *Roots* trafficked in stereotypes and idealizations, however, which further helped to cleave this "saga of an American family" from "the white family" all the more powerfully. Conjure some more of these television families: just to name a few, the Goldbergs, the Hansens (of *Mama*), the Ricardos, the Cleavers, the Bunkers, the Flintstones, the Jetsons, the Munsters, the Bradys, the Partridges, the Jeffersons, the Huxtables, the Simpsons, and the Conners. Prime-time serial drama provides the other generic home: the Carringtons, the Ewings, the Waltons, the Sopranos, and so on. It is impossible to say it bluntly enough: television *is*, *defines*, and *constitutes* family life.

Real-life ingredients and interludes have fed the character-based domestic format from the beginning, fusing public life and the interiority of television households, conjoining, as the networks would like us to believe, lifetimes and Lifetime. These fusions sustain imaginative links between viewers and these fictions of family, links that conceptually become crucial to television's normative ideals (that is, its politics of representation) and historically, beyond the terrain of representation, become crucial to television's implantation of segmented time for *family viewing*, a term that came to have a legal life in regulatory schema later in the twentieth century.[2] It would be folly to take these "real-life" elements as unmediated: they are fully the products of the entertainment industry's promotion and publicity. But they nonetheless extend an invitation from one home, one family, to another. The first network-broadcast situation comedy, on the DuMont network, *Mary Kay and Johnny* (1947–50), for example, featured real-life married couple Mary Kay and Johnny Stearns, who had a child in 1948. The child was written into the script. Ozzie and Harriet Nelson, with real-life sons David and Ricky, went on TV in 1952, and *The Adventures of Ozzie and Harriet* (1952–66) became the longest-running, live-action sitcom in American history. Ozzie Nelson also kept production costs low by creating, producing, scripting, directing, and starring family members (unions beware). Danny Thomas's show *The Danny Thomas Show* (aka *Make Room for Daddy*) (1953–64) was based on Thomas's life as a performer. The little orphan sister on *The Donna Reed Show* (1958–66) was played by Patty Petersen, the real-life younger sister of the cast member Paul Petersen. Paul Petersen and Shelley Fabares became recording stars, and the show was produced by Donna Reed's real-life husband Tony Owen. The town of Mayberry in *The Andy Griffith Show* (1960–68) was based on Andy Griffith's real hometown of Mt. Airy, North Carolina. The list goes on and on.

A particularly prominent example involves the fictional marriage between Lucy and Ricky Ricardo, Lucille Ball and Desi Arnaz. Studio executives "didn't think people would believe that a typical American girl would be married to a Cuban bandleader. 'What do you mean nobody'll believe it?' Lucy retorted. 'We *are* married!'"[3] Lucy gave birth twice on January 19, 1953: to her son, Desi Jr. (who was also featured on the cover of the very first issue of *TV Guide*), and to the baby of Lucy and Ricky in the episode broadcast on that date. Lucy and Desi/Ricky and little Desi/little Ricky refute racist assumptions with the real: we *are* married. But of course these circuits invert with the temporal object that is television, repeated and reviewed in reruns, in syndication, and now on DVD. Lucy and Desi divorced. We have fused our time with theirs.

Explicitly gay characters began to appear on sitcoms and variety shows in the seventies, and many gay and lesbian actors played queer characters long before. Spring Byington's role as a widow on the Desilu Productions' *December Bride* (1954–61) converged with the rumor that she was a lesbian, attached in her later life to actress Marjorie Main.[4] Nancy Kulp appeared on *The Beverly Hillbillies* (1962–71) as Miss Jane Hathaway, a sustained joke about her own lesbian identification. Lily Tomlin, on *Rowan and Martin's Laugh-In* (Tomlin was a regular from 1970–1973), spun a number of characters (Edith Ann, Ernestine, Susie the Sorority Girl) into a feminist and queer commentary that ran from her initial television appearance in 1969 through her continuing career. (In an interview that Lance Loud conducted with Tomlin for *Details* magazine, Lance asked whether Ernestine is gay, to which Tomlin replied, delightedly it would seem, "You know, I should have Ernestine come out. That would be great."[5]) *Bewitched* costar Dick Sargent (the second Darrin Stephens) was closeted during the very long run of that series but appeared with Elizabeth Montgomery (who of course starred as Samantha) as grand marshals at the Los Angeles Gay Pride Parade of 1992. On the other hand, their costar Agnes Moorehead (Endora), rumored to be a lesbian by tabloid journalists (and Boze Hadleigh), may have exuded camp appeal but donated her estate to Christian conservatives via Bob Jones University. To this brief list one should add many more, including Charles Nelson Reilly, Paul Lynde, Liberace, Merv Griffin, Elton John, Franklin Pangborn, and so on. And in recollecting Gore Vidal's affection for Pangborn, one should also recognize how important queer writers such as the pathbreaking author of *The City and the Pillar* (1948) have been in shaping these various images and personae, a topic that deserves further and sustained scholarship.[6]

In addition to the contingent queer stereotypes surveyed in the previous chapter and the presence of at least a few queer actors on television, by the 1970, a host of one-off gay characters began to make their way as criminals, uncles, teachers, drinking buddies, aunts, and cousins into American sitcoms. A partial list drawn from television archives would include the following:

> *All in the Family*, "Beverly Rides Again," November 6, 1976, "Cousin Liz," October 9, 1977 and "Edith's Crisis of Faith," December 25, 1977
> *The Baxters*, "Homosexual Teachers," October 31, 1970
> *Carter Country*, "Out of the Closet," September 29, 1977
> *Harry-O*, "Coinage of the Realm," October 10, 1974
> *Hot L Baltimore*, "George and Gordon," February 21, 1975
> *Marcus Welby, M.D.*, "The Outrage," October 8, 1974 and "The Other Martin Loring," February 20, 1973
> *Maude*, "Maude's New Friend," December 2, 1974 and "Gay Bar," December 3, 1977
> *Owen Marshall: Counselor at Law*, "Words of Summer," September 14, 1972
> *Room 222*, "What Is a Man," December 3, 1971
> *Starsky and Hutch*, "Death in a Different Place," October 15, 1977
> *The Streets of San Francisco*, "Mask of Death," October 3, 1974
> *WKRP in Cincinnati*, "Les on a Ledge," October 2, 1978

As I suggested in the introduction, the Norman Lear–produced sitcoms revel in their topicality, risking self-conscious political commentary on a range of timely issues (the Vietnam War, drugs, the counterculture, women's rights, and homophobia). Redressing the extent to which the sitcom form referenced a moment of familial ideality outside of its time (consistent with the embalming of values that Adorno observed in his analyses of programming of the 1950s[7]), Lear and Bud Yorkin's Tandem (later TAT Communications Company) and Grant Tinker's MTM Enterprises have, in the television scholar Kirsten Lentz's words, "been credited with transforming the situation comedy, making it more complex and more responsive to the social and political changes resulting from the civil rights and black power movements and the burgeoning feminist movement."[8] Lentz argues that while the much-studied discourse of quality (linked to representations of women and to feminism) attaches to the MTM productions, particularly *The Mary Tyler Moore Show* (1970–77), the discourse of *relevance* more often became linked to the Lear sitcoms as a marker of their treatment of racial politics.[9] As Lentz demonstrates, *relevance*—a term discursively grounded in students' demands for university learning that was more connected to the social and political transformations of the 1960s—migrates into debates about television as a representational commitment, "a new sense of responsibility to the public."[10] Realism is one key marker of such sentiment. (Of course, what appeared to be a debate about the politics of representation can also be read as an alibi for a demographic struggle to attract young viewers, those "young, urban white women between the ages of nineteen and forty-nine" who are the sine qua non of television consumers.[11]) In addition to the series *Starsky and Hutch*, which I examine in the introduction, I am taken with *All in the Family*'s (1971–79) queer appearances, especially the four episodes that include the character of Beverly La Salle (played by Lori Shannon aka Don Seymour McLean) (see figure 3.1). These serve as exemplary instances of how television began to offer a more sustained meditation on queer attachment, suggesting in response to debates over both quality and relevance that queerness intervenes in this distinction insofar as it marks Otherness neither wholly in terms of gender nor in terms of racial difference. In *All in the Family* more generally, these issues converge in striking ways: the policing of the contours of the family, gender and sexuality normativity, questions of relationality and kinship, and homophobic violence.

FEMALE IMPERSONATION ON *ALL IN THE FAMILY*

As is immediately clear from *All in the Family*'s theme song, sung by Carroll O'Connor's Archie and warbled incomparably by Jean Stapleton's Edith, the series thematizes the life and times of a throwback, someone who is out of (his own) time, or someone time forgot:

3.1. *All in the Family* (CBS, TV series, 1971–79), "Edith's Crisis of Faith: Part 1"
(1977). Shown: Lori Shannon aka Don Seymour McLean as Beverly La Salle.

Boy the way Glenn Miller played
Songs that made the hit parade.
Guys like us we had it made.
Those were the days.
And you knew who you were then.
Girls were girls and men were men.
Mister we could use a man
Like Herbert Hoover again.
Didn't need no welfare state.
Everybody pulled his weight.
Gee our old LaSalle ran great.
Those were the days.

All in the Family is all about the passage of time, that is, sociocultural
and political change, and it recursively returns to an image of stability
that is itself televisual, the 1950s sitcom, in order to challenge from

within the normative ideals (gender conformity, conservative politics) that form represented. The lyrics (themselves referring to previous popular music) attack conservative politics with the reference to Hoover, which will become relevant to my argument about the ideals of public television, and the lyrics go at gender conformity with a patriarch's repetitive vengeance: "men were men / mister we could use a man." Gender normativity and political positionality become central to the show's generational conflicts in the battle between Archie and Mike (Meathead) over the masculinity of the 1970s, wherein the generation represented by Mike, Archie's son-in-law, challenges shibboleths associated with Archie's milieu.

The ongoing conflict between Archie and Meathead helps to draw the contours of the Bunkers as bunker, the terrain over which the patronym will preside under the wobbling law of Archie. If it is to belong within the family, queerness tends to reside on the edges of the nucleus, in those maiden aunts, bachelor uncles, cousins, and other family members seen and unseen, named and unnamed, who help to cement the family's heteronormative borders, so that we can know girls as girls and men as men. "Cousin Liz," an episode that deals with the death of Edith's cousin and the subsequent revelation that she had been a lesbian, presents a named but unseen Liz, whom we come to know through her surviving "roommate"-cum-partner, Veronica (played by K Callan, whom I speculatively take as a presumptively queer actor given the paucity of information in our information-saturated world about this pseudonym that curiously lacks a period after the first initial). In this episode a number of queer dimensions around the boundaries of family seem to conflate. That is, the key dialogue and framing of the episode to follow a partner's death introduces crucial and familiar queer issues (being in the closet, mourning, inheritance, introduction and belonging to or ostracism from a partner's family) only to complicate them by making Veronica a teacher and thereby interjecting yet another topical issue of pedagogy, the political debate over banning lesbian and gay teachers from public schools (a proposition that actually appeared on the California ballot, the Briggs Initiative, in 1978). It is, to my mind, this accretion of topicality that undercuts the power of this episode's intervention.

In a beautiful moment of dialogue, Edith's humanist sympathy and capacity to align with queer feeling vies with Archie's characteristic bigotry:

> EDITH, *to Veronica*: It must have been terrible loving somebody and not being able to talk about it.
> ARCHIE: People like that teaching our kids, I'm sure God's sittin' up there in judgment!
> EDITH: Well, sure he is, but he's God; you ain't! Archie, listen, you wouldn't want to be the cause of somebody losin' their job!
> ARCHIE: Ohhhh . . .
> EDITH: Archie, she's all alone in the world now and she's got no one to take care of her like I have. And she can't help how she feels. And she didn't hurt you, so why should you wanna hurt her? Archie, I can't believe you'd do anything that mean.

Insofar as we align with Edith's consistent appeal to a blue-collar allegiance to The Job and insofar as Veronica's character appears genuinely bereft and therefore sympathetic, one might conclude that "Cousin Liz" is in fact a thoughtful and antihomophobic attempt to expand the televisual family to include queers. What prevents such a reading, in my view, involves the difficult question of Veronica as teacher, and the attribution of panicky homophobic legislation simply to a character's intentionality, to "meanness": "I can't believe you'd do anything that mean." The issue of teaching, pedagogy, takes this episode into terrain that it simply cannot manage in the brief sketch it devotes to the character of Veronica. The discourse congealed in the "topic" that is "gay teachers" convokes childhood, vulnerability, pedophilia, right-wing politics, and dyke stereotypes (the gym teacher came under special attack), but the episode is not able to sort of any of these meaningfully for the audience, returning these various issues to the interior psychology of intention. Without relying too heavily on a snippet of dialogue that likely seemed timely and perhaps politically progressive at the moment, I see a crucial leap in concern that is characteristic of the invocation of melodrama (and the melodrama of loss is at the center of this episode): from the felt responses of family members to a death of their own queer kin to public legislation that would ban queers from teaching in public schools, this leap poses an insistently political question. How are we to translate the affective microadjustments to queer lives *within* the family (those we ask of our families, for example, by the long and complicated process that is coming out) to transformations in normative kinship and generational relations in the public sphere (everything from gay marriage to custody law to protecting gay teachers and so on)? What enables a movement from "our families" to citizenship, governmentality, national, or extranational political belonging? How does queerness operate this leap?

The episodes of *All in the Family* featuring the female impersonator Beverly La Salle provide a step toward an answer. As a reminder, she had initially appeared in two episodes, "Archie the Hero" and "Beverly Rides Again," but she is most prominently featured in the two-parter "Edith's Crisis of Faith," when she is brutally murdered at Christmastime.[12] Before zooming outward again to the institutional context of 1970s television, there are four pieces to the quick argument I want to make about how the episodes with La Salle ("gee our old LaSalle ran great") stake a different claim to queer life and death than the "Cousin Liz" format of fringe familial inclusion that marks much of the televisual landscape in the 1970s: first, that the episodes feature an actor whose gayness is inseparable from his or her character; second, that they invite an affective response to homophobic violence that does *not* depend on familial belonging but rather extends affective relationality into a domain that may be specified as more properly televisual; third, that the force of their sentiment does not depend entirely on the representational domain but on their scheduling; and, fourth, that they introduce the experience of seriality.

To take each briefly in turn, what is striking about the casting of Lori Shannon (Don McLean) as Beverly is his enmeshment within notorious venues for female impersonator performance in San Francisco. A longtime performer at Finocchio's, a legendary establishment in North Beach that thrived for more than sixty years (1936–99) and attracted locals as well as tourists of San Francisco's sexual cultures, Shannon/McLean brought with him to *All in the Family* a public and out-gay persona rare for television celebrity, as Charles Pierce did in his roles (discussed in relation to *Starsky and Hutch* in my introduction).

Such attribution of Shannon's/McLean's queerness is both contemporary (Shannon/McLean had a public persona in the 1970s as queer) and mournfully retrospective (in that the female-impersonator performance venue has closed and Shannon/McLean is now dead). The synchronization, in other words, of public gayness with televisual gayness remains quite literally a matter of time (and was rewound with Ellen DeGeneres's *Ellen* as late as 1997 with "The Puppy Episode," when the lesbian actor came out). Second, the brutal murder of La Salle provokes soul searching of an order usually and televisually reserved for the effects of what I have been calling family. An affective-sociocultural economy diagrams the range of legible or legitimate responses to violence. "Edith's Crisis of Faith" raises the (again political) question of how generalized violence committed against queers may engender extrafamilial affect, rage, or despair. In a sense, "Cousin Liz" stages an inquiry into the boundaries of family in terms of "admitting" Veronica's affiliation, grief, and enduring attachment into the "bunker." More powerfully, "Edith's Crisis of Faith" wonders how grief over an insensible violent death of someone clearly *outside* the family along every vector (gender, sexuality, and kinship) can infect the norms upon which these vectors of belonging depend. Third, now moving beyond the terms of representation, the time slot for both halves of "Edith's Crisis of Faith" massively recalibrates the episode's affective stakes: they aired on Christmas night in 1977, synchronizing the episode's time (with Edith questioning her faith, as a result of homophobic violence, at Christmastime) with the time of its viewers.[13] If the secularized and commodified ritual that is Christmas in America is here recoded as a time to devote to mourning queer loss, then *All in the Family* has achieved something significant. Here, a queer character acquires density and, more significant, history: a life lived that demands recollection and narrativization. Seriality, finally, contributes to this density, insofar as Beverly had become familiar to viewers as a recurrent guest character; that familiarity is essential to enlisting understanding and sympathy in the tour de force final episode (which rightly won an Emmy award for its writing).

One final note about the grammar of the two-parter that makes it an intriguing formal intervention into the sitcom: the way that Beverly's loss is registered is a swerve from the norms of spatio-temporal orga-

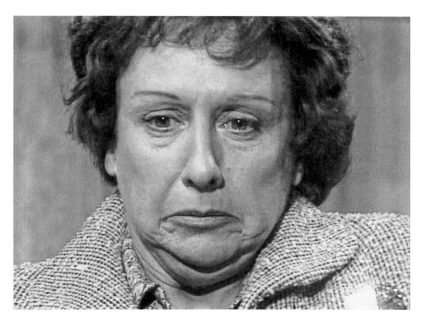

3.2. *All in the Family*, "Edith's Crisis of Faith" (1977). Shown: Jean Stapleton.

nization, both cinematographically and narrratively. In the first part, Edith receives the news of Beverly's murder—clearly specified as a hate crime by kids who "figured out what he was" in a close-up reaction shot of pure distress that moves with dripping symbolism to the Christmas tree. After two lines of dialogue with daughter Gloria (Edith: "Someone had to go kill him"; Gloria: "... just because he was different"), Edith retreats to the porch to deliver the plaintive monologue that affirms her crisis of faith ("I ain't goin' to church. I ain't goin' today. Maybe I won't go next Sunday, neither. The way I feel today, I may not go to church ever."). In an astonishing moment, the camera refutes all that the sitcom has taught it about the tempo of humor, the necessity of undercutting pathos with wit. Instead of moving quickly to Archie's ambiguous retort ("Someone from the family ought to be there representing us to God"), we simply stay with Edith's mournful face as it tries to find a way through the murder of her queer brother, sister, friend (see figure 3.2). In the second part, this kinship finds expression beyond gender confusion (which in the first part had provided a line or two of humor with Archie) when Edith seeks son-in-law Mike's consolation that we're supposed to be "all God's children." Through the trope of the gift, the narrative invokes the ghost of Beverly, whose wrapped Christmas gift for Edith conceals a card "to my lovely friend Edith." That is, a gift from the dead Beverly awaits Edith's recognition of what they meant to one another. Without getting knotted up too much again in theories of the gift, it does seem important to notice, as I did in chapter 1 with regard to the gift exchange in *Our Miss Brooks*, that this gift cannot be reciprocated (and occupies the time of the future anterior, what will have been given). The structure of the gift may be introduced as such: an economy that suspends equivalence and that also suspends the capacity for understanding based on exchange. Mike's assurance to Edith seems apropos: "Maybe we're not supposed to be understanding everything all at once. We need you." This narrative refusal of closure and seeming acceptance of a gift of queer love that undoes sitcom timing results in a second close-up on Edith's face that, in my screening notes, I marked as lasting "forever." Maybe not quite, but almost.

To be sure, the sitcoms and dramas of the 1970s continued to trade in stereotypes, but these series transform the stereotypes through more sustained encounters with queer friends and family. This happened through familiar forms (the sitcom) even as these queer appearances caused the shows' rules to shift, their laughs occasionally to subside, for this was still network-television time, the time largely devoted to the big three (ABC, CBS, NBC). As Joe Wlodarz argues in proposing the notion of cross-textual seriality, "network television of the 1970s provides *the* crucial site for exploring the emergence, expansion, and development of denotative gay imagery in mainstream American media."[14] A fourth network, however, solidified in this decade. Public television, like cable television, had been part of the American television experience for many decades, but the Lyndon Johnson administration helped cement public television's funding through key institutions. These made possible new programming experiments that explicitly sought to produce public discussion and debate over the massive changes that were taking place in America at the end of the 1960s (the Vietnam War, the civil rights movement, the counterculture, feminism, homosexuality, drug use, student protests). *An American Family*, to which I turn shortly, belongs to this short-lived (indeed momentous) spate of programming.

By launching the Public Broadcasting Act of 1967 (which established the Corporation for Public Broadcasting), Johnson explicitly opposed commercial interests to the goals of public television in America: "[The Act] announces to the world that our Nation wants more than just material wealth; our Nation wants more than a 'chicken in every pot.' We in America have an appetite for excellence, too. While we work every day to produce new goods and to create new wealth, we want most of all to enrich man's spirit. That is the purpose of this act."[15] Referencing a campaign ad from 1928 for Herbert Hoover by the Republican National Committee, which said that he would put "a chicken in every pot and a car in every garage,"[16] Johnson importantly looked backward (though in a different direction than Archie Bunker's savior, Hoover!) to those two key institutions of the twentieth century that form the basis of public television in the United States: land-grant-university cooperative-extension efforts (formalized in 1914 as a national network) and college and university broadcasting efforts, begun in the early part of the century and formalized as early as 1930 with the first annual conference of the Institute for Educational Radio/Television.

Unlike public broadcasters elsewhere, such as in Britain and Canada, where the institutions for both public radio and public television were at least initially highly centralized (in the BBC and the CBC, respectively, both of which remain key today), the United States has seen a radically decentralized network of broadcasting entities and initiatives emerge over the course of the past hundred or so years. But public television's history is firmly rooted in education and educational outreach along the university extension model developed to reach farmers and rural populations with the innovations in agriculture, veterinary sciences, nutrition, and so on that were advanced at the great land-grant universities. Johnson makes the analogy explicit, again in the Public Broadcasting Act of 1967: "In 1862, the Morrill Act set aside lands in every State—lands which belonged to the people—and it set them aside in order to build the land-grant colleges of the Nation. So today we rededicate a part of the airwaves—which belong to all the people—and we dedicate them for the enlightenment of all the people." Thinking about the airwaves as the campus of land-grant enlightenment helps to place emphasis on the pedagogical remit of public television, of course, but it does something further. The model of cooperative extension cleaves the population into two precisely to unite it into one, "the people," through populist rhetoric; in dividing, extension creates a center (the campus, the urban, the educators and the educated) and a periphery (farmers, rural people, those lacking formal education or degrees), and the land-grant university seeks to unite the center and periphery through the dissemination of enlightened research. The knowing and the unknowing are united through the diffusion and dissemination of something clearly constituting knowledge. This is a spirit I like to call *pragmatic pedagogy*, and it is central to the early efforts to unite "public television" in the late 1960s and early 1970s (here exemplified by Johnson's rhetoric about the creation of the Corporation for Public Broadcasting, but it is also linked to the creation of a national network for distribution in the Public Broadcasting Service [PBS] in 1969 and that entity's merging with the Educational Television Stations in 1973).[17]

An American Family (1973) emerged within this spirit of entrepreneurial station-driven pragmatic pedagogy (funded, it should be said, by the Ford Foundation). Drawing on the comprehensive resource represented by Jeffrey Ruoff's monograph on the series (the sole and authoritative academic work on *An American Family*), I cite a longish summary of the particular moment in which the series emerged:

> To understand *An American Family* is, in part, to understand the history of public broadcasting, for the series was produced by NET [National Educational Television], at a cost of $1.2 million, and distributed by the new Public Broadcasting Service to member stations in 1973. *An American Family* would never have been produced by the commercial networks ABC, NBC, or CBS, which, by the early 1970s, had scaled back documentary production in the race for audience ratings. Unlike the commercial networks in the 1970s, public television was not driven to seek the largest possible audience of potential consumers for advertisers. As a result, producers could explore innovative styles and subject matter. Some critics, including James Day, former president of NET, doubt that an innovative series such as *An American Family* could have been made *at any other time* in the

history of public TV, given the administrative structure of PBS and the turn to corporate underwriting for individual programs after President Nixon vetoed the 1972 Corporation for Public Broadcasting budget. After 1973, staff producers at member stations were bound, through ties to corporate funding, to conventional styles and non-controversial subject matter.[18]

If "quality" and "relevant" television such as *The Mary Tyler Moore Show* and *All in the Family* emerged at a moment, the beginning of the 1970s, when it became possible to fulfill the representational agenda of venturing into the sociopolitical realm, ostensibly beyond TV, for sitcom fodder *while at the same time* attracting desirable demographics, then *An American Family* emerged with its own audience successes from the matrix of public and educational television at the very moment *before* PBS swerved toward a more commercial model. Both the profitable model of MTM and Tandem/TAT and the noncommercial alternative that was PBS, if only for a moment, entangled definitions and borders of the family (along with the gender and sexual norms that sustain it) in this time of extraordinary televisual innovation.

But what of queer time in 1970 or thereabouts? Why is it that by the 1970s, gay men and lesbians had generated a whole new procedure of disclosure and a foundation for "gay liberation" called "coming out"? What accounts for a lag or delay of almost one hundred years between Karl Heinrich Ulrichs's passionate exhortations to tell queer stories (in the 1860s) and the mid-twentieth century's founding of an inner gay truth to be visibly, publicly, monumentally, melodramatically revealed within a complex social web? I think the answer has to be TV. And while I'm willing to qualify by saying "in part," my guess is that it's a massive determination on the reshaping of gayness in these years. Television's mode of existence, the systemic implantation of social time, has to have been one of the most significant reorganizations of precisely this string of visibility, publicness, melodrama, and monumentality — in short, real life — in the American midcentury (and here, retroactively as it were, one must mark the specificity of these speculations to that restricted grid that fed the Loud family's televisions in Santa Barbara and, more important still, imagined that family as its ideal viewer). And I think we can begin to draw the contours of the impact of these new forms of publicness—the prehistory of reality TV—through Lance Loud and the formal possibilities of observational television. I begin in the next section to detail this operation of coming out (which Lance most certainly does *not* do on *An American Family*) through the controversies spawned by this innovative series. Although I mention it only briefly in the coda, the series was remade in 2011 as a Showtime made-for-TV movie, called *Cinema Verite*. Real life indeed.

COMING OUT: LANCE EXCEEDS TV

The deadly elasticity of heterosexist presumption means that, like Wendy in Peter Pan, people find new walls springing up around them, even as they drowse: every encounter with a new classful of students, to say nothing of a new boss, social worker, loan officer, landlord, doctor, erects new closets whose fraught and characteristic law of optics and physics extract from at least gay people new surveys, new calculations, new draughts, and requisitions of secrecy or disclosure.
—Eve Kosofsky Sedgwick, *The Epistemology of the Closet*

If Eve Kosofsky Sedgwick carefully specifies the repetitive and exhausting temporality of the procedure of coming out (one must calculate, decide, and utter anew and again, each time and forever), it is nonetheless difficult to pinpoint *historically* the emergence of the metaphor or idea of the closet in relation to lesbians and gay men.[19] Michael Brown's cultural geography puts it near 1968, the eve of public television:

> The subsequent origins of a sexualised metaphor based on domestic architecture remain unclear, however. [George] Chauncey's historiography of gay New York up to the 1940s [*Gay New York*] notes that the term "closet" did not seem to be used to describe hidden sexuality. He argues that a closet emerged later in that city, and submits that the term itself was coined only in the mid- to late 1960s. Confirming this general history, Banhardt suggests closet came to mean hidden, covert, or secret somewhere around 1968. Interestingly, however, Beale documents the use of the term in Canada during the 1950s. And speculation abounds as to whether the metaphor emerged from the British "water closet" to connote cottaging or the expression "skeletons in the closet."[20]

By conjoining covert sexual practices (cottaging, or public sex in concealed spaces such as toilets and parks) with sexual secrets (the idea of the interior truth of one's being as located in one's hidden homosexuality), the metaphor of the closet, like television, transcodes the public and private, stringing together a calculus of what-can-be-said-when with the ongoing melodrama of its revelation and the apparent access to inner truths. Sedgwick emphasizes these procedures of knowledge as epistemology. Insofar as *An American Family* prompted a public discourse around the revelation of homosexuality and the impact of such revelation not only on a family but The Family, indeed on imperiled civilization more generally, the show provides among other things a way of understanding the circulation of public queerness around the early 1970s.

Recall yet another version of the dominant claim about queer representation (this one drawn from a much-taught and well-respected anthology in television studies):

> Until the late 1980s, explicit representations of lesbians and gay men were rare in television programmes. Where they did occur, they usually repeated the same old stereotypes: limp-wristed sissies like Mr. Humphries in the British situation comedy *Are You Being Served?* (1972–84); confused and unhappy young men like Steven Carrington in the American soap opera *Dynasty* (1981–89); or aggressive butch lesbians like Frankie in the Australian prison drama *Prisoner: Cell Block H* (1979–86). Lesbians and gay men were represented as deviant, tragic, predatory, and/or comic figures. Their presence on the small screen was intended to elicit horror, laughter, pity or disgust from a mainstream heterosexual audience.[21]

As previous chapters have sought to argue, not so. And certainly not so Lance. He is popularly, but wrongly, known to most as the first person to come out on television, or the first gay person on television. (The former reductively mischaracterizes what I will argue was in fact a sustained queer appearance rather than a moment or repetition of revelation, and the latter just isn't so if we believe, from *Our Miss Brooks* to *All in the Family*, that those limp wrists as well as some other wonderful characters were capable of signifying "gay.") These two myths of Lance derive largely from his absence. *An American Family* was broadcast first in January of 1973, and was rebroadcast only once in its entirety, for the tenth anniversary in 1983 (before PBS screened a follow-up program, *An American Family Revisited*). Subsequently, it has only been available through archives and personal copies of videocassettes (and pirated DVDs). By the time I first saw him, again thanks to Ruoff's loaning me his videotapes of the series, Lance was dead and his memory compromised by neglect.

Two qualifications are necessary before performing some closer analysis of *An American Family*. First, strictly speaking, the series was shot on film, not on videotape. It might be better referenced, therefore, as a broadcast serial film, indebted to its producer's training in nonfiction television and its filmmakers' experience in observational cinema (particularly with the Maysles brothers, a connection to which I return in this chapter's closing). Innovations in lightweight cameras and portable sound-recording equipment had transformed the field of observational cinema and cinema verité, and videotape had not entirely replaced film in the television industry, particularly its nonfiction divisions.[22] (*All in the Family*, incidentally, was shot on tape.) Alan Raymond, the principal cameraman, shot with an Éclair NPR 16 mm camera with a 12/120 mm Angenieux zoom lens. Susan Raymond, Alan's partner and wife, recorded sound with a Nagra tape recorder with Sennheiser 805 shotgun and 404 omnidirectional microphones, and she installed Sony ECM-16 mikes throughout the Louds' home and recorded particularly intimate conversations (including many of those of Bill and Pat at restaurants) with Vega wireless lavalier microphones.[23] Some way through the series, she tapped the telephones. If the medium (material substrate, apparatus) was in some sense film for this early version of reality television (for it was structured and broadcast for and on television), the medium for my own viewing of television straddled the recording formats that have intervened in television's broadcast temporality. I saw *An American Family* first on videotape and, later, transferred (or, rather, depended on a graduate student to transfer) the twelve hours of another source videotape to DVD. If anything, my phenomenological experience of viewing *An American Family* returned it to cinema and my time; rather than tuning in once a week when I was ten years old, I watched almost continuously when I was forty-four, in order to return and later to capture a notoriously evanescent physical object, the VHS tape. Such detail is certainly meant not simply as personal disclosure but rather to capture how multiple media and multiple times inhere in a text that we might take to be situated in or relegated to the past of broadcast television.

Second, as Ruoff nicely phrases it, in the reception of *An American Family*, "newspaper and magazine reviewers asserted that the Louds had 'lived their lives on television,' thereby perverting boundaries between TV and everyday life." I hope to have made it clear throughout this book that such "perversion" is indeed central to television's own operations, its "reality effect," as Ruoff puts it elsewhere in regard to the series.[24] To cleave the televisual from its reality effect requires a greater deal of contortion than perversion; a few details of the producer Craig Gilbert's process of developing the series testify to the extent to which television in fact structured the everyday life that *An American Family* sought to record and broadcast. In the crucial process of selecting a family, Gilbert wanted, in effect, a sitcom family: "In all these shows [such as *Father Knows Best* (1954–60) and *The Donna Reed Show* (1958–66)], the family was middle-class, attractive, and lived in a house."[25] Ideal nuclear families with their origins in the culture not of the 1970s but of the 1950s thus provide the model of the good, or at least affluent, life on which *An American Family* drew. And in the process of creating a title sequence — in which each member of the family is highlighted for purposes of individuation while a snappy theme song plays — Gilbert sets the stage for what is in effect a multiple-character, narrative television show with a number of different foci possible for each episode. In a reading that is spot on, Ruoff compares the title sequence to those of the contemporaneous situation comedies *The Brady Bunch* (1969–74) and *The Partridge Family* (1970–74), both of which, like the later *Eight Is Enough* (1977–81), *enlarge* the idea of family.[26] Families, in other words, can expand to encompass the extrafamilial, to include maids (like Alice in *The Brady Bunch*) or managers (like Reuben in *The Partridge Family*), but they must involve lots and lots of kids: all those kids! How do they do it? One "kid" stands out, however, in *An American Family*: oldest son Lance.

The Louds consist of: mother Pat; father Bill ("William C. Loud" on the patriarchal publicity); sons Lance, Grant, and Kevin; and daughters

Delilah and Michele (see figure 3.3). For most of the twelve-hour, twelve-part initial series, the family lives sans Lance at 35 Wooddale Lane in Santa Barbara, California; later, after the parents separate, Bill moves into an apartment. While the domestic interior of the Louds' home (a ranch house, the largely Eastern reviewers can't help but noticing) provides the central mise-en-scène, the Raymonds follow the Louds wherever they go: whether simply to the garage where the brothers play in a band, or outside to the pool, or to Bill's office, to restaurants, Delilah's dance performances, Michele's horse riding and tending, Grant's job sites, the airport, the beach, and so forth. An entire crew followed Lance, who begins his sustained time in the series living at the Chelsea Hotel, notorious for its underground scene, in New York; he then travels with companion Kristian to Europe and returns, broke, to California.

Opening on New Year's Eve of 1972, the first episode of the series begins with an appearance by the producer, Gilbert, to lay out the terms of the cooperative venture between the makers and the Louds. (Gilbert was subsequently parodied in Albert Brooks's film that pokes fun at the series, *Real Life*, from 1979.) The stipulations were as follows: that the filmmakers shoot for seven months, until January 1, 1972, and that the family had an effect on the filmmakers and vice versa. Gilbert gives some history of the family (Bill and Pat's origins in Eugene, Oregon, and their subsequent move south to Santa Barbara) and wryly sets the stage that is apparently nirvana: Santa Barbara (population then about 72,000; on the Pacific coast ninety miles north of Los Angeles; average temperature seventy-five degrees Fahrenheit in the summer, sixty-five in the winter). This first episode also gives away the ghost suggested by the animated shattering of the word *family* in the title sequence: as the family prepares for their New Year's Eve party, Gilbert informs us in voice-over that this is the first time that the family will not be together for the holiday, as Bill and Pat separated four months earlier (three months, we calculate, into the filming process). Cut to Bill in his office in downtown Santa Barbara, having just returned from spending the Christmas holiday in Honolulu, and cut to a photograph on Bill's desk of Lance, who we learn is living in New York. Although Lance phones in from the Village on New Year's Eve, our introduction to him essentially comes in the second episode, which marked the filming of the series proper, as Ruoff documents:

3.3. *An American Family* (PBS, TV series, 1973), directed by Alan Raymond and
Susan Raymond. Shown standing, from left: Grant Loud, Kevin Loud, Delilah
Loud, and Lance Loud; shown seated, from left: Michelle Loud, Pat Loud, and
Bill Loud. © PBS; courtesy Photofest.

The shooting of *An American Family* began when Pat Loud arrived in New York City in late May 1971 to visit Lance at the Chelsea Hotel. Gilbert and the Raymonds knew the milieu of the Chelsea better than Pat did. During this visit, the producer discovered that Lance was gay, "a ready-made point of tension," in Gilbert's words. The Raymonds started filming Mrs. Loud at the hotel before they had even been introduced. Pat's self-consciousness did not let up for weeks and probably contributed to her reserved character in the series. She held back her emotions in reaction to the camera, "that eye of half-truth. It scared me at first. I didn't know what to do with it."[27]

The second episode of the official series, chronicling Lance in New York, has lived longer than the serial as a whole; it alone was rebroadcast in anticipation of the "final episode" (discussed at length later), and it is one of only two episodes of the original serial taken up largely with a single member of the Loud family (in the other, Pat returns to Oregon to visit her mother). I am interested in how queerness and television collide in this episode as *An American Family* enunciates its pedagogical remit while at the same time attempts to contain this complicated and sustained queer appearance on American television.

As Ruoff begins to detail, and as I hope to explore more deeply in departing from his work, the series elaborates what I call a pragmatic pedagogy of queer life. It chronicles, and depends on, an insistent insider-outsider tension, between the straight world and all that was associated with Lance and his milieu, that is, bohemianism, the underground, Warhol's Factory, and, of course, homosexuality.[28] This tension animates later episodes that involve Lance (in Europe, back in Santa Barbara), but it is most evident in the second episode of the series, which is devoted to his New York stay. Pat's visit to the city, beginning with her entering the Chelsea Hotel, confirms that she has entered a world that failed to conform to her expectations, as she later (with gentle humor) verifies in the final episode: Lance introduces Pat in the hallway to Warhol Factory transvestite superstar Holly Woodlawn, who later rejoins Lance and a collection of friends in Lance's small room. Holly would later replace Candy Darling in the performance at the La Mama Experimental Theatre Club of *Vain Victory*, the Jackie Curtis play to which Lance and "roommate" Soren subsequently take Pat in the second episode, and she had also been immortalized the year before the series aired in Lou Reed's terse lyrics for "Walk on the Wild Side."[29]

The camp spectacle of La Mama's *Vain Victory* performance provides a key intertext for *An American Family*, which opposes the artifice, marginality, and apparent frivolity of a chain that includes homosexuality, New York, the underground, bohemianism, and trans and queerness in favor of the claims to reality, seriousness, and critical commentary staked by bourgeois family, Santa Barbara, television, and straightness. If Pat's dis-ease in the presence of the camera and sound operators was not already palpable in the New York footage in general terms, it intensifies and becomes thematized in her response to the *Vain Victory* performance. "I just don't like things that make me feel uncomfortable," she says at a café following the show, trying at the same time maternally to indulge Lance's and Soren's gushing enthusiasm for the "transvestite variety show." (What is more, she seeks to tolerate the presence of the camera and microphone.) Before the show, Lance lists the roster of stars in what he calls the "ultimate of the underground," to which Pat replies, "All these people I've never heard of." Lance, not missing a beat, quips, "Oh you've dreamed of them." But after the show, Pat still doesn't quite understand: "Was there a message that I didn't get?"

The centerpiece of the second episode is an extremely long conversation between Pat and Lance as they walk on a beautiful spring day through Central Park. Lance seeks to explain, and Pat seeks to get, "it." I've transcribed this as faithfully as I could and apologize for its duration, but I think every bit is necessary in order to experience the stunning temporal complexity of queer adolescence and the process of coming out, which can be a very different matter from the utterance "I'm gay." Subsequent citations of this sequence in *An American Family Revisited* and in the final episode, moreover, edit it significantly to eliminate the stumbling, inarticulate, stunted nature of Lance's disclosure and Pat's encouraging yet uncomfortable response (elements that were importantly preserved in the re-creation of this sequence in Cecelia Dougherty's experimental video about Lance, *Gone*, from 2001).[30] Insofar as Pat and Lance interrupt and work together in this conversation, it feels more like a pas de deux than a monologue, with the camera initially following their walk in the park, arms around each other:

PAT: Well I kinda wanted to . . .

LANCE: Yes?

PAT: Talk to you and find out, this is maybe the only time we're alone together . . .

LANCE: I know.

PAT: Find out, um, oh, when you think you'll be moving out of the Chelsea and um . . .

LANCE: Oh!

PAT: What, you know, just a few little plans so that Daddy and I know . . .

LANCE: I want to live there forever.

PAT: That you have . . .

LANCE: I love it there. There are all these individual little cells of people, and they're all famous and all exciting, and they all know what to do, and . . . I don't know, they're just terribly interesting.

PAT: Well, I truly believe that that's the place for you. I mean New York is, and I think that you have found an area that . . .

[*The camera has now swirled to record the conversation from the front.*]

LANCE: I know. Do you know what is so weird? That now that I look back in my life, as far as I've gotten, I keep thinking: god, I sure did some things that if I had been a grown-up and known about the things that I do, or I did then . . .

PAT: That you have done? Well you know . . .

LANCE: There seemed to me like there was so much room for, um, you know . . .

PAT: Improvement? [*laughs*]

LANCE: No, no, no, no, no. You're getting the wrong idea.

PAT: I'm sorry.

LANCE: Um, there was so much, I mean, I stood apart from so . . . everybody I could imagine, I stood apart from.

PAT: Yeah.

LANCE: Like, you know, when I was thirteen I dyed my hair silver and did all that jazz.

PAT: Yeah.

LANCE: And just think, it was energy that was being wasted because . . . [*sigh*] I don't know, it was like being a little mouse and trapped in a box or something in a little white room. I'm not saying that we were . . . led such a super average ordinary life but . . .

PAT: But you went into your room one year, and you didn't come out for about two more years . . .

LANCE: I know.

PAT: Except at night when you lurched out the window.

LANCE: I know, but it was all frustration. I felt so frustrated at being . . . I don't know, there's always been something in me that I could never understand, like I couldn't judge anything that I did or thought. I couldn't judge it on the standards that were given to me, because, um, I mean they just didn't fit. It was like . . .

PAT: I know that.

LANCE: Two different pieces of a puzzle. But then again I didn't have anything else to judge anything on, you know, and didn't understand the standards in the first place.

PAT: [*small laugh*] But um . . . well, you were pretty hard to understand yourself.

LANCE: Um, well anyway, I feel, I think if I had kids, you know, um, there was so much that you guys could have done with me . . .

PAT: Like what, hon?

LANCE: If you'd known. I don't know. It just all, I really do feel that I'll be telling someone about my life or what I did when I was younger . . .

PAT: Uh huh.

LANCE: And even though it might sound boring to them, all of a sudden as I'm talking I'll realize, well, oh Lord! I was much more interesting than anybody I ever knew. I was much more exciting than all those dull people.

PAT: Well.

LANCE: If I was me today and I met me when I was, oh you know, any younger age, I'm sure I'd much rather talk to *that* person than any of his boring friends.

PAT: You mean that automatically you'd choose you for fascinating conversation?

[*They become distracted by the curb, as well as the horseshit in the street and the descending steps. Lance propels himself down the steps ahead of Pat.*]

PAT: Do you want to go on and tell me what you were telling me about what you thought that . . . Come back

[*She commands the adolescent now flinging himself away, and she follows him to the lower side of the stone banister on which he is, childishly, balancing.*]

PAT: We could have done or didn't do and all that jazz? That fascinates me.

Let me pause over a few moments of this conversation for emphasis, noting more generally how stunning it is to discover that it—in all of its length, banality, poignancy, and adolescent awkwardness—appeared on American broadcast television in 1973.[31] While I will return to, and emphasize further, the swirling recursivity and conditionality of the temporal structure of Lance's closet ("now that I look back," "if I was me today," "there was so much you could have done with me . . . if you had known"), I want to begin with the little cells of people who "all know what to do."

Lance's screen image becomes increasingly flamboyant and queeny as *An American Family* progresses, a tendency that he retrospectively notices, if not laments. In the tenth-anniversary program, he contends that in his appearances throughout Europe and on return to Santa Barbara he truly believed that he was fabulous, au courant, and sartorially with it, rather than staging extravagant homosexuality for the Raymonds' recording and American television viewing. "I really didn't do those things to be like a woman or to be femme," he says. "I really thought," he continued, "that I was doing things that were terribly avant-garde and very different, and they were lined up in a way that there I was, a big fag." In his enthusiasm for those who "all know what to do," Lance gives the audience a preliminary indication of what it means to become enfolded into queer culture as an effect of homo-hetero division. In the world of Santa Barbara and the Loud family, Lance is epistemologically and affectively at sea. Judgments and standards and houses and bedrooms and friends and family and even speech and time themselves: none of these work for him. But in the moment when he ventures to New York and finds the Chelsea and its denizens (many of them, like Lance, young gay men who have just arrived, such as the buff boy in overalls featured in Lance's room just before his walk in the park with

Pat), there is certainty and, even more, knowingness. As with Beverly La Salle's character importing queer subcultures from the performance scene in San Francisco into the Bunker bunker in *All in the Family*, *An American Family* brings the Chelsea Hotel, and all that Gilbert and the Raymonds know it to mean, to their documentation of the Louds.

What the series therefore must struggle with is the representation of epistemological division. The show is enormously interested in Lance's appeal as a character: he attracts viewers who delight in his outrageous energy (wit, self-indulgence, self-reflexive campiness, and sheer movement that exceeds the televisual frame). But in following Lance as a character, the series must ultimately attribute to him a perspective, a way and path of knowing in relation to what others in his family (and, by extension, the straight world) can and do know. What is most remarkable to me about *An American Family* is its reversal of the dominant order, at least in this episode: that the series ultimately privileges Lance's queer epistemology, and it seeks to center that epistemology for presumably straight viewers, themselves requiring pragmatic pedagogy in the ways of the queer world of the 1970s.

In the long sequence between mother and son, Lance obviously struggles to name a whole ensemble of social effects (isolation, alienation, longing, boredom, desire, style, at-home-ness) associated with queer adolescence. These effects are knowable, intimately, and palpable to the many gay suburban kids who thanked Lance in their letters to him following the broadcast. While Lance walks with his mother, he enacts a familial bond that serves as the possibility, the very ground, of his social recognition: see me in this moment for who and what I have been and have now become. But in the telling, the present and the past become harder to distinguish. To paraphrase a lines from Gilles Deleuze in *Bergsonism*, the past is not behind, and the present *is* not;[32] in fact, Lance is already retrospective in the present, looking back on his life (at the "present" tender age of twenty) to try to understand what someone (who could be him or another) might make of what he did, had done, was. He seems to me most interested in becoming. He is wondrous: he wonders about how he comes to be and to know. In seeking to return to speak to the childhood version of Lance (in his fantasy all the more interesting than the dullards who surrounded him), Lance seems less concerned with what might be said to *be* his homosexuality that is revealed to his mother (as the definitive act of coming out that has been attributed to this episode) than with how queerness *becomes*, how and what grown-ups know (for shouldn't they know what a thirteen-year-old's fascination with Andy Warhol means?) and what they do to nurture or to thwart queer becoming. Such retrospection takes on ominous and melodramatic overtones when Lance later remarks that at age nineteen, he already felt dead. In a later episode, while applying lipstick and mascara with sister Delilah (of whose 1970s-style blue eye shadow Lance camps, "it looked like part of the kitchen had bit you"), Lance paints himself a death mask: "There, see, I look dead." With death haunting his image even in his youth, the becoming that is thus investigated in the long walk with Pat seems all the more urgent, if only articulated in the gaps and interstices of adolescent speech.

Taking the time on television to give this halting utterance its due, centering queer becoming and queer knowing in such an overt and sustained way, seems to have been a crime for which the series had to atone, at least according to its most severe critics. Before turning to the final installment of the series, *Lance Loud! Death in An American Family*, I sketch some of the terms of the critique of *An American Family*, arguing that the homophobic fear of the dissolution of family is likewise at the center of what the show's perhaps most famous critic, Jean Baudrillard, calls "simulation."

"BE IT EVER SO HOLLOW, THERE'S NO PLACE LIKE HOME"

Anne Roiphe's long article in the *New York Times Magazine* that was contemporaneous with *An American Family*'s broadcast, begins with a promising will to thoughtfulness:

> I felt despair and fascination watching the Loud family, and this could only have been caused by vibrations ricocheting down through my own experiences. The Louds are enough like me and mine to create havoc in my head, and I had to fight a constant strong desire to push away those Louds, dismiss them as unique, empty, shallow, unlike others, and yet on serious reflection, we can all learn from them, perhaps just enough to begin understanding that saddest of mysteries, the American family.[33]

A few paragraphs later, the dismissals nonetheless come, and they focus essentially on how Lance, the family's "evil flower" (8), renders the very institution of the family, indeed American civilization itself, hollow, wounded, and in need of a return to culture, values, and life as we knew it. (These are perversely, to mind, signified through *handicrafts*.) In the process of this reading of the eleven episodes that Roiphe saw in a press screening, framed by comments from the producer, Gilbert, her homophobia can barely be contained and indeed emerges in a string of name-calling that responds precisely to the show's willingness to align itself with Lance's queer epistemology.

In New York, according to Roiphe, Pat is confronted, "brutally and without preparation, with the transvestite, perverse world of hustlers, drug addicts, pushers, etc., and watches her son prance through a society that can hardly be comprehensible to a 45-year-old woman from Santa Barbara" (8). This is familiar stuff: in Pat's name, Roiphe the New York journalist (whom we might expect to seek to educate her readers) refuses to make this perverse "society" intelligible, instead collapsing the underground, the counterculture, queer culture, and youth more generally into an exasperated "etc." Next, through further identification with Pat, Roiphe distorts the text: "As Pat calmly watched a transvestite performance, I felt her straining to accept all the variety of choices in life, to act and be a worldly woman" (9). Never do we have a counter-shot of Pat watching the performance of *Vain Victory* from which to read either calm or straining toward acceptance. Why? Because the footage was shot on a different evening; there was no camera present to record Pat's response at the theater.[34] Here a generalized feminism overtakes journalistic responsibility, again pressing the distinction between the insider and outsider into the service of homophobic fear: *worldly* in this case is a synonym for calmness in the face of perversity. At another point, Roiphe turns her scorn toward forms of life that are neither productive nor reproductive, symptoms of families without compasses, into high venom: "[Lance] is so busy playing in his world of backward genders" (9). And summarizing Lance's return to Santa Barbara, in tour de force display of linguistic nastiness, Roiphe says that the camera "shows him visiting his father in his office, lying about going to school to study journalism, camping and queening about like a pathetic court jester, a Goyaesque emotional dwarf" (9). As if this were not enough, finally, the gay son just becomes poisonous slime: "But I suspect getting close to Lance must have always been like swimming next to an electric eel" (41). Lance, among other members of the family, managed to shrug off what was hurtful in Roiphe's long article, but I reproduce some of her comments here because they have rarely been understood as symptomatic of a larger question, to which I now turn: the sociopolitical function of the television family as an anchor for representational certainty. Roiphe loses her ground when *An American Family* turns out *not* to look like *The Partridge Family, My Three Sons,* or *The Brady Bunch*: "Reality turns out to bear no resemblance to a typical TV comedy" (8).

In its initial reception, as I have mentioned, it was the dissolution of Pat and Bill Loud's marriage that signified the death of the family form, the death of an American family. The ethical question that loomed largest then (meaning, in the text's reception when broadcast) involved the role of the cameras in provoking their divorce: would it have happened if the cameras hadn't been there? Although Gilbert's voice-over that introduces the first episode recognizes that there is no question that the cameras' presence had an impact on the couple, the press evidenced panic around the relationship between the fact of the Louds' participation in this television experiment and Pat and Bill's separation and eventual divorce; that panic derives from a worldview in which authentic relationality, that is, marriage, exists apart from its representation on television.

Baudrillard, I would now like you to recall, puts the Louds at the center of his inquiry into representation, likeness, authenticity, and media (the question of simulation and the hyperreal) in *Simulations*. It is fitting that *Simulations* is a simulated book, one that did not exist before it became translated into English from two different source materials: the first essay, "The Precession of Simulacra," came from *Simulacre et simulations* (Editions Galilee 1981), and it is this essay that features the Louds. It panics over the "dissolution of TV into life, the dissolution of life into TV" through *An American Family* (which Baudrillard may or, I rather suspect, may not have in fact seen, much less in its entirety, during his travels to the United States).[35] The second part of *Simulations*, "The Order of Simulacra," comes from *L'echange symbolique et la mort* (Gallimard, 1976), which was not published in English until 1993 as *Sym-*

bolic Exchange and Death.[36] Containing some of his most stunning and complicated writing, *Symbolic Exchange and Death* also contains essays on fashion and the body, which would provide, in a longer analysis of *Simulations* beyond the purview of the present chapter, crucial intertexts for the investigations in "The Precession of Simulacra" into the invaginated logic of simulacra (in which in summary, in his speculative responses to advertising and consumer culture, Baudrillard finds a society where signs — the currency of the semiotic order — no longer refer to anything but themselves but are generated by, ruled by, the code or the matrix).

Many readers of *Simulations* predominantly reference Baudrillard's discussion of Disneyland in the first essay, which has a kind of pop-culture authority in its endurance and continued culture presence that the Louds simply cannot claim. As the Semiotext(e) editors put it: "In his celebrated analysis of Disneyland, Baudrillard demonstrates that its childish imaginary is neither true nor false, it is there to make us believe that the rest of America is real, when in fact America is a Disneyland." But, like Disneyland, television comes under scrutiny as belonging to the order of the hyperreal or the simulacrum, that is, a "'deterrence machine,' just like Disneyland, meant to reveal the fact that the real is no longer real and *illusion no longer possible*. But the more impossible the illusion of reality becomes, the more impossible it is to separate true from false and the real from its artificial resurrection, the more panic-stricken the production of the real is."[37]

Here is a representative paragraph (Baudrillard actually devotes nine pages to *An American Family*), in which he poses this very question:

> It is again to this ideology of the lived experience of exhumation, of the real in its fundamental banality, in its radical authenticity, that the American TV-verite experiment on the Loud family in 1971 refers: 7 months of uninterrupted shooting, 300 hours of direct non-stop broadcasting, without script or scenario, the odyssey of a family, its dramas, its joys, ups and downs — in brief, a "raw" historical document, and the "best thing ever on television, comparable, at the level of our daily existence, to the film of the lunar landing." Things are complicated by the fact that this family came apart during the shooting: a crisis flared up, the Louds went their separate ways,

etc. Whence that insoluble controversy: was TV responsible? What would have happened *if TV hadn't been there.*[38]

Note that *broadcast* is an odd term, since the audience saw only twelve of those three hundred hours, over a period of several weeks rather than the seven months of filming. In the midst of these multiple temporalities, Baudrillard here makes the time of reception equivalent to the time of recording, when in fact it is the ideological valence of "live" television overwhelming its miniaturization to which Baudrillard is responding. Like Roiphe, his rhetoric requires him to depart from the phenomenon at hand in order to drive home the point. In any case, however, he ultimately suggests that the question about television's responsibility, insoluble as it is, is in fact posed with the wrong emphasis. Under the ruse of claiming to film as if "TV hadn't been there," television presents the Louds, in Baudrillard's view, "as if you were there." Thus quite a different problem, one represented by the aesthetics of the hyperreal. Baudrillard again:

> It is this utopia, this paradox that fascinated 20 million viewers, much more than the "perverse" pleasure of prying. In this "truth" experiment, it is neither a question of secrecy nor of perversion, but of a kind of thrill of the real, or of an aesthetics of the hyperreal, a thrill of vertiginous and phony exactitude, a thrill of alienation and of magnification, of distortion in scale, of excessive transparency all at the same time. The joy in an excess of meaning, when the bar of the sign slips below the regular water line of meaning: the non-signifier is elevated by the camera angle. Here the real can be seen to have never existed (but "as if you were there"), without the distance which produces perspective space and our depth vision (but "more true than nature). Joy in the microscopic simulation which transforms the real into the hyperreal. (This is also a little like what happens in porno, where fascination is more metaphysical than sexual.)[39]

I don't think he's got it right about the metaphysics of pornography, but even if we let that slide, the hyperreal is tricked out in familiar metaphorics of post-Marxist regret coupled with a strong disinterest in perversion. Perspective and depth yield to the elation of simulation, produced through the particular apparatus of filming (not, significantly, of broadcasting). For Baudrillard, the camera angle, itself a stand-in for cinematic signification, operates this emergent aesthetics of hyperreality. We, the viewers, become the problem, as our pleasure drives the motor converting the real into the simulation, the hyperreal. But Baudrillard's very next paragraph contradictorily suggests that the very "content" of the Loud family, not their signification through or as cinema or television, is somehow already hyperreal:

> This family was in any case already somewhat hyperreal by its very selection: a typical, California-housed, 3-garage, 5-children, well-to-do professional upper middle class ideal American family with an ornamental housewife. In a way, it is this statistical perfection which dooms it to death. This ideal heroine of the American way of life is chosen, as in sacrificial rites, to be glorified and to die under the fiery glare of the studio lights, a modern fatum. For the heavenly fire no longer strikes depraved cities, it is rather the lens which cuts through ordinary reality like a laser, putting it to death. "The Louds: simply a family who agreed to deliver themselves into the hands of television, and to die from it," said the producer. So it is really a question of a sacrificial process, of a sacrificial spectacle offered to 20 million Americans. The liturgical drama of a mass society.[40]

The Louds are, in other words, a *television* family (both too ideal, too perfect, and too normal, "simply a family"), with Pat as the "fated" character cast into some sort of mixed-metaphor death machine that is television (a hand, a lens, a laser, and, for Lance, a mouth that ate his family). But why is Baudrillard committed to a reading in which Pat figures as the sacrificial character?

I think it's fair to conclude that he neither actually watched *An American Family* (otherwise he would have understood the impossibility of broadcasting three hundred hours of footage on public television) nor followed the fate of which he's fond to its conclusions. Such lack of attention contributes to one's impatience with cultural theory that rests on breezy associations and fleeting analyses. (I have a similar response to Fredric Jameson being lost in the Los Angeles Bonaventure Hotel as the basis for a full-on theory of postmodernism, but that's another book.) If my interest thus far in the interpenetration of life and television has not uttered the word *simulation*, it has nonetheless been interested, more than Baudrillard, in how heteronormative ideals sustain this fiction of the real on which late capitalist, informatic, and neoliberal regimes depend. But I have not wanted to sacrifice any of the members of the Loud family in so doing. Pat is, at this writing, alive and well. She reunited with Bill late in life after living through the death of their son, Lance. The reunion of his parents was his last wish. That final episode of Lance's life and this series concludes my own chapter here.

DEATH IN AN AMERICAN FAMILY

The final installment, *Lance Loud! A Death in An American Family*, was shot by Susan and Alan Raymond (the original documentarians who shot and recorded the initial series) in 2001 and 2002, mainly in the months before Lance's death, of hepatitis C and HIV co-infection, at the age of fifty. (In marking the transition into the digital era, they titled their production company Video Verité.) The Raymonds and the Louds remained friends for the thirty years between the original broadcast and Lance's death, which he himself requested that they document and air as closure to and for the Louds' drama. In previous sections I looked closely at how the ostensible moment of Lance's coming out is structured by complicated temporalities of retrospection and becoming. Here I want to argue that coming out is later constructed as a retrospective *fiction*, driven by the changing discourses of gay liberation, human rights, and queerness over the three decades of the 1970s, 1980s, and 1990s, respectively, as it is circulated in new contexts and situations. In seeing how Gilbert and his editorial team shaped the first twelve hours of television from more than three hundred hours of footage, we see how in the 1970s new forms of queer reality *and* new forms of family emerged by virtue of the new horizon that was public broadcasting, that is to say, in the possibilities for serial form opened in the early 1970s by the conjunctions of funding and opportunity that I describe in the foregoing discussion. Broadcast three decades later, in 2003, however, this final episode in the story of the Louds introduced an even more complicated structure. Through a voice-over by Susan Raymond, the makers look back to the televisual experiment that was *An American Family*, condensing, contracting, and editing it for a new moment (of its broadcast in 2003). If parents Bill and Pat Loud's marriage woes and eventual divorce dominated much of the public discourse around the series in the 1970s (to be sure, with plenty of scorn for Lance, even beyond Roiphe's article), Lance "now" takes center stage. He reflects on the appearance in 1973 and during the tenth-anniversary follow-up, and he comments in this episode's present about his past, just as he approached his queer past in 1973 through a structure of retrospection.

The final episode combines footage such as (1) material from the series of 1973; (2) material from *An American Family Revisited*, the tenth-anniversary follow-up for PBS; (3) interviews shot before Lance's death (like with Beverly La Salle, at Christmastime) in 2001; (4) interviews and material shot after Lance's death, primarily of Bill and Pat, both saturated with grief, as well as his memorial service; and (5) elements added by the Raymonds such as a voice-over narration (and perhaps some establishing shots) that became necessary in postproduction. It is, like the previous episodes, a highly mediated and layered text that deserves careful attention. I treat only a few of its distinguishing characteristics in conclusion, following in particular the multiple temporalities of Lance that I have been describing all along.

Our introduction to Lance comes in footage that is simply shocking, in that if we have come to know him through television, we have not seen him since 1983. At that moment in the 1980s, admittedly at a low point after the breakup of his band, The Mumps, Lance prepares to return to Los Angeles. Subdued and reflective, he looks back on his time with the Raymonds in the 1970s as among the better moments of his life thus far, in Baudrillardian terms acknowledging how his life meshed with television temporality: "I feel at home in the vernacular of real time, the time that you guys create." Almost twenty years later, Lance is ravaged by the effects of a twenty-some-odd-year drug addiction to crystal methamphetamine and by disease: his body distorted and disabled, teeth missing, hair thinned, face elongated. Lance is dying, and his image, as he says in "the twilight," is powerfully affecting. All participants seem aware of the potentially sensational nature of the episode, including the filmmakers.

My initial observation: more forcefully in this episode than any moment before in the series or the "film," the TV makers, the Raymonds, are seen to shape our picture of this American family though voice-over, through their dominating presence in the image (via Alan's obsessive interest in mirrors), through the inclusion of their interview questions, and through their own assertions of their connection to the Loud family, confirmed it would seem by Lance's request that they return to film and to anticipate his death. In part, their insistent presence is a product of a long-standing feud between the Raymonds and the show's producer, Gilbert, over the right to "sign" *An American Family*. Ruoff chronicles these production battles at some length in his monograph on the series.[41] But another uncanny effect of the Raymonds' presence in this final episode is to give the fictional impression (like Roiphe's line about Pat's response to *Vain Victory*, like Baudrillard's assertion of a three-hundred-hour *broadcast*) that the Louds have been living, now dying, on television not for fourteen hours but for *thirty years*. The Raymonds stretch the time of transmission into the time of their self-declared friendship, in turn naturalizing their presence as well as the presumption of living *as* television.

Indeed, recollection in this installment is entirely televisual: through a structure of nested autoreferentiality between the original series of 1973, an interview Dick Cavett conducted with Lance in 1973, a public television appearance by Margaret Mead who championed the powers of observational television on television, the makers' and Lance's commentary from 1983 on the image of 1973, Pat's commentary in 2002 on the original series, and so on. Other media make brief appearances, such as Roiphe's scathing article, but mostly this is life lived entirely *within* television's frame. Importantly, this episode returns to Mead to emphasize the Louds' *consent* (and, not inconsequentially, to promote *An American Family* as "reality TV avant la lettre"), because the question of Lance's sensational desire to die on television is this installment's central problem.

Lance's own mode of living is retrospective. As a young adult, he already thinks back on his life, as I have foregrounded in my reading of the second episode. That moment, misread as "coming out," is not a proud declaration of identity but a refashioning and reprocessing of a troubled, alienated, lonely queer childhood lived almost wholly in self-conscious emulation of Andy Warhol, further wanting to be redeemed by a mother's conditional understanding of what she "could have done had she known" and the attempt to inhabit that childhood as an adult. At age fifty, Lance now looks back to the version of his family represented in the initial series and wishes for that most televisual closure, a happy ending (if not for him, then for his family). To Lance, the Louds of television in the 1970s were not a happy family; his chance comes in the final episode to unite them ideologically and literally: "I was always a very family-oriented guy, even though I didn't know that," claims Lance, reworking television history to put family and queer back together again. "But I thought family was a part of life that you moved through and that you went on from, but for me that wasn't true, and neither was it true for any of my family." Bill's overwhelming and moving grief at the loss of his son becomes the verification of this retrospective transformation (in the show from 1983, he had said of Lance simply, "I detest his way of life").

Which in turn produces a kind of visual, serial haunting: Lance will die, and therefore the serial cannot be experienced as a forward march without knowing and seeing the outcome of its final episode. The now-signature image of the Lance who millions loved flying down the Santa Barbara hills on his bike cannot *not* be invoked without the companion image of the snaggle-toothed, emaciated, and bent Lance about to die. *An American Family* thus remakes seriality into the measure of an ending, or, better, it reveals this to be the very structure of televisual seriality. The final episode is a kind of death and sometimes, though not always, requires death in order to make narrative stop. (The final episode of *M*A*S*H*, "Goodbye, Farewell, and Amen," which aired the same year as the tenth-anniversary episode of *An American Family*, remains the most-watched television episode in history, with nearly 106 million viewers. Although no cast member died in that episode, the entire series had studied the insensible deaths of war.)

In revisiting Baudrillard and taking his description of the dissolution of Bill and Pat's marriage as the first instance of death, death then comes a second time to the Louds with Lance's, and it is really this final episode that we could describe as a liturgy. So should we pose the same insoluble question? Is it television that causes Lance's death? Was the burden of fame on this ordinary upper-middle-class gay kid too much to bear? Not according to Lance, in his essay "Coming Out: It Separates the Men from the Boys," in which he delights in his public persona, circulated it as much as he could, and realizes how ravenously he embraced a queen's life:

> It was a pleasure to be a gay eyesore. I—or rather my sexual preference—became a cause célèbre, and I greedily capitalized on the situation with such generous flourishes as going on a national media tour, "gaily" provoking callers on radio talk shows across the Midwest, and appearing on *The Merv Griffin Show* with Ronnie Spector-style mascara. I rubbed everyone's nose in my gayness. Why? Because it was there.
>
> The social Armageddon I'd gloomily envisioned descending on me as a result of my decision never materialized; in fact, with my highly publicized reputation preceding me, all kinds of doors swung open as if I were a cuddly extraterrestrial. In my family and in society, my gayness became quietly accepted and—shock of all shocks—life went on. In retrospect, the most unnerving aspect of being openly gay was that it turned out to be as disappointingly normal as being straight.[42]

No, what killed him was normality, to which he opposed the sensational thrills of provocation, self-display, and fame right until the end. Rufus Wainwright and his mother, Kate McGarrigle, sang "Somewhere over the Rainbow" at Lance's memorial service, and it is almost impossible to make it to the end of the final episode without crying along.

What, then, is the take-home argument? *An American Family* may properly be said to have featured the first sustained engagement with a real-life gay person on television. In 1973, not the "late 1980s." If that person was comedy and caricature, he was also the self-conscious architect of his own flamboyance as well as its critic; stereotypes of queer people circulated on television right from the start, and queer people remade themselves in relation to these images. Lance Loud was not an anomalous figure for his time; to the contrary, he represents his time, as many gay men of his generation did, for it was a time that began, in the 1970s, with the full-scale transformation of queer relations to visibility, public life, and the melodramatic structures of disclosure. It was a time of HIV/AIDS infection that has not yet ended, and therefore it remains our own. But it was also television time, or rather times: a mesh of temporalities of real life, recording, transmission, repetition, and seriality in which Lance lived, in which we all live.

In 2008 Walter Newkirk published a book that celebrates and recollects the life of a different gay icon, Edith Bouvier Beale, or "Little Edie," whose story the Maysles brothers, David and Albert, first captured in a landmark observational film, *Grey Gardens* (1975), two years after the first broadcast of *An American Family*. As with *Hairspray*, another queer film that traveled the circuits of commodity entertainment, the story of the Beales continued in a Broadway musical production and made its way to Hollywood. Newkirk's book, titled *MemoraBEALEia*, is a more personal collection of fragments, and it contains an essay by Pat Loud (with whom the author speaks once a week). Pat finds herself surprised to meet Edie, but sees in her a comrade: "Two undefeated survivors of America's first television and film documentaries."[43] Newkirk's book is movingly dedicated to Lance as well as Edie.[44] Of Lance's televisual image, Newkirk writes: "The relationship with his mother Pat that was broadcast as part of *An American Family* was more genuine than anything ever offered on *The Brady Bunch*."[45]

In 2010 HBO announced that it was remaking *An American Family*, or making a film about its making, to be called *Cinema Verite*. The result pays homage to the original series in a number of innovative ways. It embeds original broadcast footage, most notably in sequences that provide segmenting titles for *Cinema Verite*. It visually mimics important moments in the original broadcast, such as Pat's entry into the Chelsea Hotel, when she met the crew for the first time (see figure 3.4). Even while mimicking these, however, *Cinema Verite* edits them, such as the walk Lance takes with Pat that I've endeavored to describe; in the HBO film, that loping, recursive discussion is shortened to a forty-second exchange. The logic, as I read it, is that for audiences in the early twenty-first century, Lance is already known to be gay, especially as he's played by Thomas Dekker, who imitates Lance's speech patterns almost precisely and flamboyantly prances in costumes imitative of Lance's original wardrobe (see figure 3.5).

Where *Cinema Verite* most departs from the texture of the second episode of *An American Family*, the episode that follows Lance's life in New York, is notably in its loving re-creation of the *Vain Victory* drag-show performance. In this remake, Pat's discomfort is materialized on

3.4. Pat Loud entering the Chelsea Hotel, *An American Family*. Shown, from left: Diane Lane, Shanna Collins, and Patrick Fugit.

3.5. Dual monitors from *Cinema Verite* (TV movie, 2011); Shown, from left: Lance Loud, Pat Loud, Thomas Dekker, and Diane Lane.

her face (she's played wonderfully by Diane Lane), as though taking Roiphe's feminist-inspired rant and translating it to the screen. Here, we watch Pat watch, and, as she becomes more and more distressed by the thought of America watching Lance watch *this*, she leaves. For those who haven't seen the original, or who don't remember the structure of the segment, the series of reverse shots of Pat's painful response won't mean much. But for those of us who appreciate the intervention by which *An American Family* centered Lance's queer experience as a televisual locus of knowledge, *Cinema Verite* marks a clear departure from the practical pedagogy of PBS to the commercial registers of pay cable (which is also the subject of my next chapter). Still, the remake gives Lance the final word: "Family is eternal. You can see it in the shape of the ears, or the initials carved into hearts, on trees. Divorce can't destroy it. Television can't devour it. We're still standing. Loud and proud."

CHAPTER 4

Queer Ascension

Television and Tales of the City

The title "Queer Ascension: Television and Tales of the City" means to conjure the television adaptation from 1993 of Armistead Maupin's *Tales of the City* (1978), a fictional chronicle, indeed its own sort of history, of queer life in San Francisco. If during its second episode *An American Family* peeked in real time at the scene in downtown New York circa 1972, *Tales of the City* recursively returns to the 1970s through the changing medium that is television near the beginning of the twenty-first century, that is, a medium increasingly defined by proliferation via multichannel delivery platforms, such as cable and satellite, and by time shifting, or the capacity to record programs from the multichannel environment of cable television on a videotape recorder or, later, digital recorder. The term *time shifting* suggests that it is also a helpful figurative rubric for describing these very temporal displacements of *Tales of the City*. As I noted in the introduction, the franchise began as a serial column by Maupin in the 1970s and moved from one newspaper to another; the columns appeared collected in book volumes, and the first book was adapted for public television in the 1990s. Then pay cable television (Showtime) produced the two sequels. The series continues to thrive in the format of further novels, such as *Michael Tolliver Lives* (2007) and *Mary Ann in Autumn* (2010). Along the way, what initially took shape as a coeval series of observations or sketches on gay San Francisco morphed into a retrospective meditation on a time that had definitively passed, that is, a time before HIV/AIDS.

The term *time shifting* disappoints, however, in capturing the ways in which *Tales of the City* renders *in space* these temporal displacements. I am drawn to *Tales of the City* as what I would like to call a text of ascension. Not quite utopia, but on the way: rising. Using the imagery immanent in this televised serial, an imagery largely consisting of stairs, I address more explicitly the spatial arrangements of queer and televisual temporalities that converge in these moments of technological and industrial innovation that structure my previous chapters. Consistent with the method of those chapters, I do not consider *Tales of the City* in isolation; it would be difficult indeed to conjoin in one breath *San Francisco* and *heights* without understanding, as the series does, a much broader mediatized world (a world in which Alfred Hitchcock's *Vertigo* [1958] is only one among many intertexts), and so I am interested much more broadly in these mediatized versions of urbanity. Similarly, one cannot invoke San Francisco's televisual landscape without noting its stunning visual presence, in *The Streets of San Francisco* (1972–76), for example, not to mention scores of films and television programs locating San Francisco at the center of queer America. And not to mention additional scores of television programs and sites of popular culture—from *Days of Our Lives* to the royal wedding—obsessively and lovingly cited in various televised installments of *Tales of the City*. But my frame of reference is both smaller and much larger than these intertexts would suggest: smaller, first, because San Francisco was my queer city of the 1970s, after our family moved north from Los Angeles. It was where I, with my fake ID, first went to an actual lesbian bar (Amelia's), learned to wear painter's pants and Lacoste shirts, and learned how (by becoming a boi) to accompany my best gay boyfriend, Ernie, to the Castro. My queer adolescence converged with the young adulthood of Michael Tolliver, a protagonist in *Tales of the City*, and I am constrained, or rendered breathless, by the accumulation of details that *Tales of the City* insists on nailing, from the outfittage (add Levis 501s, tube socks, work boots, All American Boy) to the music, the drugs, the mood, the politics, the textures, the light.

My frame is larger, however, for different reasons. Given the persistent actuality of queer migrations to cities (and their representation and documentation) at the beginning of the twenty-first century, I am struck by the paucity of critical thinking about the *specificity* of "the city" both sociologically and in terms of media analysis. Rarely have televisual versions of cities (from the Boston of *Cheers* to the New York of *Sex and the City* to the Pittsburgh of *Hill Street Blues* to the Baltimore of *The Wire*) borne a burden of scrutiny beyond journalistic or touristic site mapping, but rarer still has been the attempt to situate these cities of free migration and relatively open movement in relation to those queer destinations of the global South (Rio, Manila, Lagos) that more properly define "the city" in this era of megacities and urban domination of global populations than these comparatively small cities of the global North. (To take but a single illustrative example: in the textbook *Cities and Cinema*, separate successive chapters are devoted to "the city as queer playground" and "the global city and cities in globalization," reproducing the very disturbing cleavage between discourses of sexuality and those of globality that I want to challenge here.[1]) I want to wonder what *the* city could possibly mean for queer life in the new millennium and, second, how we might ascend to it. I want to take seriously the possibility that cities could provide promising spaces for queer world making without presuming that a model of normative inclusion extends generally to the city. My presentation in this chapter has sections on walls, sidewalks, stairs, and, in a much longer treatment of the serial, windows. I close with a section on Showtime and the sequels, which, as you will see, I find far less interesting than the initial *Tales of the City*.

WALLS

Questions regarding media and urban publics have proliferated in cinema and media studies. Films set in European cities in the 1920s and 1930s, Weimar "street films," postmodernist virtual cities produced in films like *Blade Runner* and *The Matrix*, sociohistorical contexts for urban sites of production, film noir: all of these have been useful rubrics for exploring, to borrow Ed Dimendberg's title, "spaces of modernity" (the literature here includes Dimendberg's *Film Noir and the Spaces of Modernity*, James Donald, Sabine Hake, David Clarke, the chapters in Linda Krause and Patrice Petro's *Global Cities*, among others).[2] I share with John David Rhodes, the author of a wonderful book about a particular filmmaker (Pasolini) and a particular city (Rome), the sense, however, that often these discussions about cities and cinema, in Rhodes's words, "assume a rather abstract, diffuse character; often the 'city' might even be only an imagined city—a fabrication of set design and cinematography."[3] This concern about specificity preoccupied me in the writing I had done on the Brazilian film *Bus 174* (2002), a documentary about a bus hijacking in Rio de Janeiro.[4] I want to elaborate on Rio, Latin American cities, and these megacities more broadly for a moment in a sort of prolegomenon to frame, in both senses (that is, to outline but also to cast suspicion on), the bulk of this chapter on queer urban life and media publics: I want to ask preliminarily and in a broad sense, that is, *which* cities, *what* media, and in what ways tied to *having been, being*, and *becoming* (the possibility of a future)? What drew me to *Bus 174* initially was television: the multihour ordeal of the hijacking was telecast "live" and earned the highest ratings of the year on Brazilian TV in 2000. José Padilha, the director of *Bus 174*, manipulates the now-archival television footage to reveal, or at least to probe, that which the television cameras could not, would not record: that is, the lives of the young people (children and adolescents), such as the hijacker, Sandro Nasciemento, who hail from the favelas and populate the streets of cities like Rio and São Paulo. Television—preoccupied with the drama of the event, the hypervisibility of the hijacker waving his gun for the cameras—was blind to the everyday invisibility of and violence against street children. Broadcast television was also deaf to the collapse of a Brazilian civil society capable of redressing the effects, congealed in these young citizen-bodies, of globalization and neoliberalist expansion. In *Expediency of Culture*, George Yúdice reminds us in stark terms that

in Rio, as in other major Latin American urban centers, poor black and mulatto youth have no citizenship rights to speak of. They are not protected by the police; on the contrary, the police, often in cahoots with *justiçeiros* or vigilantes, harass them in the best of cases, and in the worst, murder them and leave their corpses on the street to serve as a warning to others. Human rights organizations' records show that in 1991 in São Paulo alone, the military police killed 876 "street youth." That number was expected to increase to 1,350 in 1992. In comparison, 23 youth were killed in similar circumstances in New York, a city about the same size as São Paulo. The point is not so much that in São Paulo the police kill thirty-eight times as many youth as in New York (although that itself is a telling statistic), but that the method of dealing with unemployment, lack of educational opportunity, hunger, and racism is "social cleansing" of the poor.[5]

Yúdice and other writers on Latin American geography, such as Teresa Caldeira in her wonderful book *City of Walls*, confront an urban landscape in which processes of social differentiation, as Yúdice puts it, "render commonality difficult if not impossible."[6] This is a world in which invoking even the more Gramscian notion of a "subaltern public" may be to strain the potential for a national collectivity, and in which it may be more germane to witness, as Giorgio Agamben puts it, how "the capitalistic-democratic plan to eliminate the poor not only reproduces inside itself the people of the excluded but also turns all the populations of the Third World into naked life."[7] Purposeful and not so purposeful acts of occupying space in these cities (that is, being seen and being heard) might performatively assert belonging to a fractured and dissolute polity, but, as with any performative, there is no guarantee of success in those acts. Similarly, media responses can easily be folded into complicit spectacle.

These kinds of analyses and alternative genealogies not of "the city" as undifferentiated urban space but of cities under siege, cities to which we are umbilically linked in global networks, in other words, powerfully chart the fraying of normative ideals of modern city life, which include a sense of openness, fluidity, and coexisting unassimilated differences. Caldeira provides a snapshot of the contours of the normative ideal:

> Although there are various and sometimes contradictory accounts of modernity in Western cities, the modern experience of public life is widely held to include the primacy and openness of streets; free circulation; the impersonal and anonymous encounters of pedestrians; spontaneous public enjoyment and congregation in streets and squares; and the presence of people from different social backgrounds strolling and gazing at others, looking at store windows, shopping, sitting in cafes, joining political demonstrations, appropriating the streets for their festivals and celebrations, and using spaces especially designed for the entertainment of the masses (promenades, parks, stadiums, exhibition spaces).[8]

In contrast to this modern ideal, and to remain within the Americas for a moment, megacities display an *aesthetic of security* (in different ways that would need to be specified), where fortresses, barriers, walls, surveillance cameras, dogs, barbed wire, codes, armored cars, and machine guns enforce social differentiation and grant prestige.[9] This aesthetic recognizes the possibility of permeability (let's call that an index of the modern city), and it armors itself precisely against it. The wall creates a zone of relative safety that peremptorily denies social integration.[10] Public spaces harbor threat. To walk is to challenge the hegemony of the elite. Spaces calibrate affect in new rhythms; the wall cannot extend everywhere, and so anxiety and fear become dispersed. According to a text cited by Yúdice with respect to Rio, "Dark strollers in sandals and shorts fill the streets of the Zona Sul. They intuit the fear of the 'middle classes' and promenade with pride. White *cariocas* become indignant, as if only they were the true native city dwellers."[11] Examples could be multiplied, mutatis mutandis, from Mumbai, Delhi, Mexico City to Karachi, Lagos, Jakarta, Manila, Bogotá. And Baghdad, where new walls seek to contain what we've come to call "insurgency." Or the long wall that literalizes the draconian severity of the occupation of Palestine, documented in Simone Bitton's meditative film *Wall* (2005). These *are not cities that legislate inclusion on the model of distributive justice*; by the 1990s, the normative ideal of city life proposed, for example, by Iris Marion Young (in "City Life and Difference") of a "being together with strangers" seemed out of reach for many of the world's largest cities.[12] Violence and poverty create new cartographies of the global city, traced in media of the past decades, including *Bombay, Our City* (Anand Patwardhan, 1985), *City of God* (Fernando Meirelles, 2002), *Carandiru* (Hector Babenco, 2003), and *Favela Rising* (Jeff Zimbalist, 2006). These instances, like *Bus 174*, trace the movements of and constraints on *young people*: workers, hustlers, prisoners, addicts, street dwellers, lovers, artists, musicians. And they have of course moved to television and other platforms, as with the adaptation of *City of God* into TV's *City of Men* (Meirelles, 2006) and back again into another *City of Men* (Paulo Morelli, 2007) film. Whether redemptive, despairing, or critical, these visual mappings foreground the violence of social differentiation and explore obstacles to meaningful forms of social life, if not to life, that is, then adulthood itself.

These are the conditions of queer migration to urban spaces in this moment. What are we to make of them, and how do they press upon the time and spatial logic of a re-creation such as *Tales of the City?*

SIDEWALKS

A subgenre of these phenomena specifically treats queer young life in the cities of the global South: hustling on the streets and in the bars of Manila (in Lino Brocka's now seemingly ancient *Macho Dancer*, 1988) or surviving in its slums (in *The Blossoming of Maximo Oliveros*, Auraeus Solito, 2006); haunted by love in Mexico City (in *A Thousand Clouds of Peace*, Julián Hernández, 2004); tracing individual stories of urban India in *Bomgay* (Riyad Vinci Wadia, 1996), or seeing how the cities of the North are themselves reconfigured by both migration and exclusion in something like Sébastien Lifshitz's *Wild Side* (2004). You might add a number of your own examples.

What I would like to propose, now turning to the central text of this chapter, *Tales of the City* and its sequels, is that we not take the city of the queer North as an isolated example—because here I wish to concentrate on one of two cities in the United States that might qualify for the designation of "*the* queer city," that is, San Francisco. I am therefore trying to avoid the tendency to confuse specificity with hermeticism. As I noted at the outset, I want instead to let the cartography of the globe and its migrations (a more macro perspective of the embattled cities of walls) seep into the cartography of the queer street (a more micro perspective) that informs relatively recent histories of queer cities, including George Chauncey's *Gay New York*, Morris Kaplan's *Sodom on the Thames*, and Matt Houlbrook's *Queer London*. Lest my leap to these histories seem abrupt, I seek to trace a series of connections—away from the walled cities of the South to the promenades of the queer North, whose complicated micropractices of urban life these histories collect— because they provide a critique of normative inclusion from another perspective that can be, to a calculable extent, aligned with that of post-colonial reason. For the sake of maintaining control over the exegesis, I focus on Chauncey and Houlbrook, since both (at least until Chauncey's next book is published) concentrate on the transformations of the early twentieth century. It is also true that the television version of *Tales of the City* is a U.S.-British hybrid, conjoining these two histories into a fantasmatic or mythological response to Chauncey's and Houlbrook's queer historiographies, queer sidewalks. And it is true that I know intimately the San Francisco of which *Tales of the City* tells its tales. It is only more recently (and through cinema and television, among other conduits) that I've come to know how cities of walls look and feel.

The first take-home message of both Chauncey and Houlbrook, that is, the first lesson of queer history of these particular cities (New York, London) and doubtless others like them, is that the sexual binarism represented by the homo-hetero distinction is an astonishingly recent creation. Both scholars' explorations of the city and sexual difference emphasize instead how the nomenclature of *gay* occludes the variety in types of sexual actors and practices of the twentieth century and leads to misconceptions wrought by Whiggish history. Chauncey insists, contra the kind of history that assures us of progress across the march of time, that "gay life in New York was *less* tolerated, *less* visible to outsiders, and *more* rigidly separated in the second third of the century than the first, and that the very severity of the postwar reaction has tended to blind us to the relative tolerance of the prewar years."[13] At the same time, the assertion of a respectable homosexual subject in the midcentury in both cities (as the deserving beneficiary of inclusion in public life and of reform) "effaced—and continue to efface—multiple and inalienable sexual and social differences."[14] The poof, the pansy, the queen, that is, all sorts of effeminate men who had sex with men (and all varieties of these men, in turn): these queers and these practices suggest forms of difference that "cannot be mapped straightforwardly onto the modern categories 'gay' or 'homosexual.'"[15] Houlbrook and Chauncey, that is, provide a critique of the ideal of normative inclusion from the perspective of excluded and demonized genders and sexualities.

Produced as much through as on the city's social grid, queer life articulated this stunning variety spatially within the tensions of the public and the private: in the streets of the West End or the Bowery, in urinals, in bars and clubs, in alleys or parks, in apartment buildings and YMCAs, in baths, and, I'll return to this in a moment, in cinemas. I've wanted to use the designation *sidewalk* to mark this section not in order to homogenize these very different sorts of spaces and practices but to foreground the one most fraught as an index of modernity.

The sidewalk is an emblem of visibility and safety (to repeat Caldeira's list): "The primacy and openness of streets; free circulation; the impersonal and anonymous encounters of pedestrians; spontaneous public enjoyment and congregation in streets and squares; and the presence of people from different social backgrounds strolling and gazing at others, looking at store windows, shopping, sitting in cafes, joining political demonstrations, appropriating the streets for their festivals and celebrations."[16] In short, being seen and being heard openly, freely, without violence: an aesthetic, if you will, of circulation and contact. As much as both historians focus on the early twentieth century, they want their work to serve very much as a history of this present, indeed offering a kind of reparative model of a more visible, more tolerant, and more fluid queer city than we now occupy.

The second take-home message of these histories is that sexual and spatial practices converge along a number of social forms. (Houlbrook alone lists "modern forms of expert knowledge, municipal government, the urban crowd, a mass media, consumerism, new understandings of selfhood, economic change, and the separation of public and private space."[17]) Both books invoke sexual topographies, on the one hand as practices or "tactics by which gay men appropriated spaces not identified as gay,"[18] and on the other hand as forms of inscription, countermapping or cognitive mapping, "maps etched in the city streets by daily habit."[19] (Henri Lefebvre would similarly distinguish among spatial practices, representations of space, and representational spaces.[20]) To supplement macrolevel analyses of the homosexual and the modern city, microlevel analyses conceive of the city, in Houlbrook's terms this time, "as a series of related but discrete sites of interaction, danger, and pleasure: the flux and transience of the urban crowd—that public world of streets, parks, and urinals; the sites of modern consumer culture— the commercial realm of bars and nightclubs; the unique commercial space of London's bath houses; residential spaces and the separation between public and private life."[21] No doubt the forms of appearance of queer life in these sites were heavily policed, but it is also true, as both historians note, that a variety of sexual and social forms flourished beneath the gaze of the law and reformers, leading to splendidly defiant flaunting, a complex semiotics of sartorial minutiae, exciting intermixing, and modes of traversing urban spaces that marked them as queer. One queen described his London neighborhood as "a huge homosexual kingdom just below the surface of ordinary life with its own morals and codes of behaviour." "When I walk through Notting Hill Gate," he gushed, "I feel I'm at a gigantic homosexual party."[22]

Another site for gigantic homosexual parties was, of course, the cinema itself. Houlbrook describes the policing efforts of cinemas of "doubtful reputation" in London from the 1910s to the 1950s, studying how licensing provisions led to architectural modifications that eliminated darkness and the possibility of contact in seats or along what the British colorfully call "gangways" or aisles.[23] The cause for such surveillance came in the desire to constrain a different, particular, and historically marked public form of intimacy or pleasure: that is, female prostitution. And the cinema is but one urban site in the first half of the twentieth century where the boundaries anxiously policed in the case of "streetwalkers" correspond to the boundaries challenged by lads in dark cinemas with mackintoshes over their arms, concealing their "actual" and, we hope, potentially erect, movements. (If I had time and could even sketch the careful work of Samuel Delany's *Times Square Red, Times Square Blue*, I would corroborate how the discourses of urban reform seize on the apparently troublesome and exploitative exchange of sex for money in their mapping of sexual deviance and, conversely, how little they seem to understand that there are some who pay, some who don't, and some who, like Garbo, just want to be left alone.[24]) In any case, it seems important that the cinema—in its darkness, in the distance from the sidewalk marked by a commercial transaction and the space of the lobby, and in its sexual practices under the cover of a kind of public privacy—nonetheless extends the contact of the sidewalk: being with strangers in urban space. Intimately. Pleasurably. That form of participatory interaction valued by writers from Jane Jacobs to Iris Young to Chauncey and Houlbrook to Delany for its cross-class, cross-racial, incidental, fluid, and open possibilities. But, it would seem, not its cross-gender possibilities. Here is the stumbling block.

What I've learned from both Chauncey's and Houlbrook's books is more than considerable. This example of the cinema as a site of urban public sexual life, however, helps to address a methodological question that lies at the heart of both accounts of queer urban history, that is, how to account for these complex spatial productions such as the cinema, in which parts of the bodies of both genders conjoin with policing and reform and their defiance, with coats and seats and lights, with a wide variety of sexual and nonsexual alliances, and with a history of representations (the projected films themselves) in bizarre machines of urban sexualities *without addressing questions of gender*. Here's Houlbrook:

> This book is about men, not women. Certainly, queer men and women inhabited many of the same commercial venues, and their sense of self took shape within overlapping understandings of gender and sexuality. While men were able to move through the public city by day or night, women's access to public space was more problematic. The association between femininity and domesticity, familial and neighborhood surveillance, anxieties surrounding the moral status of public women, and the city's very real dangers constrained women's movements. Women's marginal position in the labor market lessened their ability to access commercial venues or private residential space. In London, queer women negotiated a very different set of problems. While female sexual deviance—particularly prostitution—was inscribed within forms of surveillance that echoed the regulation of male sexualities, lesbianism remained invisible in the law and, in consequence, in the legal sources on which this book draws. Lesbian London deserves its own study.[25]

Chauncey, by the way, excludes women in the name of feminism, in the name of doing justice to lesbians: "The book focuses on men because the differences between gay male and lesbian history and the complexity of each made it seem virtually impossible to write a book about both that did justice to each and avoided making one history an appendage to the other."[26]

What interests me in these protestations, coming from historians rigorously interested in what we might call queer gender (the spectrum of types of queer lives, practices, and identifications that can't be mapped easily onto either the masculine-feminine binary or the homo-hetero distinction), is that they immediately conflate the question of gender with sexuality, women and femininity with "lesbian" (presumably a stable historical category that would easily be mapped onto the early twenty-first-century creature?). Sorry, they seem to say in the name of specificity and equality, I'm writing on men, not on lesbians. But what then of women? Of femininity when not identical with effeminacy on presumably male bodies? Not to mention that historical catalog of prostitutes, fag hags, trannies, beards, hostesses, landladies, and so on: those women or even "women" or sometimes perhaps "lesbians" whose own maps overlaid and I suspect often determined or rewrote the cartographies of these queer men's cities are simply absent.

I am not a historian. I am limited to pointing out that the surveillance of the cinemas provides but one instance in which these histories seem pressured by their own findings to think sexuality through even more detailed topographies *alongside* gender, while not, however, forsaking the lessons of Eve Sedgwick, Gayle Rubin, and others about the specific grids and modalities of sexual life. The consequences of such thinking would augment rather than detract from the specificity of queer gender (the types of practices, self-stylings, desires, and embodiments made possible through struggles for queer urban life), seeing instead how forms of women's sexual outlawry inspired and, in turn, were nourished by men's, or seeing, even better, how difficult it sometimes might be to tell one from the other. The flourishing of urban sexual cultures seems, in some instances at least, to depend on routes traveled by men and women who put pressures on the normative confines—moral and spatial—of urban sexual life. Under the threat of policing and violence, carving out avenues for public practices of sexual dissidence, creating the modern city of sidewalks, is no small feat, and yet it seems to have frequently been one shared by men and women alike, in a world in which masculinity and femininity refuse to map neatly onto categories of modern queer life.

STAIRS

Where better to mythologize the modern city of queer sidewalks than on television, our cherished site for transcoding public life into intimate and manageable proximity? I read *Tales of the City* as simultaneously inheriting and refusing, in good melodramatic fashion, this queer historiography that I've just encapsulated. On the one hand, *Tales of the City* displays a post-Stonewall ebullience about gay progress, reveling in the ubiquity of gay male culture and its almost-total saturation of San Francisco's urban spaces. Even if we acknowledge that such exuberance is a product of openly avowed nostalgia for pre-AIDS gay male sexual cultures, it nonetheless circulates — at the point of crisis for publicness itself that I've suggested obtains in many of the world's urban spaces — a dream of sexual and urban intimacy *untroubled by antagonism, undivided by walls*. In this way, *Tales of the City*, like much U.S. popular culture of the last third of the twentieth century, reproduces and consolidates the sexual binaries that our queer historians have revealed precisely as constraint. On the other hand, *Tales of the City* produces an alternative history, now of a more recent era of queer urban life (that is, the 1970s and 1980s) that attempts at the very least to acknowledge women, gender, and feminism (all three!) and not relegate them entirely to the gutters of the extraneous (if truth be told, however, *Tales of the City* isn't really interested in lesbians). I don't want to argue that it's triumphant, neither subversive nor hegemonic, but that it routes real questions of queer being through women, femininity, and trans cartographies, interestingly mapped. (Here I should also pause to apologize for not including in this chapter detailed discussions of a host of other queer TV shows of this moment that have contradictory and oblique relationships with femininity, such as *Queer Eye, Queer as Folk*, and others you might nominate.)

In the introduction, I've noted the production history for *Tales of the City* and its sequels, enabled by American and British collaboration. It's also worth noting that the miniseries appeared through *American Playhouse*, an anthology venue that, under the stewardship of Lindsey Law, offered television opportunities for independent filmmakers and queer innovation for almost two decades.[27] Let us turn now to the convergence of story and history in this drama that follows a group of characters who converge at 28 Barbary Lane in San Francisco, a fictional address that cites the Barbary Coast, a real San Francisco neighborhood known by the beginning of the twentieth century as a hotbed of perversion, as well as prostitution, gambling, and crime. This is a delicious extended snippet from a social history of the neighborhood in 1933:

The Barbary Coast is the haunt of the low and the vile of every kind. The petty thief, the house burglar, the tramp, the whoremonger, lewd women, cutthroats, murderers, all are found here. Dance-halls and concert-saloons, where blear-eyed men and faded women drink vile liquor, smoke offensive tobacco, engage in vulgar conduct, sing obscene songs and say and do everything to heap upon themselves more degradation, are numerous. Low gambling houses, thronged with riot-loving rowdies, in all stages of intoxication, are there. Opium dens, where heathen Chinese and God-forsaken men and women are sprawled in miscellaneous confusion, disgustingly drowsy or completely overcome, are there. Licentiousness, debauchery, pollution, loathsome disease, insanity from dissipation, misery, poverty, wealth, profanity, blasphemy, and death, are there. And Hell, yawning to receive the putrid mass, is there also.[28]

Such a criminal, salacious stew makes for good stories, from the Howard Hawks film *The Barbary Coast* (1935) to the William Shatner television vehicle of the same name forty years later, with countless versions in between. The immoral frisson of the Barbary Coast makes for an odd graft, however, onto Macondray Lane, that very real pocket of multimillion-dollar urban heaven on Russian Hill, which inspired Maupin and Victoria Paul, the production designer of the set that serves as 28 Barbary Lane. The Macondray steps allow access to this enclave, described by tourist literature as "quaint," "charming," "idyllic," and "woodsy."

But for "woodsy," these are apt descriptors for the world of the fictional number 28. Licentiousness, if it is to be found, must be unearthed (and unearthed it will be) beneath a surface of Victorian charm, gleaming fresh and brightly painted wood, blooming gardens and lush trellises, and a stack of apartments linked by more staircases that relay the unfolding melodrama. An enclosed, enchanted world, rising into the sky, 28 Barbary Lane will recode the stew of perversion, Orientalism, and debauchery of the Barbary Coast as "charming." Perhaps also as "generous." And without risk.

As opposed to an aesthetic of security associated with the wall or an aesthetic of circulation and contact associated with the street, the first staircase, then, modeled after the Macondray steps, establishes what I'd like to call an aesthetic of *curiosity*, one that toys with the distinctions

4.1. Macondray steps, San Francisco. Courtesy of
Larry Rhodes, http://www.toursofthetales.com.

of publicness and privacy, outside and inside, ostracism and belonging,
gay and straight, man and woman, around which the serial will build
its material. Steps that rise from the street in San Francisco are largely
public, but like those in the Berkeley hills, they generally access houses,
not parks or businesses. Or, better, they traverse public streets and private houses, instilling in the intrepid climber the occasional sense that
one is trespassing. Unlike walls or fences, they present no prohibition
or physical obstacle, and frequently the hidden or secret space that one
accesses by ascending the steps repays the often-considerable physical
effort involved in the climb. Unlike sidewalks, they do not invite the
intermixing and gazes of many strangers: they, like the television, exist
only for you. The art directors for *Tales of the City* take the Macondray
steps and graft the imaginary Barbary Lane directly onto them. First,
take the Macondray steps (see figure 4.1). Next, the very same steps of

Tales of the City, with Mary Ann Singleton descending (see figure 4.2). And now the exterior steps of the Barbary Lane set, traversing its own levels of intrigue (see figure 4.3).

The camera in *Tales of the City* furthermore acts in your stead, as though it is discovering a magical land each time it enters from the position of these ostensible exterior steps. It frames the house on Barbary Lane frequently through foliage, poking its way through a space that seems oversaturated, bountiful, obscenely lush. The aura of magic drenches the space through an unusual vehicle, not one restricted to mise-en-scène but extending into a typology of character, that of Mrs. Anna Madrigal, Barbary Lane's landlady. Given to flowing, knee-length linens and silks, headbands, Orientalist interior decorating, and copious amounts of marijuana, Mrs. Madgrial, played by Olympia Dukakis, seems designed to breathe new life into the word *enchanting* (see figure 4.4). Harboring her own mysteries (spoiler alert), she presides at the top of the exterior stairs and thus functions formally as a gate-

4.2. *Tales of the City* (PBS, TV miniseries, 1994). Shown: Laura Linney as Mary Ann Singleton.

4.3 *Tales of the City* (PBS) TV Miniseries 1994.

4.4. *Tales of the City*. Shown: Olympia Dukakis. © PBS, courtesy Photofest.

keeper, monitoring entries and exits. She is repeatedly foregrounded as a sentry in dialogue referring to her, for example, as a keeper of a lighthouse. Whatever class antagonism might arise from the structural relationship of landlord to tenant vanishes, too, by the assertion of a Barbary Lane "family," over which Mrs. Madrigal presides as "the mother of us all."[29]

She also resides in the ground-floor apartment and is alone among the cast in only rarely venturing above, through the network of staircases that join the apartments on the upper two levels. This second kind of staircase, within the complex of (the set that is) Barbary Lane, stitches together the narrative arcs of an ensemble-cast drama featuring Mary Ann Singleton (in one of Laura Linney's first major roles), an ingenue from Cleveland who flees her conventional and cloying parents to make a life in the city; the resident bohemian Mona Ramsey, initially played by Chloe Webb (who, despite the Quaalude popping and mantra chanting, is an account executive at an advertising agency); Mona's best gay boyfriend Michael "Mouse" Tolliver, initially played by Marcus D'Amico, a flannel-and-501-clad clone searching for true love; the Halcyon family (Edgar, owner of said ad agency; Frannie, his sauced society wife; DeDe, initially pouty and then interestingly complicated daughter; and Beauchamp, his scofflaw son-in-law); and an assortment of lovers tossed in to create surprises mostly in sexual identity.

The stairs that link this cast together serve as exchange points in the relay of individual dramas, and each step can thereby provide a platform on which to pause, to convey some necessary narrative information, or to take into shared space that which unfolds in the privacy of each apartment. The stairs exert some centrifugal force on the domain of the relatively private, *drawing out*, leaking domestic and intimate details into the quasi-public but protected space of Barbary Lane. (In passing, I should note that there is a third, almost-hidden staircase revealed by the infrequent reverse shots that greet visitors entering into this mythical bower. It rises alongside one of the few impermeable walls that help to constrain the cascading garden, suggesting that every possible obstacle or obstruction harbors paths of exploration and further adventure. Uh oh, and I need to mention how the entire mystery of the first sequel, *More Tales of the City*, traverses the theme of vertigo produced by a series of steep stairs in a landmark San Francisco church.)

By virtue of its staircases, *Tales of the City* lifts the queer gaze from the streets into the air, so that every aspect of San Francisco becomes tinged with happy gayness bathed in surprising sunshine for a city usually smothered by fog: a pan of the view from the Bay Bridge to Coit Tower to Alcatraz, the aerials of the Financial District and its streets and canyons of industry, the Ghirardelli Square sign, or the beaches (waves crashing, kites flying) and parks with clean and empty benches inviting trysts and gay leisure. (The ability to map these spaces is important to the serial, as witnessed by Maupin's "Atlas" on his website or by the even more impressive site curated by Larry Rhodes, Tours of the Tales.[30]) Gayness parades openly and proudly, without fear or risk, whether on a crowded Castro Street in evening, on a stretch of nude beach, on a cable car with Michael decked out in a Halloween costume as the god Pan, in a roller rink with disco blaring, or in the remaining wonderfully perverse baths. Again, one wants to appreciate with what care this gayness is encoded through details of casting and mise-en-scène: to relish the presence of virtually every in-joke and representative of the queer and radical San Francisco scene, from Syd Straw, Country Joe McDonald, drag queens, and Rod Steiger to Vaginal Davis, Ian McKellen, Karen Black, Lea DeLaria, Parker Posey, Mary Kay Place, and even our own Lance Loud. One wants also to notice more details of costuming, including the presence of the fictional ad agency's campaign for Dittos pants, the ample distribution of Lacoste shirts, and the aforementioned 501s but also painter's pants, striped tube socks and work boots, a long discussion about Bass Weejuns and rugby shirts (the period coincided with "preppy"), clone mustaches, and coded bandanas ("robin's egg blue"), as well as a roster of cues about "outsider" status in every single garment worn by Mary Ann (who further signifies an "insider" knowingness regarding the queer vernacular or queer colloquial, in which the name Mary Ann is a synonym for poof).

This happy gayness flows from the staircases of Barbary Lane to pervade the city more generally, extending to the borders of wherever belonging can be coded (it definitely does not extend to Cleveland, or even to "the Peninsula" or Atherton). In other words, the enchanting bower or boudoir curated and ruled by Mrs. Madrigal is without boundaries insofar as it admits the transgression that *is* Anna Madrigal: the trans secret revealed in the anagram of her name is "a man and a girl."[31]

In other words, *Tales of the City* quite explicitly draws its own maps: of insider and outsider, the world of "us all" and the world of "them," the land of decent, quirky, anything-goes Barbary Lane and the land of the truly malicious (such as the character Norman, a pornographer and blackmailer who meets a very camp demise in the last episode), not to mention the truly boring (Cleveland, which is the butt of many jokes). Mary Ann's initial reaction to Mrs. Madrigal is that she's weird: "We don't have people like that in Cleveland." To which Mona replies: "Too bad for Cleveland."

But *Tales of the City* draws these maps in two women's stories: in the naïveté and bumbling gradual education of Mary Ann, the explicit motor of the majority of the narrative action, and in the invisible ink, as it were, of Mrs. Madrigal's past, the history of her childhood (raised in her mother's whorehouse, the Blue Moon brothel, in Winnemucca, Nevada), her war years, and her sex change. Together these stories balance the self-satisfied and perhaps unappealingly celebratory story of privilege and privacy at the heart of the gay intrigues that wind around the Halcyons, Michael, and other characters.

WINDOWS

The initial and controversial installment of *Tales of the City* might be said to be about framing, one of the terms with which I began. It seeks to demarcate without constricting, to render permeable and as transparent as possible a world that is frequently mystified—San Francisco's queer world of the 1970s and 1980s, before it was ravaged by HIV/AIDS—for a television audience nursed on the quality drama of *American Playhouse* literary classics of accepted value. How to tell that story, or better, those stories in the plural, through the televisual form of the prime-time serial or quality soap opera? Let me explore three windows before turning to the sequels that appeared on *Showtime*.

First, the windows of *Tales of the City* domesticate. The story of the street, of the historical Barbary Coast and its perversions and vice, becomes the fictional story of a house, of its inhabitants and their domestic tribulations. This, again, is melodrama. As outrageous as these transgressions may be (from joints passed at every gathering to casual sex to betrayals of every order), they are located, as melodrama operates, in individuals and managed as personal crises. What some viewers found objectionable about *Tales of the City* seems to be the extent to which the public materials that were translated into private narratives themselves were visible on the screen: in addition to some gay male sex and naked men (including, in a risky move, genitalia and jokes about balls), viewers caught glimpses of bathhouses, bars, and cruising scenes for public sex. The sex-positive message of the serial, one that intensified in the sequels, functioned as a powerful antidote both to condemnations of (especially) gay male promiscuity and to the ongoing attempt to render some forms of sex and desire pathological and degraded. In loud response, in its narrative, mise-en-scène, and casting, *Tales of the City* embraced queer San Francisco in all of its variety; if the show ultimately ends just as heterosexual sentimental fiction does in *Further Tales of the City* ("reader, I married him"), it nonetheless presents quite an array of queer culture on its way to that ending and condemns only *one* sexual practice along its route, exploitative sex with a nonconsenting child by the blackmailer and pornographer Norman. Framing straight exploitation as real perversion, *Tales of the City* puts counterpressure on cultural myths about homosex and its nefarious effects on children.

That said, its windows also feminize. By focalizing the primary narrative arcs through the dual poles of Mary Ann and Mrs. Madrigal, *Tales of the City* frames two decades of gay male urban history as the story of women's lives. To the extent to which Olympia Dukakis succeeds in being enchanting (and I admit to being seduced), the question of her "passing" as a woman onscreen is never in doubt and in fact adds to the butch allure she manufactures in "letting the man out" of her character.[32] And Mary Ann, about whom it might be said that she stands in for legions of gay male migrants to San Francisco, is overcoded as proto-feminist ingénue, working for a crisis switchboard and ultimately making her way as an investigative reporter in *Further Tales of the City* by tracking down Jim Jones (the charismatic millenarian of the Jonestown massacre) who fictionally turns out to be surviving in a shack in Golden Gate Park. She may work as a surrogate for suburban, but not for clone. Insofar as the narrative centers its women, it moves perhaps so freely with its melodramatic transformations that it is hard to tell who's who or who's what.

For my purposes, the question is really to do with how insistently the narrative wants to complicate what we see (in knowing that Anna was "Andy," hints of which are scattered throughout five episodes preceding the "real" revelation) and how part of the appeal of melodrama always lies in disavowal ("I know but nevertheless . . ."). There is a great deal of pleasure to be had in watching Anna cavort in Bohemian Grove, that playground of privilege, with Edgar Halcyon, thinking of how a trans woman trammels generations of rigidly conservative gender politics with her dancing shoes. There is a great deal of pleasure to be had in watching a story unfold that has as its telos the upsetting of fundamental sexual and gender common sense, watching characters in whom we have invested hours of interest ultimately transform from landlord and tenant into father and daughter (Anna and Mona, if you haven't already guessed). This feminization is at the heart of the project of melodrama that I want to press upon in turning now to the sequels, for I want to argue, finally, that the windows in *Tales of the City* as a whole are oddly, impossibly, *placed*. In evoking marginal and radical cultures through the melodramatic mode, they create points of view that are as interesting as they are untenable.

Maupin describes the work of all three televisual tales as the pursuit of family—a family melodramatically configured through surrogates and avatars. *More Tales of the City*, Maupin thinks, is all about the pursuit of the mother, while *Further Tales of the City* "is about working things out with fathers."[33] We aren't far from the textual universe of programming of the 1970s that I treated in chapter 3; in fact, we're so close that all three tales cite and revisit sitcoms, soaps, and televisual events not simply to summon the period but also to pay homage to their own genealogy. Some examples of televisual tidbits that are conjured as interlocutors in *Tales of the City* and the two sequels include *Sonny and Cher, McMillan and Wife, All in the Family, The Jeffersons*, Angie Dickinson, *Days of Our Lives, Mary Tyler Moore* (through the casting of Ed Asner), Anita Bryant and her vile Save the Children campaign, and the royal wedding. These references become nested in other paeans to melodrama, whether through movie allusions (e.g., Ingmar Bergman and Douglas Sirk's *Magnificent Obsession* [1954]), television events (e.g., the Bryant campaign and royal wedding), or moments of television history (e.g., the ascendance of Asian American women to news-anchor positions on major affiliates and network programs—Connie Cheung and Kaity Tong, to take two prominent examples).

What makes these more than in-jokes, a game of trivia, or cameo spotting (although this is surely part of the fun) is that the television world cited by *Tales of the City* results, as I have begun to suggest, in an odd superimposition of marginal cultural figures in the San Francisco scene onto an almost entirely white, middle-class, familial sphere. In some cases, the graft seems to take, breeding figures, such as Mrs. Madrigal, who combine an openness that is never moralistic with queer gender that is never ever close to *homonormative*. As I understand that term, associated with Lisa Duggan's work, the homonormative appears as a neoliberal logic that upholds and sustains normative values while abandoning queer commitments to economic redistribution, social justice, and sexual freedom.[34] At the same time, homonormativity fragments queer cultures, as Gayle Rubin has argued, by hierarchizing and demonizing some sexual cultures and practices while centering and exalting others.[35] The grafts produced through the many strands of *Tales of the City*, alongside their formal and figurative logics, seem to me less decidable in the peculiar reflexivity of the serial and, to take the word at its biological root, hybridity. That is, these tales compulsively return to normative images, scenarios, narratives, and lives by framing the serial as domestic melodrama, while they convoke radical challenges simultaneously. How then are we to read the serial's political will toward something like retrospective aspiration, a look backward at a more promising time from the point of view of a disturbing present?

Let me cite an example from *Further Tales of the City* to illustrate the spatio-temporal and generic density I am noticing and as a way to get into some of the narrative issues. (Remember that *Further Tales of the City* opens in 1981, not the 1970s of the first two versions, but just on the cusp of HIV/AIDS.) The image is, of course, of a window, in what is ostensibly a gay bar. Michael is in the midst of a period of what we might delicately describe as intense sexual activity. Regarding that clichéd promiscuity, Dr. John Fielding, Michael's erstwhile boyfriend, returned to reunite, tells Michael, "You're not living a life, Michael. You're fucking the Village People." At this bar, Michael leans next to another man he will pick up and who will turn out to be a cop, Officer Bill Rivera (Village People joke). Rivera, who happens not to be Hispanic at all (identity-politics joke), serves as a thread stitching several different plotlines and characters together: Michael, Prue Giroux (the society gossip columnist whose lost poodle, Vuitton, leads her to Jim Jones's cabin), and Father Paddy (a gay, not pedophile, priest who is a companion to Prue). In the bar, Officer Rivera listens to his Walkman (which debuted in Japan in 1979), and Michael asks to listen through his headphones to the then-new technology. As often takes place in the two sequels, because Showtime's budget allowed for it, a period song plays on the soundtrack, serving as diegetic sound in the bar. Here, it is the inimitable Grace Jones's "Love Is the Drug." Elsewhere we have everything from Anne Murray, in a nod to the serial's Canadian production provenance, to disco hits serving as droll commentary: Martha Quinn's "I Know What Boys Like," France Joli's "Come to Me," and the essential Sylvester, with "Do You Wanna Funk?"

This encounter between "Michael" and "Officer Rivera" takes place "actually" in a studio interior, in Montreal, the setting for filming most of the entire series, including everything that takes place on the 28 Barbary Lane set. "Virtually," an establishing shot of San Francisco looking north from Russian Hill initially seems to locate the bar, watching over the bridge and bay, but the shot reverses to a point of view vaguely suggesting the financial district, finessing contradictory directions simply by populating the world outside of the bar with city lights, an abstract Lite-Brite array of dots against a black background.[36] But the actual and the virtual are not separate domains, as teachings from Spinoza and Deleuze to their better readers would have us know: this is a televisual version of what Tom Conley calls a "film hieroglyph," a form of media writing that did not simply refer representationally to things and phenomena in the world but, "more compellingly, drew attention to and enabled a glimpse of unforeseen relations that flickered in the movement of its aural and graphic form."[37] In Anne Friedberg's terms, it is a *virtual window*: "A *virtual* window is reliant not on its transparency but on its opacity; its highly mediated modulation of light provides an aperture: not to a reality but to a delimited *virtuality*."[38]

What is it we're seeing?

What we're seeing is corporate vision, a virtual mapping of the world made possible by Viacom. If *Tales of the City* took a route from Channel Four to PBS in its initial installments, the sequels depended on the resources and possibilities of subscription television, namely through Showtime and its parent company, Viacom.

Viacom is a self-described "leading global entertainment content company."[39] Its media networks include BET Networks, Addictinggames, CMT, Comedy Central, Gametrailers, Logo, MTV, MTV2, mtvU, Tr3s, Neopets, Nickelodeon, Nick Jr., Nick at Nite, Nicktoons, Parentsconnect, Scratch, Shockwave, Spike, TeenNick, TVLand, VH1, and VH1 Classic. Among Viacom's properties in the Paramount Pictures Corp. are Paramount Pictures, Paramount Vintage, MTV Films, Nickelodeon Movies, and Paramount Home Entertainment. And in addition to digital assets and Simon & Schuster publishing group, Viacom owns Infinity Broadcasting, which operates 185 radio stations that reach seventy-six million listeners daily.[40] According to Viacom, their brands are seen globally in approximately 700 million households, in approximately 170 territories and 37 languages, via more than 200 locally programmed and operated TV channels and more than 550 digital and mobile TV properties.[41] Viacom is part of a television industry in which cable advertising alone generated a mind-boggling $27.3 *billion* in 2010, according to the statistics from the National Cable and Telecommunications Association.[42] Nearly all homes in the United States have televisions, and a vast percentage of those homes (up to 90 percent) subscribe to a form of pay television according to the Nielsen Cross-Platform Report.[43]

A staggeringly large conglomerate such as Viacom is subject to the regulatory framework for television enforced by the FCC, a framework that includes broadcast and cable-ownership limits (or "caps") set in order to ensure that no single cable company dominates the marketplace or monopolizes the channels made available to subscribers. These caps function both to ensure competition and to foster a diversity of content. While Viacom has contested in court some of the congressional limits on ownership, it remains subject to the local rule that specifies that a company may own two stations in the same market as long as eight independent voices still exist and neither station ranks within the top four. At the same time, at the national level, Viacom's broadcast stations may not reach in excess of 35 percent of the nationwide audience; its ownership of cable stations faces similar caps still to be determined in litigation, namely in testing the effects of the key case of the past decade, *Prometheus Radio Project v. FCC* (Federal Communications Commission).

As I suggested in this book's introduction, this regulatory framework is based on a "public trustee" model for broadcasters. Because the broadcast spectrum is limited, and because the spectrum is allocated by government decision to a finite number of broadcasters in an environment of increasing and acute competition, each broadcaster assumes some share of the public interest. "When broadcasters embrace their roles as journalists and protectors and proponents of the public interest," a key report on digital television policy suggests, "we benefit far beyond what TV stations can recover in advertising—people are engaged as citizens; government power is checked; waste and fraud are exposed; and we can value our televisions as much as broadcasters value our well-being."[44] Public policies aimed at strengthening the fiduciary or trustee responsibilities of commercial broadcasters have included initiatives with the following aims:

to foster diversity of programming
to ensure candidate access to the airwaves
to provide diverse views on public issues
to encourage news and public-affairs programming
to promote localism (local news)
to develop quality programming for children
to sustain a separate realm of high-quality, noncommercial
    television programming
to promote access for the disabled (e.g., closed-captioning)[45]

The presumption that policymakers have of "diversity" of programming or views has only the slightest relationship to the language of the academic humanities; the strengthening of fiduciary responsibility is largely to do with ensuring localism and access. To the extent that queer-media scholars can intervene in this long-standing model of the public trustee, they can insist on funding for public (noncommercial) television and for children's programming, and advocate local news that responds to local concerns rather than simply promote queer visibility as an aspect of so-called diversity.

Industrial analysis helps us to understand why Viacom's plans to start a gay cable network, Outlet (subsequently changed to LOGO and now surpassed by other streams of gay-oriented cable programming), might have been a boon for independent producers of LGBTQ media and for careful readings of new films and series but it also cemented these types of industrial production arrangements that limit how queer media moves in corporate circuits. Hollis Griffin, a scholar whose own work has emerged at the same moment as these forms of queer media, has glossed the tensions inherent in networks such as LOGO:

> The cultural industries' attempts to attract queer publics are, perhaps, still something of a new phenomenon, and there have been fewer scholarly interventions in the many questions raised by these practices. Recurring issues in all debates about the fairly recent allure of sexual difference in attempts to court media audiences include the fundamental discrepancies between consumerhood and cultural citizenship and, relatedly, distinctions between mainstream gay rights efforts and an ostensibly more radical queer activism.[46]

These tensions persist as scholars turn to the proliferating offerings on channels such as LOGO, including *RuPaul's Drag Race* and reruns of *Absolutely Fabulous* (for which I'm particularly grateful). As much as one may want the ostensible freedom to watch unlimited reruns of *Queer as Folk* or *Drawn Together*, then, the programming on offer, like Dana (the tennis player) on *The L-Word*, demands the prior approval of its advertisers. "Entertaining a social, savvy audience of gay trendsetters" LOGO's programming is precisely the kind of savvy queer TV the new digital world will bring to us.[47]

Why might a gay channel be profitable to Viacom? Cable requires lower ratings than network television for advertising revenues. While a prime-time series (*Ellen, Will and Grace*) needs to sustain ratings above 2, cable programming, including *The L Word*, can generate revenue with ratings below 1. Remember that a rating point is equivalent to a single percent of all television households, which means one percent of roughly 105.5 million, or 1,055,000. Second, despite significant academic evidence to the contrary, corporate television executives seem to

accept market research that mistakenly claims that both the median income and amount of disposable income is actually *higher* for gay couples'
households than it is for straight households. Various estimates of "gay
buying power" or "gay spending power" (Google either of these) claim
to measure the capacity of LGBTQ adults to spend, essentially assessing
the personal disposable income of LGBTQ people, but most economic
research puts the actual *earnings* of LGBTQ adults below their straight
counterparts.[48]

My second point is to suggest that queer studies needs rigorous economic analysis and intervention into audience research policy not to
bolster corporate organization but to subject those forms of organization to critical scrutiny. The chapters in the volume *Homo Economics* and
Queer Economics[49] offer a starting point for a queer social science that
explodes normative and positivist assumptions, and we need that work
desperately in queer media studies, for it seems that we or our queer organizations have abdicated. The Gay and Lesbian Alliance against Defamation (GLAAD) no longer supports academic research on media and
instead counts characters in its annual "Where We Are On TV" report.[50]
That is, instead of instigating and supporting studies of queer media
in which we pursue critical questions, experimental answers, and complex representations, GLAAD may be seeking to support commercial in-
vestments in queer media that promise class mobility and simplified
politics. Queer-media studies needs more work like Katherine Sender's
book *Business, Not Politics* to generate an economic analysis of stratification that can redress the so-called research undertaken by market studies and polling groups who benefit from overemphasizing the
riches of the gay market.[51] The move by GLAAD to discontinue funding
of such research further imperils the production of accurate and dense
understandings of discrimination and stratification. It is in the interests of market researchers to paint a picture of white male suburbanites
with money to burn.

A third point, related to my remarks about queer migration and
cities of the global South, is that queer-media studies requires a global
and comparative watchfulness. Viacom's other big deal in the first half
of 2005 was with China: Viacom announced a joint venture that has
brought Viacom products (in this case the Nickelodeon programs *Cat
Dog* and *The Wild Thornberrys*) to the largest television broadcaster in

the world. China Central Television reaches 386 million households in China, a market into which Viacom plans to move increasingly, incrementally adding its brands to the Chinese broadcast grid, a strategy that has now bred management case studies of the hurdles Viacom faces in regulation and cultural differences.[52] Like it or not, our queer representational future is tied to the peculiar collar of *Cat Dog*.[53]

But here at home, Showtime's catchy slogan "no limits" mainly pertained to the serial's changed relationship to sexual explicitness and nudity. In *Further Tales of the City*, Laura Linney bares her breast in the opening sequence, an index of the new visual world of the series. Other characters, such as Michael, offer full-frontal shots, and sexually explicit scenes at bars and bathhouses become more commonplace. (The additional DVD commentary reveals two loving details: The sex scenes were all planned for the shoot's first week, so the crew came to believe that they were shooting pornography! And the bathhouse scenes were shot at an actual bathhouse in Montreal's Gay Village, creating visual links between Montreal's gay topography and San Francisco's.) A party at a Rock Hudson–like star's house—where his lover is played by Joel Grey (a relationship that is based on Maupin's own relationship with Hudson)—is a wonderful excuse for beefcake and for Michael to seduce the Hudson figure, Cage Tyler (John Robinson), in another sexually explicit encounter. Maupin even appears in a cameo (outside the Glory Hole).

There are no limits indeed to where the series can literally travel, thanks to the sponsorship of Carnival Cruises for *More Tales of the City*, so Mary Ann and Michael (now played by Paul Hopkins) can light out on the seas to search for true love. Mona (now played by Nina Siemaszko) is narratively swept into the wilds of the Nevada desert to the Blue Moon Brothel, where she "finds herself" in the person of her grandmother, Anna's own mother, also named Mona Ramsey but referred to by her brothel name, "Mother Mucca" (Jackie Burroughs); the brothel allows for outrageous sexual humor and scantily clad prostitutes bonding in suggestively flirty ways. Closer to home, in a touching plotline, HIV/AIDS is figured through Michael's sudden illness with Guillain-Barré syndrome, and he is tended to by the charming Dr. Jon Fielding (Billy Campbell). In *More Tales of the City*, and even more strikingly in *Further Tales of the City*, editing between the different story lines starts to stitch these locales together into ever more outrageous concatenations, enfolding Guyana, Cuba, Alaska, California, Nevada, and God knows where else, all tentacles of the big queer family that the series has spawned.

It's my sense that the series starts to rely on increasingly silly plotlines and a lot of naked bodies to hang on to its viewers, most of us already fans of the series from its first iteration and therefore up for anything it offers. If Jim Jones being alive and well and living in Golden Gate Park doesn't seem wacky enough, try Dede and Dor returning from an attempt to be lesbian revolutionaries in Cuba (after having survived Jonestown), only to parent twin Asian babies then captured by Jones and brought to Alaska. Oy. Emphasis on character shifts to emphasis on story, and emphasis on mise-en-scène shifts to emphasis on editing, so that the text can maintain some control over its parallel story lines. We still get up in the air, in an airplane flown by comic Lea DeLaria (k.d. lang, the first choice for the part, wasn't available), and we still return to Barbary Lane, celebrating Mary Ann Singleton's wedding to Brian Hawkins (Whip Hubley). There is just less in the way of ethico-political *aspiration*. We're more on the ground, uneasily, in the city of San Francisco, or its gorgeous three-walled facsimile, the set at 28 Barbary Lane.

I have wanted to argue that there is a great risk entailed in taking this urban world, its elegant windows and gleaming staircases, as a stand-in for other or all experiences of migration by queer young people seeking a future in this world. In that sense, the windows of the series can never yield a transparent glimpse, only a partial one, located in a history and geography mapped as much by televisual convention (from genre to production constraints to set design) as by the San Francisco I remember of the latter part of the twentieth century. The frame simultaneously casts suspicion: there are other worlds in which living itself is imperiled for seekers such as I was, such as you might be.

CODA

Becoming

Television has so much spare time that everyone will be on it in the end.
—Tim Fountain, *Resident Alien: Quentin Crisp Explains It All*

We, or television, would appear to be looping back onto the preceding reflections, as the objects I've been examining morph before my eyes. The Louds and the experiment that was *An American Family* became a movie for HBO, *Cinema Verite* (2011), starring Thomas Dekker as Lance. Fittingly, as Lance was, Dekker is also a musician and a sexually complicated renegade, "playing gay" here for the second time.[1] *Tales of the City* became a theatrical musical, with a brief run (also in 2011) and mostly negative notices; even the *New York Times* prefers the TV version.[2] During the time of this book's writing, *Our Miss Brooks* became available on a weirdly amateurish DVD release, in a "collector's edition" that looks as though it may have been made by Chinese pirates. Television, in other words, has so diversified and diverged from the network model with which I began this book that it is now wreaking definitional havoc, and not only in the halls of universities. More than one television producer with whom I've recently spoken calls the industry the "wild west," referring less to Los Angeles—since the high costs of union labor there are sending production crews to cheaper locales—than to a state of lawless invention and experimentation. Remakes, rip-offs, and repackaging seem to be workable alternatives to genuinely new ideas and strategies, some of which are, however, emerging through the smog.

Stunningly good scholarship on this industry in flux is also circulating, required reading that would include, for starters, John Caldwell's *Production Culture* and Amanda Lotz's *The Television Will Be Revolutionized*.[3] Both respond to the changes wrought in the entertainment industries by globalization and digital developments; both find severe limits with the paradigms of textual analysis that dominate humanities-based approaches to media. Even if I have shared their impatience, I increasingly find myself wondering, methodologically, how best to proceed in this contradictory climate of overabundance (textual detail) and narrowcasting (an increasingly fragmented archive). Ethnography, industry analysis, working papers on production niches and material cultures, comparative analysis, close reading, studies of intermedia and new media, and performance: all seem crucial and messily imbricated with one another, at least when I've attempted to write on queer television in the past.[4] This is especially the case with studies that are appearing with a vengeance on series such as *The L Word*, since the production personnel, including writers, directors, and actors; the story arcs and characters; the changing industrial landscape; and the actual landscapes of Los Angeles and Vancouver (where the serial was shot) all converge in the unfolding of the critical history of that series.[5] Rather than try to select a single program as exemplary for these closing thoughts on what television is becoming in its digital iteration, I want instead to reflect, quite briefly, on something more ineffable, more ethereal: that is, what may television be in its potentiality rather than its actuality, what it may enable us, ourselves, to become. For me, that means the domain of gesture, silence, longing, muted expression, and the inchoate: in short, melodrama, "an illusion . . . grounded in eroticism."[6] This is where my interest in television began, where the familiar and the unfamiliar lock horns: seduction, revelation, betrayal, romance, control, illness, the glance, the touch, the caress, and the kiss.

It is the unspoken core of this book, and in speaking it here, I am perhaps able to look forward at what may become of television's arguments, to make some of them explicit anew. First, melodrama is a mode, a way of life, a commonsense way of processing the unspoken dimensions of social relations by granting privilege to "situations, feelings and emotions which everyone has experienced at one time or another," including family, work, cherished poles of gender and sexual behavior, and so on.[7] As a powerful processor of a shared sensorium, melodrama, like television, is *productive*: it is a mode of transformation that strains to express the inexpressible, whether anguish, pessimism, despair, conflict, antagonism, or, conversely, pre-Oedipal utopia, resolution, or bliss. Melodrama, like television, capitalizes on the uncertainties of address, the lacunae of chance, the mute and silent realms of longing, the dissatisfaction too close to name, which are constitutive of both specific subject positions (lesbian, gay, mother, son, to name but a few) and televisual discourse as a mediator whose function may be guaranteed but whose success never is.

As respondents, we can point to moments, and this is what I've endeavored to do over the course of the preceding chapters, not exhaustively (exhaustingly) to catalogue television's queer appearances but to notice when they render forces, positions, and desires dynamic, as the very best readings of melodrama have done. In noticing them, I have sought to retain that dynamism by following particular lines of flight or inquiry, whether theoretical, historical, contextual, geographical, or, sometimes, autobiographical. Television *requires* that we shuttle between the macroindustrial and the microindividual; it is a machine that produces its value from that very movement. In Richard Dienst's terms, the logic of television as such a machine involves "a process of abstraction, an original form of reification performed in time rather than through finished things, where relations between people are now absorbed by the passage of countless overlapping slices of images that replace the possibility of shared interests or mutual subjective recognition."[8] What I've tried to suggest as a corrective to such a sweeping view of television's valorizing work is an emphasis on the *differential* nature of the strategies of or drives toward condensation in image and narrative in the myriad spatial and temporal organizations constitutive of social relations under capitalism. Queer forms of life congeal differentially in the spatio-temporal modalities of television.

This is not to celebrate reception, or reading television, as a form of queer choice; to the contrary, the most forceful element of Dienst's argument for me is his insistence that the time of the imagination is offered to television as a "free contribution to capitalist power," especially redistributing pleasure time and household time (also parenting time and childhood time) for capitalist imperatives.[9] What I've wanted to do is to watch *how* those temporal rhythms have shifted over time, and how they retain connections in different ways to our shared experiences and desires, here named *queer* to nominate something that television has produced from its early years that was not yet assimilable as gay or lesbian *and* something encompassing enough today to gather many of us under its inquiry.

Still, in appreciating melodrama's pursuit of the ineffable, I am not wishing to settle on a name for an image, any image, its spatio-temporal organization, its affective register, or its palpable effects as queer, for it has also been equally my interest in the ether that has mobilized this project. *Ether* here indexes a number of forces simultaneously: it marks a historical era, now seemingly over, when television signals traveled through the airwaves, in the seventy years from television's birth in 1939 to June 12, 2009.[10] Departing from the time of this technological periodization, I rely on scholars such as Jeffrey Sconce who have shown how broadcast images are always potentially haunted by other transmissions, how the images of our likenesses on TV harbor other ghosts: "Wherever streams of consciousness and electrons converge in the cultural imagination, there lies a potential conduit to an electronic elsewhere that even as it evokes the specter of the void, also holds the promise of a higher form of consciousness, one that promises to evade the often annihilating powers of our technologies and transcend the now materially demystified machine that is the human body."[11] In the ether, transmissions may be overcoded, but they are never fully determined. In moving from *ether* to *ethereal*, then, I am looking upward and playing with a range of meanings, from a descriptive sense of pertaining to the ether to more celestial aspirations or ascensions to the very sense of the impalpable that I have been pursuing here.

You can see what I mean on YouTube. I want to close with two more morsels of queer TV that have haunted me for years, two made-for-TV movies: the first is *Losing Chase* (1996), an overwrought melodrama directed for Showtime and Hallmark by Kevin Bacon, starring his wife, Kyra Sedgwick, and the unbelievably dreamy Helen Mirren. Here's the plot: once Beau Bridges as Mirren's husband is dispatched to his job in Boston, Sedgwick and Mirren fall for one another on Martha's Vineyard, amid gorgeous wooden sailboats (see figure C.1). Who wouldn't love this? It would have taken me some pages to generate a narrative of

C.1. *Losing Chase* (TV movie, 1996). Shown, from left: Kyra Sedgwick and Helen Mirren.

their encounter, but that has been done on YouTube by a fan who has assembled the Sedgwick-Mirren lovefest to the late Whitney Houston's "I Have Nothing." The exposition with the soundtrack is much better than I ever could have generated in prose! (The video was called "Losing Chase—I Have Nothing," by deltarose1, and it appears to have been deleted from YouTube: such is the ethereality and ephemerality of our digital archive!)

On YouTube, the narrative is clearly not the point, and neither, therefore, is conflict. Where *Losing Chase* requires quite a bit of effort to bring Chase Philips (Mirren) and Elizabeth Cole (Sedgwick) together—effort that has to overcome conflicts between generations, employer and employee, illness and wellness, and insanity and sanity—"Losing Chase—I Have Nothing" cuts, as it were, right to the chase of lesbian desire, pulling shot-reverse-shot sequences out of *Losing Chase* and building others to drive home the point. We get all of the good stuff—sailboat, smoking, sailboat, foot stroking, sailboat, wine, sailboat, longing stares—plus Whitney, and almost none of the bad stuff, which is that

C.2. *Losing Chase*. Shown: Helen Mirren.

Chase ends up, at the end, without Elizabeth, alone (see figure C.2). Before YouTube, in fact, I saw *Losing Chase* as an ode to loss, as a way of grieving lost forms of intimacy, creativity, and expression and dying visions of equity, intimacy, and connection that were articulated in the cultural feminist and lesbian-feminist practices of the previous two decades (the 1970s and 1980s). But "deltarose1," who mashed *Losing Chase* and Whitney Houston, reads the film as a baldly declarative lesbian love story: "I Have Nothing" begins, "Share my life / take me for what I am." And she does, they do.

Mobilizing what is potentially available in *Losing Chase*, deltarose1 teaches me something about the immanent field of digital platforms, and yet . . . I want to stay with the time of the original and with the loss for a moment longer, since what deltarose1's radically condensed version of *Losing Chase* obliterates is the paternal law whose iteration is the generative force of the lesbian desire celebrated via Whitney. That is, in banishing the figure of the father in order to make room for the lesbian to emerge, *Losing Chase* strives for a terrain of transformation, intimacy, and proximity, all intuitively grasped but inaccessible. And yet the movie is caught short of that desire through what returns, must return, as symbolic investment but is displaced from the actual *figure* of the father: namely, the demand for respectability (crosshatched by class determination) and the return of the law and surveillance involving the paternal surrogates who are Chase's sons. (I would cite as evidence here the many, many scenes in which "little Richard" reprimands or chastises his mother.) *Losing Chase* shows us the constraints on the very vision of love between the women deltarose1 celebrates. The movie splits the figure of Chase, the dissatisfied mother, into two entities: a movement toward women, nature, and art as substitutes for the alienated labor of the family and of social reproduction, and the movie reveals what stalls that movement, namely, obligation and respectability. *Lesbian* ultimately means what is stabilized only as a settlement. Television understood as a conduit of affective value, as a conduit indeed of melodrama, can help us understand precisely these kinds of settlement and loss *as much as* it can reveal new forms of desiring production, to borrow a more Deleuzian term.

The other example was consigned, I thought, not just to the past but to memory: a television program made for Channel Four called *Wild Flowers* (Robert Smith, 1989). At the end of the 1980s, it had made the rounds of film festivals, and I think Ruby Rich and I were the only ones who thought we remembered it scene by scene. Miraculously, the program's director teaches at Goldsmiths, University of London and agreed to make a digital transfer from his video master. (Thank you, Robert!) And *Wild Flowers* could now be in reruns on my HDTV. It's even better than I had remembered. Like *Losing Chase*, it is a melodrama invoking *lesbian* and *mother*, and like *Losing Chase*, it also a story of loss and grief. Beatie Edney stars as Sadie, girlfriend of Angus McFarland (Stevan Rimkus), who returns to his hometown village in Scotland on a university holiday. Sadie falls in a doomed way for Angus's mother, Annie (Colette O'Neil), whose shameful lesbian affair thirty-odd years before haunts the village and has poisoned Annie's own mother, Marguerite (Sheila Keith), against her (see figure C.3). As with *Losing Chase*, the chemistry between the top-notch actors becomes infectious, with O'Neil luminously inspired by the gorgeous Edney (daughter of Sylvia Syms, who starred, among other important roles, in the queer classic *Victim* [Basil

C.3. *Wild Flowers* (TV movie, 1989). Shown, from left: Colette O'Neil as Annie and Beatie Edney as Sadie.

Dearden, 1961]). There are boats, too, in *Wild Flowers* and two sons, a lovely kiss, and many looks and caresses. Mostly what there is, however, is a swirl of time, and in this swirl, I will want to close with how this made-for-TV movie finds "queer."

Set in a picturesque historic town, Largs, on the Scottish seaside, the story unfolds in two moments: Annie's death and the visit home, which is the bulk of the narrative action. The time of Annie's girlhood affair is only implied, but it haunts the action in both subsequent moments. Smith intercuts Sadie's return to the town for Annie's funeral in the present with her first visit with Angus, creating another layer of ghosting, as if the force of her loving memory could actually rewrite the loss to come. In *Wild Flowers*, the psychic forces, such as this one, all belong to women, complicating how we understand the law and symbolic investment; the men and the boys, including a fiery priest, are ultimately impotent when faced with the more formidable women. As Deleuze reads masochism, so may we read *Wild Flowers*: it is an exploration of the results of investing "the mother-image with the symbolic power of the law."[12]

This is a story about passion and mothers, divided by those Manichaean lines required by the melodramatic imagination. Annie's mother, Marguerite, is the most direct embodiment of injunction, articulated as a living memory erected to shame under God's eyes. Annie will never escape her sin; neither will she ever outgrow the affective power of her mother's wrath ("I'm nigh fifty," she says, "and my mother can still make me cry"). Annie, in turn, would appear to be the good mother: while she wields power over her boys, including her husband, she nurtures music, fun, occasional naughtiness, and deeply felt passion. When she turns that spirit toward Sadie, however, we witness another fracturing of the mother-image: *Wild Flowers* lovingly paints a picture of Annie's vivacious, artful, queer desire (including peeping and scandalizing, in addition to loving women) at the same time as it insists on settlement and constraint. Some of that settlement is here marked as age: in a line I thought I remembered precisely as "my time for loving is over," Annie actually tells Sadie, sending her on her way from the village, "I'm long past the loving stage." Some of that settlement involves history: Annie's affair took place in a moment when it could not be sanctioned, while for Sadie's generation, it just isn't a big deal.

The way that *Wild Flowers* marks time, however, complicates even the reading we might bring to it of a forbidden love in a buried past now flourishing, if briefly, in an enlightened present. The marking of time kills Annie before our story begins, but that structure allows Annie's spirit to hover over not just the narrative but the entire town. The two village busybodies, for example, monitor Annie and Sadie throughout the narrative, as a sort of omniscient and omnipresent comic chorus. Through Ina and Maisie we feel propriety, scorn, and judgment, as they embody the look of the village at Annie and her exploits. Very quickly, though, it is hard to resist seeing them as a lesbian couple: they are always together, arm in arm, whispering to one another and sharing each other's world. As Annie and Sadie clearly become lovingly close, their pleasure starts to have a melancholic effect on the ladies, as watching a sparkler can make a stick seem dull. Stern judgment turns to affectionate grief by the moment of Annie's funeral: "She was a queer one, Annie McFarland." If Annie's spirit haunts the village, it is neither dead nor consigned to a past of homophobic hatred and Kirk-enforced (Church-enforced) wrath. It suffuses the Glasgow apartment to which

Sadie returns after the funeral with what would appear to be a girlfriend waiting to help her arrange the flowers that covered Annie's coffin.

It is a queer spirit that is, finally, seen retroactively to *begin* to transform the Bad Mother, to soften Marguerite but not, after all, to banish or kill her off. It's Annie who dies, of what we do not know, and that death is meant to be grieved. The values with which *Wild Flowers* concludes come with that grief, with an admiration for Annie's spirit. The two traits that seem most powerful to me in that spirit are the refusal of pity and the taking of responsibility, both of which are narratively associated precisely with the refusal of Sadie. When Marguerite has reduced Annie to tears, Sadie runs to her and brushes Annie's face with her hand, a gesture that would seem to open onto seduction but harbors pity, which Annie refuses. When Sadie asks Annie to leave with her, Annie asks, "You think I'm not content? I'm content." These values then spill into the resolution, in which Marguerite moderates her fierceness toward Sadie at Annie's funeral, in the end urging her to take the coffin's flowers. In the name of Scottish frugality ("I hate waste"), the mother condones something, ineffable, ethereal, queer.

INTRODUCTION

1. Raymond Williams, *Television: Technology and Cultural Form* (New York: Schocken Books, 1975).

2. The title of J. A. Yelling's book dates "the" enclosure movement from the fifteenth century to the nineteenth: *Common Field and Enclosure in England, 1450–1850* (Hamden, CT: Archon Books, 1977). Analyses of the "new enclosure" movements include Michael Hardt and Antonio Negri's *Empire* (Cambridge, MA: Harvard University Press, 2000), and also the Retort Collective's *Afflicted Powers: Capital and Spectacle in a New Age of War* (London: Verso, 2005).

3. Advisory Committee on Public Interest Obligations of Digital Television Broadcasters, "The Origins and Future Prospects of Digital Television," Benton Foundation, accessed 3/25/13, http://benton.org/initiatives/obligations/charting_the_digital_broadcasting_future/sec1.

4. GLAAD, "Where We Are on TV Report: 2006–2007 Season," September 2007, accessed 3/25/13, http://www.glaad.org/publications/tvreport07.

5. See Amy Villarejo, *Lesbian Rule: Cultural Criticism and the Value of Desire* (Durham, NC: Duke University Press, 2003).

6. Mary Ann Doane, "Information, Crisis, Catastrophe," in *Logics of Television: Essays in Cultural Criticism*, edited by Patricia Mellencamp (Bloomington: Indiana University Press, 1990).

7. John Corner, "Television and the Practice of 'Criticism,'" *Flow*, September 22, 2006, accessed 3/25/13, http://flowtv.org/2006/09/television-and-the-practice-of-criticism.

8. Douglas Kellner, "*Beavis and Butt-Head*: No Future for Postmodern Youth,"

in *Television: The Critical View*, 6th edition, edited by Horace Newcomb (New York: Oxford University Press, 2000), 322.

9. David Rodowick actually makes this case about photography in his book *The Virtual Life of Film* (Cambridge, MA: Harvard University Press, 2007), in which he tweaks a beautiful reading of Stanley Cavell into a reflection on the limits of photographic representation: "We may attribute qualities of image or representation to both paintings and photographs, but a deeper examination shows that they present very different modes of existence to our acts of viewing. In speaking of modes of existence, I am less interested in how paintings and photographs function as 'representations' than in how they indicate their states of being, or how they disclose (or not) their genesis in past acts of making. Indeed if photographs provoke in us an 'ontological restlessness,' in Cavell's fine phrase, this may be because in spite of their uncanny isomorphism photographs are not 'representations' at all. The more we think about photographs, the more difficult it is to place them ontologically and to understand how they bridge the world and our perception. Photographs, in fact, confront us with conundrums of being, of our place in the world and our perceptual relation to the world and to the past" (55).

10. C. Lee Harrington, "Lesbian(s) on Daytime Television: The Bianca Narrative on *All My Children*," *Feminist Media Studies* 3, 2 (2003): 207.

11. David Marc jokes that episode 29, season 3, of *Father Knows Best* "might as well have been titled 'Betty Meets the Lesbians,'" rather than "Betty, the Track Star." David Marc, *Comic Visions: Television Comedy and American Culture* (Malden, MA: Blackwell, 1989), 50.

12. To take but one example, Rodowick contributes to an important discussion regarding the grounding of the discipline of cinema and media studies in *The Virtual Life of Film* (Cambridge: Harvard University Press, 2007), in which the persistence of "desire" as such remains unaccountably vague: "Throughout the twentieth century, the technological processes of film production have innovated constantly, its narrative forms have evolved continuously, and its modes of distribution and exhibition have also varied widely. But what has persisted is a certain mode of psychological investment — a modality of desire if you will" (22).

13. Steven Capsuto has written such a popular history in his *Alternate Channels: The Uncensored Story of Gay and Lesbian Images on Radio and Television* (New York: Ballantine Books, 2000).

14. A few texts on television temporality, other than those focusing on televisual liveness, have shaped an emerging discussion. See Paul Booth, *Time on TV: Temporal Displacement and Mashup Television* (New York: Peter Lang, 2012); Jennifer Gillan, *Television and New Media: Must Click*

TV (London: Routledge, 2010); Sarah Kozloff, "Narrative Theory and Television," in *Channels of Discourse, Reassembled: Television and Contemporary Criticism*, edited by Robert C. Allen (Chapel Hill: University of North Carolina Press, 1992); and William Uricchio, "TV as Time Machine: Television's Changing Heterochronic Regimes and the Production of History," in *Relocating Television: Television in the Digital Context*, edited by Jostein Gripsrud (London: Routledge, 2010).

15. Miriam Bratu Hansen, *From Babel to Babylon: Spectatorship in American Silent Film* (Cambridge: Harvard University Press, 1991); Miriam Bratu Hansen, "The Mass Production of the Senses: Classical Cinema as Vernacular Modernism," *Modernism/Modernity* 6, 2 (April 1999); Miriam Bratu Hansen, "Room-for-Play: Benjamin's Gamble with Cinema," *October* 109 (2004); Philip Rosen, *Change Mummified: Cinema, Historicity, Theory* (Minneapolis: University of Minnesota Press, 2001); and Hanns Zischler, *Kafka Goes to the Movies*, translated by Susan H. Gillespie (Chicago: University of Chicago Press, 2003).

16. Jeffrey Sconce, *Haunted Media: Electronic Presence from Telegraphy to Television* (Durham, NC: Duke University Press, 2000); and Siegfried Zielinski, *Audiovisions: Cinema and Television as Entr'actes in History* (Amsterdam: Amsterdam University Press, 1999).

17. Jane Feuer, "The Concept of Live Television: Ontology as Ideology," in *Regarding Television: Critical Approaches*, edited by E. Ann Kaplan (Frederick, MD: University Publications of America, 1982).

18. See James Friedman, ed., *Reality Squared: Televisual Discourse on the Real* (New Brunswick, NJ: Rutgers University Press, 2002).

19. Peter Dews offers the paraphrase in his helpful chapter "Adorno, Post-structuralism, and the Critique of Identity," in *The Problem of Modernity: Adorno and Benjamin*, edited by Andrew Benjamin (London: Routledge, 1989), 19.

20. Regarding scheduling, see John Ellis, "Scheduling: The Last Creative Act in Television?" *Media Culture Society* 22 (2000).

21. Amy Villarejo, "TV Queen: Lending an Ear to Charles Pierce," *Modern Drama* 53, 3 (Fall 2010).

22. C. Lee Harrington, "Lesbian(s) on Daytime Television: The Bianca Narrative on *All My Children*, *Feminist Media Studies* 3, 2 (2003): 215.

23. See Lynne Joyrich, "Epistemology of the Console," in *Critical Inquiry* 27, 3 (Spring, 2001). She helpfully explores "the ways in which U.S. television both impedes and constructs, exposes and buries, a particular knowledge of sexuality" (440).

24. Dialogue transcribed by me from recorded sources throughout unless otherwise noted.

25. Gilles Deleuze, *Bergsonism*, translated by Hugh Tomlinson and Barbara Habberjam (New York: Zone Books, 1991), 86; and Bliss Cua Lim, *Translating Time: Cinema, The Fantastic, and Temporal Critique* (Durham, NC: Duke University Press, 2009).

26. Elizabeth Freeman, "Introduction," GLQ 13, 2–3 (2007): 159.

27. Elizabeth Freeman, "Introduction," GLQ 13, 2–3 (2007): 162.

28. Lee Edelman, *No Future: Queer Theory and the Death Drive* (Durham, NC: Duke University Press, 2004).

29. Lynne Joyrich reads *Far from Heaven* in terms of media temporalities in her wonderful article "Written on the Screen: Mediation and Immersion in *Far from Heaven*," *Camera Obscura* 19, 3 (2004).

30. Mary Ann Doane, "Information, Crisis, Catastrophe," in *Logics of Television: Essays in Cultural Criticism*, edited by Patricia Mellencamp (Bloomington: Indiana University Press, 1990).

31. Jeffrey Sconce, *Haunted Media: Electronic Presence from Telegraphy to Television* (Durham, NC: Duke University Press, 2000), 174.

32. Elizabeth Grosz, *The Nick of Time: Politics, Evolution, and the Untimely* (Durham, NC: Duke University Press, 2004); and Elizabeth Grosz, *Time Travels: Feminism, Nature, Power* (Durham, NC: Duke University Press, 2005).

33. Douglas Kellner, "Television and the Frankfurt School (T.W. Adorno)," in Toby Miller, ed., *Television Studies*, edited by Toby Miller (London: BFI Publishing, 2002).

34. Theodor Adorno, "How to Look at Television," *Quarterly of Film, Radio and Television* 8, 3 (1954).

35. Jean Baudrillard, *Simulations*, translated by Paul Foss, Paul Patton, and Philip Beitchman (New York: Semiotex[e], 1983).

36. *Armistead Maupin's Tales of the City*, 6-epsidode unedited edition DVD (Silver Spring, MD: Acorn Media, 2002), liner notes by Armistead Maupin.

37. Teresa P. R. Caldeira, *City of Walls: Crime, Segregation, and Citizenship in São Paulo* (Berkeley: University of California Press, 2000).

38. George Chauncey, *Gay New York: Gender, Urban Culture, and the Making of the Gay Male World, 1890–1940* (New York: Basic Books, 1994); Matt Houlbrook, *Queer London: Perils and Pleasures in the Sexual Metropolis, 1918–1957* (Chicago: University of Chicago Press, 2005); Morris Kaplan, *Sodom on the Thames: Sex, Love, and Scandal in Wilde Times* (Ithaca, NY: Cornell University Press, 2005).

39. George Chauncey, *Gay New York: Gender, Urban Culture, and the Making of the Gay Male World, 1890–1940* (New York: Basic Books, 1995), 9.

40. Matt Houlbrook, *Queer London: Perils and Pleasures in the Sexual Metropolis, 1918–1957* (Chicago: University of Chicago Press, 2005), 12.

41. George Chauncey, *Gay New York: Gender, Urban Culture, and the Making of the Gay Male World, 1890–1940* (New York: Basic Books, 1995), 23, 26.

42. Amanda Lotz, "If It's Not TV, What Is It?," in *Cable Visions: Television beyond Broadcasting*, edited by Sarah Banet-Weiser, Cynthia Chris, and Anthony Freitas (New York: NYU Press, 2007), 100.

43. Dienst is careful about the scale of this relationship: "The relationship between television and capital encompasses a great many figural operations, from microscopic mimesis to general social subsumption." *Still Life in Real Time: Theory after Television* (Durham, NC: Duke University Press, 1994), 37.

CHAPTER 1. ADORNO'S ANTENNA

1. J.M. Bernstein, "Introduction," in Theodor W. Adorno, *The Culture Industry*, edited with an introduction by J.M. Bernstein (London: Routledge, 1996), 2.

2. Theodor Adorno, "How to Look at Television," *Quarterly Review of Film and Television* 8, 3 (1954).

3. Theodor Adorno, *The Culture Industry*, edited with an introduction by J.M. Bernstein (London: Routledge, 1996); Theodor Adorno, "On the Fetish-Character of Music and the Regression of Listening," in T. W. Adorno, *Essays on Music*, selected with introduction, commentary, and notes by Richard Leppert, new translations by Susan H. Gillespie (Berkeley: University of California Press, 2002).

4. Mary Ann Doane, "Information, Crisis, Catastrophe," in *Logics of Television: Essays in Cultural Criticism*, edited by Patricia Mellencamp (Bloomington: Indiana University Press, 1990), 222.

5. Stanley Rubin describes the uncertainty of the time slot in early network television as he was poised to begin writing teleplays: "While the nascent TV networks were on the air a few hours each day, there were no filmed dramas to guide us. Checking series on radio was of little help. We finally decided on an interim length—a script that would be a little long for a 15-minute show, a little short if it turned out that shows would actually run 30 minutes. Either way an adjustment should not be too difficult [and] we were fortunate enough to make a sale." Stanley Rubin, "A (Very) Personal History of the First Sponsored Film Series on National Television," *Journal of E-Media Studies* 1, 1 (2008), accessed March 27, 2013, http://journals.dartmouth.edu/cgi-bin/WebObjects/Journals.woa/1/xmlpage/4/article/312.

6. In her reevaluation of debates on television liveness, Mimi White help-

fully insists "that history, duration, and memory are as central to any theoretical understanding of television's discursive operations as liveness and concomitant ideas of presence, immediacy, and so forth." Mimi White, "Television Liveness: History, Banality, Attractions," *Spectator* 20, 1 (Fall 1999/Winter 2000): 41.

7. Alexander Garcia Duttmann notices Adorno's capacity to inhabit multiple times in discussing Adorno's work on Proust: "Adorno hoped that with this new translation Proust would come back to life as if for the first time, and in doing so prompt the fruition of 'something crucial' in a cultural environment that had otherwise remained 'behind the times.'" Alexander Garcia Duttmann, "A Second Life: Notes on Adorno's Reading of Proust," *World Picture* 3 (2009), accessed May 12, 2010, http://www.worldpicture journal.com/WP_3/Duttman.html.

8. Robert Miklitsch, *Roll over Adorno: Critical Theory, Popular Culture, Audiovisual Media* (Albany, NY: SUNY Press, 2006), 44.

9. David Jennemann, *Adorno in America* (Minneapolis: University of Minnesota Press, 2007), xxvii.

10. David Jennemann, *Adorno in America* (Minneapolis: University of Minnesota Press, 2007), xvii.

11. It seems impossible to begin to write about Adorno without heaving against his domesticators. See Miriam Bratu Hansen, "Mass Culture as Hieroglyphic Writing: Adorno, Derrida, Kracauer," *New German Critique* 56 (Spring/Summer 1992). This extremely good issue is devoted to Adorno.

12. Fredric Jameson, *Late Marxism: Adorno, or the Persistence of the Dialectic* (New York: Verso, 1990), 142.

13. David Jennemann, *Adorno in America* (Minneapolis: University of Minnesota Press, 2007), 193, note 11.

14. My discussion, again, is limited to the United States, where Adorno was watching and writing and where I now do the same. This is, as I've said, to beg the issues of mass culture's global reach, the limits of the national model, the role of the state in the production of mass culture, and a host of similar problematic issues for which some of Adorno's work has been justifiably challenged, even dismissed.

15. Raymond Williams, *Television: Technology and Cultural Form*, 3rd edition (London: Routledge, 2003).

16. Theodor Adorno, "How to Look at Television," *Quarterly Review of Film, Radio and Television* 8, 3 (1954).

17. The two definitive examples would be Erik Barnouw, *Tube of Plenty*, 2nd revised edition (New York: Oxford University Press, 1990); and Horace

Newcomb, ed., *Television: The Critical View*, fifth edition (New York: Oxford University Press, 1994). Also see Raymond Williams, *Television, Technology and Cultural Form* (New York: Schocken Books, 1974).

18. Lynn Spigel, *Make Room for TV: Television and the Family Ideal in Postwar America* (Chicago: University of Chicago Press, 1992).

19. On the role of the programmer, see John Ellis, *Visible Fictions: Cinema, Television, Video* (London: Routledge, 1992).

20. Thanks to Jackie Byars first for assigning this to me and inspiring me to continue the practice with my own students.

21. Susan Buck-Morss, *The Origin of Negative Dialectics: Theodor W. Adorno, Walter Benjamin, and the Frankfurt Institute* (New York: The Free Press, 1977), 166.

22. Theodor Adorno, *The Psychological Technique of Martin Luther Thomas' Radio Addresses* (Stanford: Stanford University Press, 2000); and Theodor Adorno, *The Stars Down to Earth and Other Essays on the Irrational in Culture*, edited with an introduction by Stephen Crook (London: Routledge, 1994).

23. See Ernst Bloch et al., *Aesthetics and Politics*, afterword by Fredric Jameson, translated by Ronald Taylor (London: NLB, 1977), in which Jameson reframes Adorno's readings in a broader social conjuncture: "Other conceptions of realism, other kinds of political aesthetics, remain conceivable. The Realism/Modernism debate teaches us the need to judge them in terms of the historical and social conjucture in which they are called to function" (213). Peter Hohendahl also comments on Adorno's complex readings in what Hohendahl calls his "micrological" analyses in *Prismatic Thought: Theodor W. Adorno* (Lincoln: University of Nebraska Press, 1995), 146.

24. Samuel Weber, "Television: Set and Screen," in *Mass Mediaurus: Form, Technics, Media* (Stanford: Stanford University Press, 1996), 108–28.

25. Paul Bové, *Mastering Discourse: The Politics of Intellectual Culture* (Durham, NC: Duke University Press, 1992), 98.

26. *The Culture Industry*, edited with an introduction by J.M. Bernstein (London: Routledge, 1996).

27. See Jim Collins, *Uncommon Cultures: Popular Culture and Post-modernism* (London: Routledge, 1987).

28. Thanks to Johannes von Moltke for a preview. Johannes von Moltke, "Teddie and Friedl: Theodor A. Adorno, Siegfried Kracauer, and the Erotics of Friendship," *Criticism* 51, 4 (Fall 2010).

29. Theodor Adorno, "How to Look at Television," 213. Hereafter, all citations from this article will appear parenthetically.

30. Ian Watt, *The Rise of the Novel: Studies in Defoe, Richardson, and Fielding* (Berkeley: University of California Press, 2001).

31. Theodor Adorno, "The Schema of Mass Culture," in Theodor Adorno, *The Culture Industry*, edited with an introduction by J.M. Bernstein (London: Routledge, 1996), 56.

32. Tobias Wolff, *This Boy's Life: A Memoir* (New York: Atlantic Monthly Press, 1989), 209.

33. www.glaad.org/reference, accessed March 27, 2013.

34. http://www.foxnews.com/entertainment/2012/10/05/study-number-gay-characters-on-tv-at-all-time-high/, accessed March 27, 2013.

35. Karen Narasaki, press release, GLAAD, accessed October 14, 2002, www.glaad.org.

36. Stephen Tropiano, "Where Have All the Gays Gone?," *The Advocate*, October 1, 2002, 51.

37. Martha Wolfenstein and Nathan Leites, *Movies: A Psychological Study* (New York: The Free Press, 1950).

38. In this reading I am trying to tease out a less mechanistic, less surface-depth model than the one that Jennemann, for example, proposes in *Adorno in America* (Minneapolis: University of Minnesota Press, 2007): "Subjects conditioned to accepting at face value what they are presented and accustomed to receiving only glossy surfaces that invite no deeper considerations may have lost the capacity to look beyond those surfaces" (126).

39. Lawrence Rickels, *The Case of California* (Baltimore, MD: The Johns Hopkins University Press, 1991), 113.

40. Lawrence Rickels, *The Case of California* (Baltimore, MD: The Johns Hopkins University Press, 1991), 113.

41. Peter Hohendahl, *Prismatic Thought: Theodor W. Adorno* (Lincoln: University of Nebraska Press, 1995), 70–71.

42. Diana Fuss, *Identification Papers* (New York: Routledge, 1995), 1.

43. Diana Fuss, *Identification Papers* (New York: Routledge, 1995), 1.

44. Stuart Hall, "Encoding/Decoding," in *Media and Cultural Studies: Key-Works*, edited by Meenakshi Gigi Durham and Douglas M. Kellner (Oxford: Blackwell Publishers, 2001).

45. Patricia White, *Uninvited: Classical Hollywood Cinema and Lesbian Representability* (Bloomington: Indiana University Press, 1999), 147, 174.

46. André Bazin, "The Ontology of the Photographic Image," in *What Is Cinema? Volume 1*, essays selected and translated by Hugh Gray, foreword by Jean Renoir (Berkeley: University of California Press, 1967), 14–15. Hereafter, all citations from this essay will appear parenthetically.

47. Philip Rosen, *Change Mummified: Cinema, Historicity, Theory* (Minneapolis: University of Minnesota Press, 2001), 12. Hereafter, all citations from this book will appear parenthetically.

48. Thanks to Shelley Stamp at the University of California, Santa Cruz, for pressing the question of discursive context; I try to respond to it more energetically in chapter 2.

49. Monica Pearl chooses the autobiographical as the introductory indictment in her review of my *Lesbian Rule: Cultural Criticism and the Value of Desire* (Durham, NC: Duke University Press, 2003). See Monica Pearl, "Review of *Lesbian Rule*," GLQ 11, 2 (2005).

50. Many thanks to Phil Hallman for bestowing upon me just recently the whole first season on DVD.

51. The dialogue, again, is my transcription from DVD.

52. Cited in Daniel Jennemann, *Adorno in America* (Minneapolis: University of Minnesota Press, 2007), 88. Original appears in Theodor W. Adorno, *The Psychological Technique of Martin Luther Thomas' Radio Addresses* (Stanford: Stanford University Press, 2000), 55–56.

53. In terms more familiar to debates within television studies, one might distinguish in David Morley's terms, processed through Jane Feuer, between the "ideological problematic" of a text (which is to say the field and range of its representational possibilities), and the "mode of a text's address" (which is to say the text's relation to, and positioning of, its audience). The fact that these are all too frequently intermeshed if not interdependent makes this distinction perhaps condemned to the fate of "form versus content," but it does help analytically, I think, to propel an analysis of form. Jane Feuer, "The Concept of Live Television: Ontology as Ideology," in *Regarding Television: Critical Approaches*, edited by E. Ann Kaplan (Frederick, MD: University Publications of America, 1982), 17.

54. Judith Roof, *All about Thelma and Eve: Sidekicks and Third Wheels* (Urbana: University of Illinois Press, 2002), 78.

55. Christine Becker, *It's the Pictures That Got Small: Hollywood Film Stars on 1950s Television* (Middletown, CT: Wesleyan University Press, 2008), 158.

56. Grateful thanks to Amanda Anderson for this formulation and suggestion.

57. There is a real question about when and where the "closet" came to signify gayness. In his *Closet Space: Geographies of Metaphor from the Body to the Globe* (London: Routledge, 2000), Michael P. Brown finds evidence that the term began to shade (either from toilet or privacy) into queer signification by the 1960s in the United States but that there may be some reason to think, from Canadian evidence, that it migrated in the 1950s (10).

1. Bernard Stiegler, *Technics and Time, 3: Cinematic Time and the Question of Malaise*, translated by Stephen Barker (Stanford: Stanford University Press, 2011), 157.

2. Edmund Husserl, *On the Phenomenology of the Consciousness of Internal Time*, translated by John Barnett Brough (Dordrecht, The Netherlands: Kluwer Academic Publishers, 1991).

3. Daniel Bensaid, *Marx for Our Times: Adventures and Misadventures of a Critique*, translated by Gregory Elliott (London: Verso, 2002), 35.

4. Ben Brantley, "Borne Back Ceaselessly into the Past," *New York Times*, October 6, 2010, accessed September 17, 2012, http://theater.nytimes .com/2010/10/07/theater/reviews/07gatz.html?pagewanted=all.

5. Ben Brantley, "Borne Back Ceaselessly into the Past," *New York Times*, October 6, 2010, accessed September 17, 2012, http://theater.nytimes .com/2010/10/07/theater/reviews/07gatz.html?pagewanted=all.

6. Peggy Phelan, *Unmarked: The Politics of Performance* (New York: Routledge, 1993), 146.

7. Peggy Phelan, "Performance, Live Culture, and Things of the Heart," *Journal of Visual Culture* 2, 3 (2003): 292.

8. Daniel Zalewski, "The Hours: How Christian Marclay Created the Ultimate Digital Mosaic," *New Yorker*, March 12, 2012, accessed September 17, 2012, http://www.newyorker.com/reporting/2012/03/12/120312fa_fact _zalewski#ixzz1zORTvdLW.

9. The industry-standard report is the Nielsen Company's "The Cross Platform Report—Q4 2011," accessed September 11, 2012, http://nielsen .com/us/en/insights/reports-downloads/2012/the-cross-platform-re port-q4–2011.html.

10. Bernard Stiegler, "The Time of Cinema: On the 'New World' and 'Cultural Exception,'" *Tekhnema* 4 (1998): 62. It was subsequently incorporated into the third volume of Stiegler's book series, *Technics and Time: Technics and Time, 3: Cinematic Time and the Question of Malaise*, translated by Stephen Barker (Stanford: Stanford University Press, 2011). Since the latter is much more easily available, I cite from it in the text that follows; hereafter all page numbers will appear parenthetically and refer to this text.

11. See Philip Rosen, *Change Mummified: Cinema, Historicity, Theory* (Minneapolis: University of Minnesota Press, 2001).

12. Roland Barthes, *Camera Lucida: Reflections on Photography*, translated from the French by Richard Howard, foreword by Geoff Dyer (New York: Hill and Wang, 1982), 78.

13. See D. N. Rodowick, *The Virtual Life of Film* (Cambridge: Harvard University Press, 2007).

14. Edmund Husserl, *On the Phenomenology of the Consciousness of Internal Time*, translated by John Barnett Brough (Dordrecht, The Netherlands: Kluwer Academic Publishers, 1991).

15. Vivian Sobchack, "The Scene of the Screen," in *Carnal Thoughts: Embodiment and Moving Image Culture* (Berkeley: University of California Press, 2004), 147.

16. Vivian Sobchack, "The Scene of the Screen," in *Carnal Thoughts: Embodiment and Moving Image Culture* (Berkeley: University of California Press, 2004), 149.

17. Bernard Stiegler and Jacques Derrida, *Echographies of Television: Filmed Interviews* (New York: Polity Press, 2002).

18. Richard Dienst, *Still Life in Real Time: Theory after Television* (Durham, NC: Duke University Press, 1994), xi.

19. Vivian Sobchack, "The Scene of the Screen," in *Carnal Thoughts: Embodiment and Moving Image Culture* (Berkeley: University of California Press, 2004), 159. Sobchack glosses the magnitude of the essay's claims in an interview in 2009: "It's more about the dispersal or diffusion of embodiment. So in *Carnal Thoughts* I changed the essay somewhat. I am still cautionary, but obviously there is pleasure as well as threat in diffusion, which is not the same thing as disembodiment. When I initially wrote the essay, however, we were all just beginning to try to understand the structural and cultural implications of 'new media' and 'the digital' and asking the big questions and, of course, making large claims and dramatic arguments." "Vivian Sobchack in Conversation with Scott Bukatman," *Journal of e-Media Studies* 2, 1 (2009), accessed September 24, 2012, http://journals.dartmouth.edu/cgi-bin/WebObjects/Journals.woa/xmlpage/4/article/338.

20. Barbara Klinger, *Beyond the Multiplex: Cinema, New Technologies, and the Home* (Berkeley: University of California Press, 2006), 4.

21. Barbara Klinger, *Beyond the Multiplex: Cinema, New Technologies, and the Home* (Berkeley: University of California Press, 2006), 27. She notes with some horror that the industry term for obstacles to purchasing new technology is WAF: the "wife acceptance factor" (44).

22. See Uma Dinsmore-Tuli, "The Pleasures of 'Home Cinema,' Or Watching Movies on Telly: An Audience Study of Cinephilic VCR Use," *Screen* 41, 3 (2000).

23. Bernard Stiegler, *Technics and Time, 3: Cinematic Time and the Question of Malaise*, translated by Stephen Barker (Stanford: Stanford University Press, 2011), 41.

24. Bernard Stiegler, *Technics and Time, 3: Cinematic Time and the Question of Malaise*, translated by Stephen Barker (Stanford: Stanford University Press, 2011), 60.

25. Thanks to Hent Devries for his comments on "Adorno's Antenna" and all things Teddie.

26. Sobchack, who is herself an above-the-knee amputee, has movingly challenged the loose senses in which *prosthetic* is used in cultural theory, most often completely detached from embodied experience. Stiegler's use of the term *adoption* is similarly delinked from its resonance as a legal structure for kinship, the politics of which become pressing from the perspective of race, ethnicity, nation, sexuality, disability, and other vectors of inequality. Vivian Sobchack, "A Leg to Stand On: Prosethetics, Metaphor, and Materiality," in *Carnal Thoughts: Embodiment and Moving Image Culture* (Berkeley: University of California Press, 2004), 205–25.

CHAPTER 3. "TELEVISION ATE MY FAMILY": LANCE LOUD ON TV

1. Jane Feuer, "The Concept of Live Television: Ontology as Ideology," in *Regarding Television: Critical Approaches*, edited by E. Ann Kaplan (Frederick, MD: University Publications of America, 1982), 20.

2. In 1975 the three major networks adopted the "family-viewing hour" with the aim of reducing both the representation of violence and sexually explicit material. In 1976 a California federal court declared the scheme unconstitutional because the Federal Communications Commission was shown to have exercised undue pressure on the networks to adopt it. The ruling was later vacated, but the family-viewing hour never returned *formally* to dictate television regulation.

3. Marla Brooks, *The American Family on Television: A Chronology of 121 Shows, 1948–2004* (Jefferson, NC: McFarland and Company, 2005), 24.

4. A reliable source for network broadcast information is *The Complete Directory to Prime Time Network and Cable TV Shows 1946-Present*, by Tim Brooks and Earle Marsh, twentieth anniversary edition (New York: Ballantine Books, 1999). It helpfully includes information such as the rerun schedule on CBS for *December Bride*, which extended its broadcast from 1959 to 1961.

5. Lance Loud, "Lily Tomlin: The Queen of Comedy Brings Her Award-Winning Stage Show to the Screen," interview by Lance Loud, *Details*, October 1991, accessed April 1, 2013. www.pbs.org/lanceloud/lance/lily tomlin.html.

6. An oft-cited instance comes in Gore Vidal's article "Pink Triangle and Yellow Star" (*The Nation*, October 14, 1981) in which he contends that the

word *gay* is an impoverished, "ridiculous" term through which to designate "Frederick the Great, Franklin Pangborn, and Eleanor Roosevelt." In Gore Vidal, *The Second American Revolution and Other Essays (1976–1982)* (New York: Random House, 1982), 167. Also see Marcie Frank, *How to Be an Intellectual in the Age of TV: The Lessons of Gore Vidal* (Durham, NC: Duke University Press, 2005).

7. Theodor W. Adorno, "How to Look at Television," *Quarterly Review of Film, Radio, and Television* 8, 3 (spring 1954): 213–235.

8. Kirsten Marthe Lentz, "*Quality* versus *Relevance*: Feminism, Race, and the Politics of the Sign in 1970s Television," *Camera Obscura* 15, 1 (2000): 46.

9. See Jane Feuer, Paul Kerr, and Tise Vahimagi, eds., MTM: *"Quality Television"* (London: British Film Institute, 1984).

10. Kirsten Marthe Lentz, "*Quality* versus *Relevance*: Feminism, Race, and the Politics of the Sign in 1970s Television," *Camera Obscura* 15, 1 (2000): 60.

11. Kirsten Marthe Lentz, "*Quality* versus *Relevance*: Feminism, Race, and the Politics of the Sign in 1970s Television," *Camera Obscura* 15, 1 (2000): 82 note 6.

12. *All in the Family*, episode no. 113, "Archie the Hero," first broadcast 29 September 1975 by CBS, directed by Paul Bogart and written by Lou Dorman and Bill Davenport; *All in the Family*, episode no. 141, "Beverly Rides Again," first broadcast 6 November 1976 by CBS, directed by Paul Bogart and written by Phil Doran and Douglas Arrango; *All in the Family*, episode no. 171, "Edith's Crisis of Faith: Part 1," first broadcast 25 December 1977 by CBS, directed by Paul Bogart and written by Erik Tarloff, Bob Schiller, and Bob Weiskopf; *All in the Family*, episode no. 172, "Edith's Crisis of Faith: Part 2," first broadcast 25 December 1977 by CBS, directed by Paul Bogart and written by Mel Tolkin, Erik Tarloff, and Larry Rhine.

13. Rosen remarks that "cinema manifests a special relation to modern time awareness first as a matter of distribution through its status as a mass medium, and only second as a matter of representation." Philip Rosen, *Change Mummified: Cinema, Historicity, Theory* (Minneapolis: University of Minnesota Press, 2001), 100.

14. Joe Wlodarz, "We're Not All So Obvious: Masculinity and Queer (In)visibility in American Network Television of the 1970s," in *Queer TV*, edited by Glyn Davis and Gary Needham (London: Routledge, 2009), 91.

15. http://www.cpb.org/aboutpb/act/, accessed April 1, 2013.

16. A line Hoover himself did not apparently utter: see http://www.hoover .archives.gov/info/faq.html#chicken, accessed April 1, 2013.

17. Laurie Oullette and James Hay cite this tradition but see it as more dogmatic: "Conceptualized as an extension of the public university, the earliest experiments in 'education by television' were abstract, didactic, un-

adorned, and dominated by academics, journalists, and other bona fide intellectual authorities. This is not surprising, for the citizens these programs wished to 'empower' were conceived as a gullible mass that needed guidance in the liberal arts to participate in the rituals of public democracy." Laurie Oullette and James Hay, *Better Living through Reality TV* (Malden, MA: Blackwell Publishing, 2008), 3.

18. Jeffrey Ruoff, *An American Family: A Televised Life* (Minneapolis: University of Minnesota Press, 2001), 5.

19. Eve Kosofsky Sedgwick, *Epistemology of the Closet* (Berkeley: University of California Press, 1990), 68. For a social-science dossier on coming out in the classroom, see essays in R. Jeffrey Ringer, ed., *Queer Words, Queer Images: Communication and the Construction of Homosexuality* (New York: NYU Press, 1994), including R. Jeffrey Ringer, "Coming Out in the Classroom: Faculty Disclosures of Sexuality" (322–31); Elenie Opffer, "Coming Out to Students: Notes from the College Classroom" (296–321); Mercilee M. Jenkins, "Ways of Coming Out in the Classroom" (332–34); and Jacqueline Taylor, "Performing the (Lesbian) Self: Teacher as Text" (289–95).

20. Michael P. Brown, *Closet Space: Geographies of Metaphor from the Body to the Globe* (London: Routledge, 2000), 5.

21. Sara Gwenllian Jones, "Gender and Queerness," in *Television Studies*, edited by Toby Miller (London: BFI Publishing, 2002), 109.

22. "At this time, in July 1970, the use of film for television was an object of discussion for the SMPTE [Society of Motion Picture and Television Engineers]. Film was lauded for its greater flexibility in single-camera photography. In addition, when it came to editing, film with its superior postproduction capability, had the advantage. As far as the recording of news events was concerned, the CBS engineering department reported that, 'As of now, . . . it is simply not possible nor economically feasible to compete with 16mm film for this application. In this case, electronic photography must simply plead—no context.' It wasn't long before CBS would eat its words." Albert Abramson, *The History of Television, 1942 to 2000* (Jefferson, NC: McFarland and Company, 2003), 134–35.

23. Jeffrey Ruoff, *An American Family: A Televised Life* (Minneapolis: University of Minnesota Press, 2001), 31–32.

24. Jeffrey Ruoff, *An American Family: A Televised Life* (Minneapolis: University of Minnesota Press, 2001), 107, 103.

25. Craig Gilbert, "Reflections on *An American Family*," *Studies in Visual Communication* 8, 1 (1982): 24.

26. Thanks to Mimi White for the *Eight Is Enough* reminder.

27. Jeffrey Ruoff, *An American Family: A Televised Life* (Minneapolis: University of Minnesota Press, 2001), 29.

28. Ruoff provides helpful information about the importance of Alice Carey, who was working in New York at WNET as a "production secretary." She became, in her words, "the liaison between the straight population of Channel 13—anybody who was terrified of the word *homosexual*—and Lance." She knew Jackie Curtis and his production of *Vain Victory*, featured in the second episode, and she functioned as the urban intellectual organic to the queer scene who coordinated everything Lance. Jeffrey Ruoff, *An American Family: A Televised Life* (Minneapolis: University of Minnesota Press, 2001), 28–29.

29. "Holly came from Miami, F.L.A. / Hitchhiked her way across the USA / Plucked her eyebrows on the way / Shaved her legs, and then he was a she / She said, 'Hey babe, take a walk on the wild side.'"

30. *Gone* is a two-channel videotape that combines a musical performance by Le Tigre and a dance performance by Jennifer Monson with Dougherty's own reflections and obsessions on and with Lance and *An American Family*. Since *Gone* focuses on the second episode of the serial, it investigates the Central Park sequence as a crucial nexus of silence, revelation, and everyday queer life, riffing through contemporary multimedia on this thirty years later. See the page for *Gone* on Doughterty's website, http://www.ceciliadougherty.com/goneWebsite.

31. Christopher Pullen remarks, "Although Pat Loud expresses in *Lance Loud! Death in An American Family* (2003) that this was *not* the point at which Lance came out to her (she implies that she and her husband Bill had been aware for some time that Lance was likely to be gay), this sequence remains a defining moment in the representation of gay people on television. It may be considered as the first time on mainstream television that audiences became aware of a gay identity which was not mediated (obviously interpreted) by producers of drama or expository documentary. Rather through its presentation as observational documentary, it is suggested that Lance was not only likely to be gay but he was performing as himself rather than being a subject of a particular discourse or examination." Christopher Pullen, *Documenting Gay Men: Identity and Performance in Reality Television and Documentary Film* (Jefferson, NC: McFarland and Company, 2007), 41–42.

32. Gilles Deleuze, *Bergsonism*, translated by Hugh Tomlinson and Barbara Habberjam (Brooklyn, NY: Zone Books, 1988), 55.

33. Anne Roiphe, "Things Are Keen but Could Be Keener," *New York Times Magazine*, February 18, 1973, 8. Hereafter page references to this article will appear in the text.

34. See Jeffrey Ruoff, *An American Family: A Televised Life* (Minneapolis: University of Minnesota Press, 2001), 45.

35. Jean Baudrillard, *Simulations*, translated by Paul Foss, Paul Patton, and Philip Beitchman (New York: Semiotext[e], 1983), 55.

36. Jean Baudrillard, *Symbolic Exchange and Death*, translated by Iain Hamilton Grant, with an introduction by Mike Gane (London: Sage Publications, 1993). Thanks to Jeff Sconce for reminding me of this publication history.

37. http://www.semiotexte.com/books/simulations.html.

38. Jean Baudrillard, *Simulations*, translated by Paul Foss, Paul Patton, and Philip Beitchman (New York: Semiotext[e], 1983), 49.

39. Jean Baudrillard, *Simulations*, translated by Paul Foss, Paul Patton, and Philip Beitchman (New York: Semiotex[e], 1983), 50–51.

40. Jean Baudrillard, *Simulations*, translated by Paul Foss, Paul Patton, and Philip Beitchman (New York: Semiotex[e], 1983), 51.

41. Jeffrey Ruoff, *An American Family: A Televised Life* (Minneapolis: University of Minnesota Press, 2001), 26.

42. http://www.pbs.org/lanceloud/lance/comingout.html, accessed April 1, 2013.

43. Pat Loud, "Remembering Edie Beale," in Walter Newkirk, *MemoraBEALEia: A Private Scrapbook about Edie Beale of Grey Gardens First Cousin to First Lady Jacqueline Kennedy Onassis* (Bloomington, IN: AuthorHouse, 2008), 79.

44. Walter Newkirk, *memoraBEALEia: A Private Scrapbook about Edie Beale of Grey Gardens First Cousin to First Lady Jacqueline Kennedy Onassis* (Bloomington, IN: AuthorHouse, 2008), 4.

45. Walter Newkirk, *memoraBEALEia: A Private Scrapbook about Edie Beale of Grey Gardens First Cousin to First Lady Jacqueline Kennedy Onassis* (Bloomington, IN: AuthorHouse, 2008), 4.

CHAPTER 4. QUEER ASCENSION:
TELEVISION AND TALES OF THE CITY

1. Barbara Mennel, *Cities and Cinema* (London: Routledge, 2008).

2. David Clarke, ed., *The Cinematic City* (London: Routledge, 1997); Edward Dimendberg, *Film Noir and the Spaces of Modernity* (Cambridge, MA: Harvard University Press, 2004); James Donald, *Imagining the Modern City* (Minneapolis: University of Minnesota Press, 1999); Sabine Hake, "Visualizing the Urban Masses: Modern Architecture and Architectural Photography in Weimar Berlin," in *Visualizing the City*, edited by Alan Marcus and Dietrich Meumann (London: Routledge, 2007); and Linda Krause and Patrice Petro, eds., *Global Cities: Cinema, Architecture, and Urbanism in a Digital Age* (New Brunswick, NJ: Rutgers University Press, 2003).

3. John David Rhodes, *Stupendous, Miserable City: Pasolini's Rome* (Minneapolis: University of Minnesota Press, 2007), xv.

4. Amy Villarejo, "*Bus 174* and the Living Present," *Cinema Journal* 46, 1 (Fall 2006). I extend some of the arguments about Brazilian representation in my chapter "Killing Me Softly: Brazilian Film and Bare Life," in *Beyond Globalization: Making New Worlds in Media, Art, and Social Practices*, edited by A. Aneesh, Lane Hall, and Patrice Petro (New Brunswick, NJ: Rutgers University Press, 2011).

5. George Yúdice, *The Expediency of Culture: Uses of Culture in the Global Era* (Durham, NC: Duke University Press, 2003).

6. George Yúdice, *The Expediency of Culture: Uses of Culture in the Global Era* (Durham, NC: Duke University Press, 2003), 123.

7. Giorgio Agamben, *Means without End: Notes on Politics*, translated by Vincenzo Binetti and Cesare Casarino (Minneapolis: University of Minnesota Press, 2000), 35.

8. Teresa P. R. Caldeira, *City of Walls: Crime, Segregation, and Citizenship in São Paulo* (Berkeley: University of California Press, 2000), 299.

9. Mike Davis's work on the relationship between urban aesthetics and security, from *City of Quartz: Excavating the Future in Los Angeles* (London: Verso, 1990) to *Planet of Slums* (London: Verso, 2007), is an invaluable resource.

10. Here I would wish to unsettle the falsely inclusive rhetoric offered by the coeditors of *Visualizing the City*: "Walls are built to barricade in the rich and keep out impoverished migrants, but, however high and robust the barriers are, they prove porous, permeable; the poor, as well as our anxieties about them, are always with us." Alan Marcus and Dietrich Neumann, "Introduction: Visualizing the City," in *Visualizing the City*, edited by Alan Marcus and Dietrich Neumann (London: Routledge, 2007), 1.

11. Cited in George Yúdice, *The Expediency of Culture: Uses of Culture in the Global Era* (Durham, NC: Duke University Press, 2003), 138.

12. Iris Marion Young, "City Life and Difference," in Iris Marion Young, *Justice and the Politics of Difference* (Princeton, NJ: Princeton University Press, 1990).

13. George Chauncey, *Gay New York: Gender, Urban Culture, and the Making of the Gay Male World, 1890–1940* (New York: Basic Books, 1994), 9.

14. Matt Houlbrook, *Queer London: Perils and Pleasures in the Sexual Metropolis, 1918–1957* (Chicago: University of Chicago Press, 2005), 242.

15. Matt Houlbrook, *Queer London: Perils and Pleasures in the Sexual Metropolis, 1918–1957* (Chicago: University of Chicago Press, 2005), 146.

16. Teresa P. R. Caldeira, *City of Walls: Crime, Segregation, and Citizenship in São Paulo* (Berkeley: University of California Press, 2000), 299.

17. Matt Houlbrook, *Queer London: Perils and Pleasures in the Sexual Metropolis, 1918–1957* (Chicago: University of Chicago Press, 2005), 12.

18. George Chauncey, *Gay New York: Gender, Urban Culture, and the Making of the Gay Male World, 1890–1940* (New York: Basic Books, 1994), 23.

19. George Chauncey, *Gay New York: Gender, Urban Culture, and the Making of the Gay Male World, 1890–1940* (New York: Basic Books, 1994), 26.

20. See Henri Lefebvre, *The Production of Space*, translated by Donald Nicholson-Smith (Oxford: Blackwell, 1991).

21. Matt Houlbrook, *Queer London: Perils and Pleasures in the Sexual Metropolis, 1918–1957* (Chicago: University of Chicago Press, 2005), 41.

22. Quoted in Matt Houlbrook, *Queer London: Perils and Pleasures in the Sexual Metropolis, 1918–1957* (Chicago: University of Chicago Press, 2005), 118.

23. Matt Houlbrook, *Queer London: Perils and Pleasures in the Sexual Metropolis, 1918–1957* (Chicago: University of Chicago Press, 2005), 58.

24. Samuel R. Delany, *Times Square Red, Times Square Blue* (New York: New York University Press, 1999).

25. Matt Houlbrook, *Queer London: Perils and Pleasures in the Sexual Metropolis, 1918–1957* (Chicago: University of Chicago Press, 2005), 10.

26. George Chauncey, *Gay New York: Gender, Urban Culture, and the Making of the Gay Male World, 1890–1940* (New York: Basic Books, 1994), 27.

27. Among the many filmmakers whose directorial work was enabled by *American Playhouse* are Tom Kalin, Julie Dash, and Jill Godmilow, while queer plays by figures as important as Lanford Wilson and Terrence McNally were adapted for television for the series. The final installment of *American Playhouse*, incidentally, was a ten-hour observational documentary about a mixed-race family, titled *An American Love Story* (1999), modeled on — you guessed it — *An American Family*.

28. Benjamin Estelle Lloyd, *Lights and Shades of San Francisco* (San Francisco, 1876). Quoted by Herbert Ashbury, *The Barbary Coast — An Informal History of the San Francisco Underworld* (New York: Knopf, 1933).

29. I mean for this phrase simply to designate Mrs. Madrigal's maternal function, the way the serial constitutes the group at Barbary Lane as a family of Mrs. Madrigal's children. It is, of course, a biblical reference to Mary as the "mother of us all," as well as the title of Gertrude Stein and Virgil Thompson's opera about Susan B. Anthony, and echoes of both Catholicism and feminism do indeed converge in Mrs. Madrigal!

30. http://www.armisteadmaupin.com/ and http://www.toursofthetales.com /Home.html. Acccessed April 1, 2013.

31. While Armistead Maupin's own name can be anagrammatically rendered as "A Man I Dreamt Up," his name really is Armistead Maupin.

32. Armistead Maupin, *Further Tales of the City*, directed by Pierre Gang (2001; Los Angeles: Showtime Entertainment, 2002), special features, DVD.

33. Armistead Maupin, *Further Tales of the City*, directed by Pierre Gang (2001; Los Angeles: Showtime Entertainment, 2002), special features, DVD.

34. Lisa Duggan, *The Twilight of Equality? Neoliberalism, Cultural Politics, and the Attack on Democracy* (Boston: Beacon Press, 2003).

35. Gayle Rubin, "Thinking Sex: Notes for a Radical Theory of the Politics of Sexuality," in *Pleasure and Danger*, edited by Carole Vance (New York: Routledge, 1984).

36. Larry Rhodes, the tour guide of the Tours of the Tales, notices that the nighttime skyline that Brian surveys from his apartment in the "pentshack" is not San Francisco but Oakland. See his website, www.toursofthetales.com, for an astonishingly definitive geography of Maupin's worlds.

37. Tom Conley, *Film Hieroglyphs: Ruptures in Classical Cinema* (Minneapolis: University of Minnesota Press, 1991), ix.

38. Anne Friedberg, *The Virtual Window: From Alberti to Microsoft* (Cambridge: MIT Press, 2006), 138.

39. http://www.viacom.com/aboutviacom/Pages/default.aspx, accessed April 1, 2013.

40. http://www.viacom.com/ourbrands/Pages/default.aspx, accessed April 1, 2013.

41. This is Viacom's self-description in the "About Us" section of its website. http://www.viacom.com/aboutviacom/Pages/default.aspx, accessed April 1, 2013.

42. National Cable and Telecommunications Association, "Industry Data," accessed April 2, 2013., http://www.ncta.com/industrydata.

43. These data are moving targets, but the third quarter report in 2011 put the figure at 90.4%. The report can be accessed through the Nielsen website: http://www.nielsen.com/us/en/reports/2012/cross-platform-report-q3–2011.html, accessed April 2, 2013.

44. Citizen's Guide to the Public Interest Obligations of Digital Television Broadcasters, 19, prepared by the Benton Foundation and available online at their website, www.bentonfoundation.org.

45. Although this list is my own, much of the terrain of media policy is charted by Eric Klinenberg in his book *Fighting for Air: The Battle to Control America's Media* (New York: Holt Paperbacks, 2008). The most authoritative work on the political economy of media is by Robert W. McChesney, who has written extensively on media policy. See, for example, Robert W. McChesney, *The Problem of the Media: U.S. Communication Politics in the Twenty-First Century* (New York: Monthly Review Press, 2004).

46. Hollis Griffin, "Your Favorite Stars, Live on Our Screens: Media Culture, Queer Publics, and Commercial Space," *The Velvet Light Trap: A Critical Journal of Film and Television* (Fall 2008), 16.

47. This comes from LOGO's own self-description on its official website: http://www.logotv.com/about, accessed April 2, 2013.

48. See the essays in *Queer Economics: A Reader*, edited by Joyce Jacobsen and Adam Zeller (London and New York: Routledge, 2008).

49. *Homo Economics: Capitalism, Community, and Lesbian and Gay Life*, edited by Amy Gluckman and Betsy Reed (New York and London: Routledge, 1997) and *Queer Economics: A Reader*, edited by Joyce Jacobsen and Adam Zeller (London and New York: Routledge, 2008).

50. Available through GLAAD's website: http://www.glaad.org/publications /whereweareontv12, accessed April 2, 2013.

51. See Katherine Sender, *Business, Not Politics: The Making of the Gay Market* (New York: Columbia University Press, 2005).

52. The case study is published by the IBS Case Development Centre, or IBSCDC. It may be bought at www.ibscdc.org/Case_Studies/Strategy, accessed April 2, 1013.

53. Shawn McIntosh examines HBO Asia in his chapter "Will Yingfusiji Buzz Help HBO Asia?," in *It's Not TV: Watching HBO in the Post-television Era*, edited by Marc Leverette, Brian L. Ott, and Cara Louise Buckley (London: Routledge, 2008).

CODA. BECOMING

1. "The Many Shades of Thomas Dekker," *Out*, April 17, 2011, accessed April 2, 2013. http://www.out.com/entertainment/movies/2011/04/17 /many-shades-thomas-dekker.

2. "But despite the frequent interludes of soul-baring song, we never come to know them as intimately or as memorably as we do in the books, originally serialized in the *San Francisco Chronicle*, or the terrific British mini-series seen on PBS in 1994." Charles Isherwood, "When We Were Young and Gay, under the Disco Ball," *New York Times*, June 17, 2011, accessed April 2, 2013, http://theater.nytimes.com/2011/06/18/theater /reviews/armistead-maupins-tales-of-the-city-the-musical-review.html.

3. John Thornton Caldwell, *Production Culture: Industrial Reflexivity and Critical Practice in Film and Television* (Durham, NC: Duke University Press, 2008) and Amanda D. Lotz, *The Television Will Be Revolutionized* (New York: NYU Press, 2007).

4. See my own rant against textual analysis in Amy Villarejo, "Ethereal Queer: Notes on Method," in *Queer TV: Television and Dissident Sexualities*,

edited by Glyn Davis and Gary Needham (New York: Routledge, 2009); my attempt to speak overtly to performance studies scholars in Amy Villarejo, "TV Queen: Lending an Ear to Charles Pierce," in *Modern Drama*, 53, 3 (Fall 2010); and my early response to the age of digital television in Amy Villarejo, "Materiality, Pedagogy, and Queer Visibility," in *A Companion to Lesbian, Gay, Bisexual, Transgender, and Queer Studies*, edited by George E. Haggerty and Molly McGarry (Hoboken, NJ: Wiley-Blackwell, 2007).

5. See Candace Moore, "Having It All Ways: the Tourist, the Traveler, and the Local in *The L Word*," *Cinema Journal* 46, 4 (Summer 2007).

6. Christian Viviani, "Who Is without Sin? The Maternal Melodrama in American Film, 1930–1939," in *Imitations of Life: A Reader on Film and Television Melodrama*, edited by Marcia Landy (Detroit: Wayne State University Press, 1991), 181.

7. Christian Viviani, "Who Is without Sin? The Maternal Melodrama in American Film, 1930–1939," in *Imitations of Life: A Reader on Film and Television Melodrama*, edited by Marcia Landy (Detroit: Wayne State University Press, 1991), 168.

8. Richard Dienst, *Still Life in Real Time: Theory after Television* (Durham, NC: Duke University Press, 1994), 63.

9. Dienst, *Still Life in Real Time*, 62.

10. See the U.S. government's website on digital television, DTV.gov, for details of the digital conversion.

11. Jeffrey Sconce, *Haunted Media: Electronic Presence from Telegraphy to Television* (Durham, NC: Duke University Press, 2000), 92.

12. Gilles Deleuze, "Coldness and Cruelty," in *Masochism*, translated by Jean McNeil (New York: Zone Books, 1989), 74.

Abramson, Albert. *The History of Television: 1942 to 2000*. Jefferson, NC: McFarland and Company, 2003.

Adorno, Theodor. *The Culture Industry*. Edited with an introduction by J.M. Bernstein. London: Routledge, 1996.

———. "How to Look at Television." *Quarterly Review of Film, Radio, and Television* 8, 3 (1954): 213–35.

———. "On the Fetish-Character of Music and the Regression of Listening," 288–317. *Essays on Music*. Selected with introduction, commentary, and notes by Richard Leppert. New translations by Susan H. Gillespie. Berkeley: University of California Press, 2002.

———. *The Psychological Technique of Martin Luther Thomas' Radio Addresses*. Stanford: Stanford University Press, 2000.

———. *The Stars Down to Earth and Other Essays on the Irrational in Culture*. Edited with an introduction by Stephen Crook. London: Routledge, 1994

Agamben, Giorgio. *Means without End: Notes on Politics*. Translated by Vincenzo Binetti and Cesare Casarino. Minneapolis: University of Minnesota Press, 2000.

Ashbury, Herbert. *The Barbary Coast—An Informal History of the San Francisco Underworld*. New York: Knopf, 1933.

Barnouw, Erik. *Tube of Plenty*. 2nd revised edition. New York: Oxford University Press, 1990.

Barthes, Roland. *Camera Lucida: Reflections on Photography*. Translated from the French by Richard Howard. Foreword by Geoff Dyer. New York: Hill and Wang, 1982.

Baudrillard, Jean. *Simulations*. Translated by Paul Foss, Paul Patton, and Philip Beitchman. New York: Semiotex[e], 1983.

———. *Symbolic Exchange and Death*. Translated by Iain Hamilton Grant. With an introduction by Mike Gane. London: Sage Publications, 1993.

Bazin, André. "The Ontology of the Photographic Image." In *What Is Cinema? Volume 1*, 9–16. Essays selected and translated by Hugh Gray. Foreword by Jean Renoir, with a new foreword by Dudley Andrew. Berkeley: University of California Press, 1967, 2005.

Becker, Christine. *It's the Pictures That Got Small: Hollywood Film Stars on 1950s Television*. Middletown, CT: Wesleyan University Press, 2008.

Becker, Ron. *Gay TV and Straight America*. New Brunswick, NJ: Rutgers University Press, 2006.

Bernstein, J.M. "Introduction." In Theodor W. Adorno, *The Culture Industry*, 1–28. Edited with an introduction by J.M. Bernstein. London: Routledge, 1996.

Bloch, Ernst, Georg Lukács, Bertolt Brecht, Walter Benjamin, and Theodor Adorno. *Aesthetics and Politics*. Afterword by Fredric Jameson. Translation by Ronald Taylor. London: NLB, 1977.

Booth, Paul. *Time on TV: Temporal Displacement and Mashup Television*. New York: Peter Lang, 2012.

Bové, Paul. *Mastering Discourse: The Politics of Intellectual Culture*. Durham, NC: Duke University Press, 1992.

Brooks, Marla. *The American Family on Television: A Chronology of 121 Shows, 1948–2004*. Jefferson, NC: McFarland and Company, 2005.

Brooks, Tim and Marsh, Earle. *The Complete Directory to Prime Time Network and Cable TV Shows 1946-Present*. Twentieth Anniversary Edition. New York: Ballantine Books, 1999.

Brown, Michael P. *Closet Space: Geographies of Metaphor from the Body to the Globe*. London: Routledge, 2000.

Buck-Morss, Susan. *The Origin of Negative Dialectics: Theodor W. Adorno, Walter Benjamin, and the Frankfurt Institute*. New York: The Free Press, 1977.

Caldeira, Teresa P. R. *City of Walls: Crime, Segregation, and Citizenship in Sao Paulo*. Berkeley: University of California Press, 2000.

Capsuto, Steven. *Alternate Channels: The Uncensored Story of Gay and Lesbian Images on Radio and Television*. New York: Ballantine Books, 2000.

Chauncey, George. *Gay New York: Gender, Urban Culture, and the Making of the Gay Male World, 1890–1940*. New York: Basic Books, 1994.

Clarke, David, ed. *The Cinematic City*. London: Routledge, 1997.

Collins, Jim. *Uncommon Cultures: Popular Culture and Post-modernism*. New York: Routledge, 1989.

Conley, Tom. *Film Hieroglyphs: Ruptures in Classical Cinema*. Minneapolis: University of Minnesota Press, 1991.

Corner, John. "Television and the Practice of 'Criticism.'" *Flow*, September 22, 2006. Accessed March 25, 2013. http://flowtv.org/2006/09/television-and-the-practice-of-criticism/.

Davis, Mike. *City of Quartz: Excavating the Future in Los Angeles*. London: Verso, 1990.

———. *Planet of Slums*. London: Verso, 2007.

Delany, Samuel. *Times Square Red, Times Square Blue*. New York: NYU Press, 1999.

Deleuze, Gilles. *Bergsonism*. Translated by Hugh Tomlinson and Barbara Habberjam. New York: Zone Books, 1991.

———. "Coldness and Cruelty." In *Masochism*, 9–142. Translated by Jean McNeil. New York: Zone Books, 1989.

Dews, Peter. "Adorno, Poststructuralism, and the Critique of Identity." In *The Problem of Modernity: Adorno and Benjamin*. Edited by Andrew Benjamin. London: Routledge, 1999.

Dienst, Richard. *Still Life in Real Time: Theory after Television*. Durham, NC: Duke University Press, 1994.

Dimendberg, Edward. *Film Noir and the Spaces of Modernity*. Cambridge, MA: Harvard University Press, 2004.

Dinsmore-Tuli, Uma. "The Pleasures of 'Home Cinema,' Or Watching Movies on Telly: An Audience Study of Cinephilic VCR Use." *Screen* 41, 3 (2000): 315–27.

Doane, Mary Ann. "Information, Crisis, Catastrophe." In *Logics of Television: Essays in Cultural Criticism*, 222–239. Edited by Patricia Mellencamp. Bloomington: Indiana University Press, 1990.

Donald, James. *Imagining the Modern City*. Minneapolis: University of Minnesota Press, 1999.

Duggan, Lisa. *The Twilight of Equality? Neoliberalism, Cultural Politics, and the Attack on Democracy*. Boston, MA: Beacon Press, 2003.

Duttmann, Alexander Garcia. "A Second Life: Notes on Adorno's Reading of Proust." *World Picture* 3 (2009). Accessed May 12, 2010. http://www.worldpicturejournal.com/WP_3/Duttman.html.

Edelman, Lee. *No Future: Queer Theory and the Death Drive*. Durham, NC: Duke University Press, 2004.

Ellis, John. "Scheduling: The Last Creative Act in Television?" *Media Culture Society* 22 (2000): 25–38.

———. *Visible Fictions: Cinema, Television, Video*. London: Routledge, 1992.

Feuer, Jane. "The Concept of Live Television: Ontology as Ideology." In *Regard-*

ing Television: Critical Approaches, 12–22. Edited by E. Ann Kaplan. Frederick, MD: University Publications of America, 1982.

Feuer, Jane, Paul Kerr, and Tise Vahimagi, eds. MTM: *"Quality Television."* London: British Film Institute, 1984.

Fountain, Tim. *Resident Alien*. London: Nick Hern Books, 1999.

Frank, Marcie. *How to Be an Intellectual in the Age of TV: The Lessons of Gore Vidal*. Durham, NC: Duke University Press, 2005.

Freeman, Elizabeth. "Introduction." GLQ 13, 2–3 (2007): 159–76.

Friedberg, Anne. *The Virtual Window: From Alberti to Microsoft*. Cambridge, MA: MIT Press, 2006.

Friedman, James, ed. *Reality Squared: Televisual Discourse on the Real*. New Brunswick, NJ: Rutgers University Press, 2002.

Fuss, Diana. *Identification Papers*. New York: Routledge, 1995.

Gamson, Joshua. *Freaks Talk Back: Tabloid Talk Shows and Sexual Nonconformity*. Chicago: University of Chicago Press, 1998.

Gilbert, Craig. "Reflections on *An American Family*." *Studies in Visual Communication* 8, 1 (1982): 24–54.

Gillan, Jennifer. *Television and New Media: Must Click TV*. London: Routledge, 2010.

Gluckman, Amy, and Betsy Reed. *Homo Economics: Capitalism, Community, and Lesbian and Gay Life*. New York and London: Routledge, 1997.

Griffin, Hollis. "Your Favorite Stars, Live on Our Screens: Media Culture, Queer Publics, and Commercial Space." *The Velvet Light Trap: A Critical Journal of Film and Television* (Fall 2008): 15–28.

Grosz, Elizabeth. *The Nick of Time: Politics, Evolution, and the Untimely*. Durham, NC: Duke University Press, 2004.

———. *Time Travels: Feminism, Nature, Power*. Durham, NC: Duke University Press, 2005.

Hake, Sabine. "Visualizing the Urban Masses: Modern Architecture and Architectural Photography in Weimar Berlin," 51–72. In *Visualizing the City*. Edited by Alan Marcus and Dietrich Neumann. London and New York: Routledge, 2007.

Hall, Stuart. "Encoding/Decoding." In *Media and Cultural Studies: KeyWorks*, 166–76. Edited by Meenakshi Gigi Durham and Douglas M. Kellner. Oxford: Blackwell Publishers, 2001.

Hansen, Miriam Bratu. *From Babel to Babylon: Spectatorship in American Silent Film*. Cambridge, MA: Harvard University Press, 1991.

———. "Mass Culture as Hieroglyphic Writing: Adorno, Derrida, Kracauer." *New German Critique* 56 (Spring/Summer 1992): 43–73.

———. "The Mass Production of the Senses: Classical Cinema as Vernacular Modernism." *Modernism/Modernity* 6, 2 (April 1999): 59–77.

———. "Room-for-Play: Benjamin's Gamble with Cinema." *October* 109 (2004): 3–45.

Hardt, Michael, and Antonio Negri. *Empire*. Cambridge, MA: Harvard University Press, 2000.

Harrington, C. Lee. "Lesbian(s) on Daytime Television: The Bianca Narrative on *All My Children*." *Feminist Media Studies* 3, 2 (2003): 207–28.

Hohendahl, Peter. *Prismatic Thought: Theodor W. Adorno*. Lincoln: University of Nebraska Press, 1995.

Houlbrook, Matt. *Queer London: Perils and Pleasures in the Sexual Metropolis, 1918–1957*. Chicago: University of Chicago Press, 2005.

Husserl, Edmund. *On the Phenomenology of the Consciousness of Internal Time*. Translated by John Barnett Brough. Dordrecht, The Netherlands: Kluwer Academic Publishers, 1991.

Jacobsen, Joyce and Adam Zeller, eds. *Queer Economics: A Reader*. London and New York: Routledge, 2008.

Jameson, Fredric. *Late Marxism: Adorno, or the Persistence of the Dialectic*. New York: Verso, 1990.

Jennemann, David. *Adorno in America*. Minneapolis: University of Minnesota Press, 2007.

Jones, Sara Gwenllian. "Gender and Queerness." In *Television Studies*, 109–112. Edited by Toby Miller. London: BFI Publishing, 2002.

Joyrich, Lynne. "Epistemology of the Console." *Critical Inquiry* 27, 3 (Spring 2001): 439–67.

———. "Written on the Screen: Mediation and Immersion in *Far From Heaven*." *Camera Obscura* 19, 3 (2004): 186–219.

Kaplan, Morris. *Sodom on the Thames: Sex, Love, and Scandal in Wilde Times*. Ithaca, NY: Cornell University Press, 2005.

Keller, James R., and Leslie Stratyner, eds. *The New Queer Aesthetic on Television: Essays on Recent Programming*. Jefferson, NC: McFarland, 2006.

Kellner, Douglas. "Television and the Frankfurt School (T.W. Adorno)." In *Television Studies*, 17–20. Edited by Toby Miller. London: BFI Publishing, 2002.

———. "*Beavis and Butthead*: No Future for Postmodern Youth." In *Television: The Critical View, 7th Edition*, 319–329. Edited by Horace Newcomb. New York: Oxford University Press, 2000.

Klinenberg, Eric. *Fighting for Air: The Battle to Control America's Media*. New York: Holt Paperbacks, 2007.

Klinger, Barbara. *Beyond the Multiplex: Cinema, New Technologies, and the Home*. Berkeley: University of California Press, 2006.

Kozloff, Sarah. "Narrative Theory and Television." In *Channels of Discourse, Reassembled: Television and Contemporary Criticism*, 67–100. Edited by Robert C. Allen. Chapel Hill: University of North Carolina Press, 1992.

Krause, Linda, and Patrice Petro, eds. *Global Cities: Cinema, Architecture, and Urbanism in a Digital Age*. New Brunswick, NJ: Rutgers University Press, 2003.

Lefebvre, Henri. *The Production of Space*. Translated by Donald Nicholson-Smith. Oxford: Blackwell, 1991.

Lentz, Kirsten Marthe. "*Quality* versus *Relevance*: Feminism, Race, and the Politics of the Sign in 1970s Television." *Camera Obscura* 15, 1 (2000): 45–93.

Lim, Bliss Cua. *Translating Time: Cinema, The Fantastic, and Temporal Critique*. Durham, NC: Duke University Press, 2009.

Lotz, Amanda. "If It's Not TV, What Is It?" In *Cable Visions: Television beyond Broadcasting*, 85–102. Edited by Sarah Banet-Weiser, Cynthia Chris, and Anthony Freitas. New York: NYU Press, 2007.

Loud, Lance. "Lily Tomlin: The Queen of Comedy Brings Her Award-Winning Stage Show to the Screen." Interview by Lance Loud. *Details*, October 1991. Accessed March 25, 2013. www.pbs.org/lanceloud/lance/lilytomlin.html.

Loud, Pat. "Remembering Edie Beale." In Walter Newkirk, *MemoraBEALEia: A Private Scrapbook about Edie Beale of Grey Gardens First Cousin to First Lady Jacqueline Kennedy Onassis*, 79–80. Bloomington, IN: AuthorHouse, 2008.

Marc, David. *Comic Visions: Television Comedy and American Culture*. Malden, MA: Blackwell, 1989.

Marcus, Alan, and Dietrich Neumann. "Introduction: Visualizing the City." In *Visualizing the City*, 1–9. Edited by Alan Marcus and Dietrich Neumann. London: Routledge, 2007.

Maupin, Armistead. *Tales of the City*. New York: Harper and Row, 1978.

McChesney, Robert W. *The Problem of the Media: U.S. Communications Politics in the Twenty-First Century*. New York: Monthly Review Press, 2004.

McIntosh, Shawn. "Will Yingfusiji Buzz Help HBO Asia?" In *It's Not TV: Watching HBO in the Post-television Era*, 65–82. Edited by Marc Leverette, Brian L. Ott, and Cara Louise Buckley. London: Routledge, 2008.

Mennel, Barbara. *Cities and Cinema*. London: Routledge, 2008.

Miklitsch, Robert. *Roll over Adorno: Critical Theory, Popular Culture, Audiovisual Media*. Albany: SUNY Press, 2006.

Miller, Margo. "Masculinity and Male Intimacy in Nineties Sitcoms: Seinfeld and the Ironic Dismissal." In *The New Queer Aesthetic on Television: Essays on Recent Programming*, 147–159. Edited by James R. Becker and Leslie Stratyner. Jefferson, NC: McFarland, 2006.

Miller, Toby, ed. *Television Studies*. London: BFI Publishing, 2002.

Moore, Candace. "Having It All Ways: the Tourist, the Traveler, and the Local in *The L Word*." *Cinema Journal* 46, 4 (Summer 2007): 3–22.

Newcomb, Horace, ed. *Television: The Critical View*. 5th edition. New York: Oxford University Press.

Newkirk, Walter. *MemoraBEALEia: A Private Scrapbook about Edie Beale of Grey Gardens First Cousin to First Lady Jacqueline Kennedy Onassis*. Bloomington, IN: AuthorHouse, 2008.

Pearl, Monica. "Review of *Lesbian Rule*." GLQ 11, 2 (2005): 325–27.

Phelan, Peggy. "Performance, Live Culture, and Things of the Heart." *Journal of Visual Culture* 2, 3 (2003): 291–302.

Pullen, Christopher. *Documenting Gay Men: Identity and Performance in Reality Television and Documentary Film*. Jefferson, NC: McFarland and Company, 2007.

Oulette, Laurie, and James Hay. *Better Living through Reality TV*. Malden, MA: Blackwell Publishing, 2008.

Retort Collective. *Afflicted Powers: Capital and Spectacle in a New Age of War*. London: Verso, 2005.

Rhodes, John David. *Stupendous, Miserable City: Pasolini's Rome*. Minneapolis: University of Minnesota Press, 2007.

Rickels, Lawrence. *The Case of California*. Baltimore, MD: The Johns Hopkins University Press, 1991.

Ringer, R. Jeffrey. *Queer Words, Queer Images: Communication and the Construction of Homosexuality*. New York: NYU Press, 1994.

Rodowick, David. *The Virtual Life of Film*. Cambridge, MA: Harvard University Press, 2007.

Roiphe, Anne. "Things Are Keen but Could Be Keener." *New York Times Magazine*, February 18, 1973.

Roof, Judith. *All about Thelma and Eve: Sidekicks and Third Wheels*. Urbana: University of Illinois Press, 2002.

Rosen, Philip. *Change Mummified: Cinema, Historicity, Theory*. Minneapolis: University of Minnesota Press, 2001.

Rubin, Gayle. "Thinking Sex: Notes for a Radical Theory of the Politics of Sexuality." In *Pleasure and Danger*, 267–293. Edited by Carole Vance. New York: Routledge, 1984.

Rubin, Stanley. "A (Very) Personal History of the First Sponsored Film Series on National Television." *Journal of E-Media Studies* 1, 1 (2008). Accessed March 25, 2013. http://journals.dartmouth.edu/cgi-bin/WebObjects/Journals.woa/1/xmlpage/4/article/312.

Ruoff, Jeffrey. *An American Family: A Televised Life*. Minneapolis: University of Minnesota Press, 2001.

Sconce, Jeffrey. *Haunted Media: Electronic Presence from Telegraphy to Television*. Durham, NC: Duke University Press, 2000.

Sedgwick, Eve Kosofsky. *Epistemology of the Closet*. Berkeley: University of California Press, 1990.

Sender, Katherine. *Business, Not Politics: The Making of the Gay Market*. New York: Columbia University Press, 2005.

Sobchack, Vivian. *Carnal Thoughts: Embodiment and Moving Image Culture*. Berkeley: University of California Press, 2004.

Spigel, Lynn. *Make Room for TV: Television and the Family Ideal in Postwar America*. Chicago: University of Chicago Press, 1992.

Stiegler, Bernard. *Technics and Time, 3: Cinematic Time and the Question of Malaise*. Translated by Stephen Barker. Stanford, CA: Stanford University Press, 2011.

———. "The Time of Cinema: On the 'New World' and 'Cultural Exception.'" *Tekhnema* 4 (1998): 62–114.

Uricchio, William. "Television as Time Machine: Television's Changing Heterochronic Regimes and the Production of History." In *Relocating Television: Television in the Digital Context*, 27–40. Edited by Jostein Gripsrud. London: Routledge, 2010.

Vidal, Gore. *The Second American Revolution and Other Essays (1976–1982)*. New York: Random House, 1982.

Villarejo, Amy. "*Bus 174* and the Living Present." *Cinema Journal* 46, 1 (Fall 2006): 115–20.

———. "Ethereal Queer: Notes on Method." In *Queer TV*, 48–62. Edited by Glyn Davis and Gary Needham. London: Routledge, 2008.

———. "The Halting Grammar of Intimacy: Watching *An American Family*'s Final Episode." In *Political Emotions*, 193–214. Edited by Janet Staiger, Ann Cvetkovich, and Ann Reynolds. London: Routledge, 2010.

———. "Killing Me Softly: Brazilian Film and Bare Life." In *Beyond Globalization: Making New Worlds in Media, Art, and Social Practices*, 121–137. Edited by A. Aneesh, Lane Hall, and Patrice Petro. New Brunswick, NJ: Rutgers University Press, 2011.

———. *Lesbian Rule: Cultural Criticism and the Value of Desire*. Durham, NC: Duke University Press, 2003.

———. "Materiality, Pedagogy, and Queer Visibility." In *A Companion to Lesbian, Gay, Bisexual, Transgender, and Queer Studies*. Edited by George E. Haggerty and Molly McGarry. Hoboken, NJ: Wiley-Blackwell, 2007.

———. "TV Queen: Lending an Ear to Charles Pierce." *Modern Drama* 53, 3 (Fall 2010): 350–69.

Viviani, Christian. "Who Is without Sin? The Maternal Melodrama in American Film, 1930–1939." In *Imitations of Life: A Reader on Film and Television Melodrama*, 168–182. Edited by Marcia Landy. Detroit, MI: Wayne State University Press, 1991.

von Moltke, Johannes. "Teddie and Friedl: Theodor W. Adorno, Siegfried Kracauer, and the Erotics of Friendship." *Criticism* 51, 4 (Fall 2010): 683–94.

Watt, Ian. *The Rise of the Novel: Studies in Defoe, Richardson, and Fielding*. Berkeley: University of California Press, 2001.

Weber, Samuel. *Mass Mediaurus: Form, Technics, Media*. Stanford, CA: Stanford University Press, 1996.

White, Mimi. "Television Liveness: History, Banality, Attractions." *Spectator* 20, 1 (Fall 1999/Winter 2000): 39–56.

White, Patricia. *Uninvited: Classical Hollywood Cinema and Lesbian Representability*. Bloomington: Indiana University Press, 1999.

Williams, Raymond. *Television: Technology and Cultural Form*. New York: Schocken Books, 1975.

Wlodarz, Joe. "We're Not All So Obvious: Masculinity and Queer (In)visibility in American Network Television of the 1970s." In *Queer TV*, 88–107. Edited by Glyn Davis and Gary Needham. London: Routledge, 2009.

Wolfenstein, Martha, and Nathan Leites. *Movies: A Psychological Study*. New York: The Free Press, 1950.

Wolff, Tobias. *This Boy's Life: A Memoir*. New York: Atlantic Monthly Press, 1989.

Yelling, J. A. *Common Field and Enclosure in England, 1450–1850*. Hamden, CT: Archon Books, 1977.

Young, Iris Marion. *Justice and the Politics of Difference*. Princeton, NJ: Princeton University Press, 1990.

Yúdice, George. *The Expediency of Culture: Uses of Culture in the Global Era*. Durham, NC: Duke University Press, 2003.

Zielinski, Siegfried. *Audiovisions: Cinema and Television as Entr'actes in History*. Amsterdam: Amsterdam University Press, 1999.

Zischler, Hanns. *Kafka Goes to the Movies*. Translated by Susan Gillespie. Chicago: University of Chicago Press, 2003.

Page numbers in italics refer to figures and tables.

effects of, 30, 42, 126; of American values, 54–55, 114, 154; of emerging technologies, 29; of television, 2, 19, 22, 29, 35

Cavell, Stanley, 164n9

Chauncey, George, 27, 96, 128–29, 131–32

children: fears of homosexual abuse against, 87–88, 143; heterosexual abuse against, 142; real-life in sitcom families, 82–83; as viewers of television, 48, 147. *See also* adolescents and young adults

cinema: images of queer existence, 26–27; influence of on television, 4, 9, 22, 24, 75, 77–79; merging of the viewer with, 71–76; as a reflection of human existence, 44, 53–54; as a temporal object, 73–75, 175n13

cinematic time, 67, 71–76

cities: function of the sidewalk in, 27, 127–33, 136; function of the staircase in, 3, 135, 136; function of the wall in, 27, 124–28, 134–36; global networks of, 33, 124, 126; megacities, 124–25, 127–28; migration of queer individuals to, 26, 123–24, 128, 149, 151; queer life in, 125, 130–33, 134, 142; representations of life in, 26–27, 123–24, 128; use of public spaces in, 97, 127, 129–30, 132, 140; victimization of street youth in, 125–26

Clock, The, 69–71

"coming out": of Lance Loud, 96, 103, 108, 114, 116–18, 177n31; and metaphor of the closet, 96, 171–72n57; by queer individuals, 8, 24–25, 80, 89, 95–96, 114

consciousness: convergence of with

technology, 21, 35, 55, 67, 73; and memory, 11, 21, 49–50, 73–76, 79; merger of with machine, 21, 79, 155; perception of time duration, 67–71. *See also* stream of consciousness

Corner, John, 4–5

critical theory of television, 9, 19–20, 31, 34, 41, 49

cultural criticism, 5, 30, 37, 40, 43, 113

culture: American counterculture, 23, 84, 92, 109, 143; American ideals, 99, 134, 142; consumer, 58, 85, 111, 130; and mass entertainment, 30, 34; queer, 106–7, 109, 142–44; and self-identity, 48–50, 155; sexual, 89, 133–34, 144, 157; visual, 48–49

culture industry: Adorno's analysis of the, 30, 32–34, 39–46, 62; manipulative character of the, 30, 32, 43–44, 47, 50, 62; programming, 34, 148; use of stereotypes by the, 56

Deleuze, Gilles, 7, 17, 107, 145, 159

Derrida, Jacques, 7, 10, 61, 77

Dienst, Richard, 7, 29, 77, 154

digital television: conversion to from analog, 1–2, 8–9, 29; and other digital technologies, 34, 78, 122; scope and flexibility of, 10, 36, 77, 146–48, 153

Doane, Mary Ann, 3–4, 19, 31–32

Dukakis, Olympia, 28, 137, *138f*, 142

duration. *See* time: concept of duration

Elevator Repair Service performances, 67–68

homosexuals. *See* gay individuals; lesbians; queer individuals

Houlbrook, Matt, 27, 128–32

Husserl, Edmund, 21, 55–56, 66–67, 73–74

identification of viewers with televisual images, 7, 51–52, 57, 62, 72

images: case of Lance Loud, 106, 108, 115–19; cinematic, 53, 76; and consciousness, 11, 72–74, 154–55; as constructions of cinema and television, 1, 8, 42, 45, 49, 77; educational power of, 48, 81; gendered, 35, 45; as memory, 48, 54, 75, 144; photographic, 53, 164n9; of queer existence, 15, 26, 83–84, 92, 144; of reality construed by television, 8, 20, 32, 65, 79–80, 86; symbolic capacity of, 123, 159–60; temporality of, 53, 69–70. *See also* stereotyping

Jameson, Frederic, 33–34, 36, 113

Jennemann, David, 32–33

Lane, Diane, *120f*, 121

Lear, Norman, 23, 84–85

Lentz, Kirsten, 85

lesbians: actors on television, 83, 90; capture of psyches through melodrama, 63, 154, 156–58; in cities, 123; and "coming out," 9, 95–96, 103–5; Cousin Liz and Veronica on *All in the Family*, 23, 87–90; in *Losing Chase*, 155–58; politics concerning, 23, 41–42, 87, 132–33, 149; representation of on television, 2–3, 5–7, 15, 23, 41–42, 97; stereotypes of, 20, 50, 59–62, 133, 160; television programming

for, 2, 6, 148–50; in *Wild Flowers*, 158–61

liveness: and the ephemerality of performance, 68–69; and the "live effect," 77, 79; in televisual time, 10–11, 19, 31, 46, 80, 167–68n6

London, queer population in, 26, 129, 130–32

Los Angeles, queer population in, 12, 14, 83, 115

Losing Chase, 155–58, *156f, 157f*

Madrigal, Anna. *See* Dukakis, Olympia

Marclay, Christian, 69–71

mass culture, 30, 34, 41–43, 168n14

mass media, 39, 42, 47, 49–50

Maupin, Armistead, 25–26, 122–23, 135, 140, 143, 150

McLean, Don Seymour (aka Lori Shannon), 85, *86f*, 89–90

megacities, 124–25, 127–28

melodrama: power of to communicate abstractions, 56, 88–89, 97, 141–42, 153–55, 159–60; power of to transform psycho-social assumptions, 81, 95, 143–44, 158

memory of the temporal object, 11, 70, 75, 167–68n6

miniseries. *See* series: miniseries

Mirren, Helen, 155–56, *156f, 157f*

More Tales of the City, 25, 28, 139, 143, 146, 150

MTM Enterprises, 84

network television: construing of fiction and reality by, 65, 82; versus the digital spectrum, 34, 77, 146, 148, 152; major channels (grid) of, 1, 8–9, 21, 35, 37, 94; queer characters in prime time

of polymorphic meaning, 49–50; and the dynamics of identification in *Our Miss Brooks*, 50–52; fake, 40–41; the overlap of reality and illusion, 52–55; of televisual depictions, 5, 10, 45, 49, 65, 169n23

retention of memory, 73–76, 79

Rickels, Lawrence, 45–46

Rodowick, D. N., 72, 164n9

Roiphe, Anne, 108–10, 116, 121

Roots: The Saga of an American Family, 22, 24, 81

Rosen, Philip, 9, 54–55, 72

Ruoff, Jeffrey, 94–95, 99–102, 116, 177n29

San Francisco: queer population in, 13, 27, 89, 107, 123, 128; setting for *Tales of the City*, 25–26, 122, 129, 134–36, 141–45, 151

Sconce, Jeffrey, 9, 19, 155

Sedgwick, Eve Kosofsky, 96–97, 133

Sedgwick, Kyra, 155–56, *156t*

self-identification: melancholic elements of, 47–49, 51; role of television in shaping, 7–9, 47, 52, 65, 79; with an unidentified Other, 48

seriality: as an adaptation to viewer schedules, 35–36; impact of on viewer consciousness, 89–90, 118; power of to transmit queer imagery, 10–11, 19, 22–23, 92, 117

series: *An American Family* as an experimental, 23–24, 94–108, 114–17; on cable television, 148–51, 153; comedic queer content of *Our Miss Brooks*, 50, 57–63; inclusion of queer individuals in, 2–3, 80, 83; miniseries as a transformative derivative of the, 22–25; queer

characterizations in *Starsky and Hutch*, 13–16; queer characters in *All in the Family*, 85–92; *Tales of the City* as an experimental, 25, 28, 122–23, 134

sexuality: freedom of, 124, 132; homophobic responses to, 16, 42, 87–88, 108–9, 125; homosexual innuendo, 32, 60, 63–64; societal oppression of homosexuality, 96–97, 102; societal promotion of heterogeneity, 18, 46–47

Shannon, Lori. *See* McLean, Don Seymour

Showtime, 25–26, 28, 96, 122, 145–46, 150

sitcoms: of the 1950s and 1960s, 8, 36, 82, 99; of the 1970s, 22–23, 81–85, 92, 95, 143–44; character treatments in, 31–32, 56, 58; representations of the family in, 81, 84–85, 110; temporalities of, 31, 80, 91–92

Sobchack, Vivian, 76–77, 173n19, 174n26

spectators. *See* viewers

staircase symbolism, 28, 123, 133–41

Stapleton, Jean, 84–92, *91f*

Starsky and Hutch: "Death in a Different Place" episode, 12–14, 16, 84; gay topics and characters in, 12–16, *13f*, 89

stereotyping: Adorno's study of, 55–57; constraining effects of, 8, 20, 55–56; of the heterosexual individual, 57, 64; of the queer individual, 5, 17, 20, 23, 59–62, 97; as visual shorthand, 8, 14, 32, 56, 63–64, 92. *See also* images

Stiegler, Bernard: on the human need for fiction, 71–72; studies of

time: concept of duration, 17, 21, 53; and concept of liveness, 10–11, 31–32, 167–68n6; obscuring of by the temporal object, 70–76, 77; phenomenon of calendarity, 77, 79; serialization of by television, 22, 31, 37, 38t, 56, 167n5; significance of ephemerality to performance, 68–69; televisual, 12, 21, 31, 67, 71, 77–80

transgenderism: in *All in the Family*, 23, 84, 86f, 89–92; in *Tales of the City*, 28, 42, 140, 141

transvestite performances, 13, 102, 103, 109

Viacom, 146–50

viewers: Adorno's assertions concerning, 40–45, 49–50, 55, 57; attitudes of shaped by television, 37, 40, 45, 82, 107, 141–42; characters and narrators as surrogates for, 15, 67–68; consciousness of time by, 31, 67, 70–71, 73, 78; duty of to assess images thoughtfully, 65, 169n23, 170n38; familiarity of with characters, 31–32, 62, 90; identification of with characters, 48, 57, 62, 95, 107, 112–13; merging of with the temporal object, 3, 41, 46–47, 53–54, 90; programming for specific kinds of, 35–36, 44, 85; shared televisual experiences of, 32, 77, 117

wall symbolism, 96, 126–27, 134–36, 139, 179n10

Warhol, Andy, 70, 102, 108, 116

White, Mimi, 167–68n6

Wild Flowers, 158–61, *159f*

Williams, Raymond, 1–2, 35–37

window symbolism, 141–45

YouTube, 9, 29, 58, 156–57

Yúdice, George, 125–26, 127

Zielinski, Siegfried, 9